D.H. LAWRENCE

NEW ESSAYS FROM INDIA

Edited by

Bibhu Padhi

ATLANTIC

PUBLISHERS & DISTRIBUTORS (P) LTD

ATLANTIC
PUBLISHERS & DISTRIBUTORS (P) LTD
7/22, Ansari Road, Darya Ganj, New Delhi
Tel.: +91-11-4077 5252, 2327 3880
E-mail: orders@atlanticbooks.com
Web: www.atlanticbooks.com

Published by Atlantic Publishers & Distributors (P) Ltd 2024

Disclaimer

- The author and the publisher have taken every effort to the maximum of their skill, expertise and knowledge to provide correct material in the book. Even then if some mistakes persist in the content of the book, the publisher does not take responsibility for the same. The publisher shall have no liability to any person or entity with respect to any loss or damage caused, or alleged to have been caused directly or indirectly, by the information contained in this book.
- The author has fully tried to follow the copyright law. However, if any work is found to be similar, it is unintentional and the same should not be used as defamatory or to file legal suit against the author.
- If the readers find any mistakes, we shall be grateful to them for pointing out those to us so that these can be corrected in the next edition.
- All disputes are subject to the jurisdiction of Delhi courts only.

Printed & bound in India by Atlantic Print Services

In memories of

Professor V.Y. Kantak

and

Professor G.K. Das

Contents

Introduction

Today, D.H. Lawrence enjoys a popularity and respect that he did not during his lifetime. There have been many reprints of his works. With the publication of the new Cambridge University Press's publication of Lawrence's complete works, his fame has risen to new heights. There has been a significant revival of interest in his readers in his variegated works.

The present book is a modest addition to the existing Lawrencian criticism. All of its essays are written by scholars from India; its many voices have run parallel to voices from England, the North America and elsewhere. As far as this editor knows, there has not been any book of its kind in the whole gamut of Lawrencian criticism. The essays include several aspects of Lawrence's genius, beginning with *The White Peacock* to Lawrence's nonfiction/prose. Each essay tries to describe Lawrence's expressive power and indicates those subtle connections that link the verbal fabric to the immensities under the skin.

Lawrence's much-neglected first novel, *The White Peacock*, was rewritten and re-titled three times. In her essay on the novel, Anita Bhela shows how it is full of symbolic realism. Natural scenes are depicted with such "lyrical realism" that the visual scenes appear before our eyes instinctively. The uncompromising, stark symbolic realism include the presentation of characters too. They are not static. They grow, change and degenerate in consonance with basic nature and changing personal and social relationships. The man-man and man-woman relationships—beautiful, degraded, or tragic—are presented clearly and there is no attempt to hide the ugly and disturbing aspects of life or to idealize characters. At no time Lawrence is judgmental. Lettie, Leslie and George are all presented empathetically. As Bhela writes, "The novel...is not so much about mismatched marriages but about limited choices available, especially for the emerging modern woman." Women are presented as mothers and nurturers, but a different perspective on women as devourers is presented through Annable. Lettie's changing character in the role of the "powerful woman, conscious of her seductive charm," is fore grounded through a subtle comparison of Lettie to Salome in Aubrey's paintings. There are man-woman bonding, but there are scenes of perfect man-man bonding, such as those of George and Cyril; and Annable and Cyril. The characters, scenes and relationships achieve depth through a symbolism that integrates into the narrative references to songs, poets, and painters.

The essay on *Sons and Lovers* tries to show how the business of art is to reveal the relation between man and what Lawrence calls the "circumambient universe". Scenes and episodes that bring man and nature intimately close to each other remain a prominent functional feature of Lawrence's fiction. In these scenes Lawrence does not merely provide evocative nature imagery, he is concerned with larger conceptual issues. The essay discusses the symbolic nature and narrative significance of these scenes. It also tries to show how these scenes embody issues of perception and communication.

Gagan Behari Das's essay discusses the pattern of repetition in the family-chronicle novel, *The Rainbow*, which has been intimately worked out in its structure, which leads to the problem of spatial form. In its temporal progress one can observe that Will and Anna's search is a repetition of an ancient one. "If," Das writes, "a logical connection between repetition and simultaneity is established, then what one perceives as meaning will be exclusively spatial and total at a certain point of time." He argues that *The Rainbow* gradually emerges as a metaphor for such repetition in every character, image, parallelism and episode. This repetitive pattern is the characteristic technique of Lawrence.

Ursula's search for an "unknown reality" is deeply associated with two epiphanic images—those of "wild horses" and "the rainbow." The symbolic horse-chasing scene just before the final rainbow image is the culmination of her experience and knowledge as a "traveler on the face of the earth." It returns regularly with different verbal signs that do not refer to sensible objects of the real world, but to a vision-like dream-objects. In a kind of a language of absence the narrative repeats the same signified connection with different signifiers. This reductionism, writes Das, "brings together all images and symbols and turns the narrative into a complex structure."

In his essay, Nigamananda Das analyzes some aspects of the language of *Women in Love*. The essay explores a variety of vocabulary, collocation of words, repetitions, the relevance of Lawrence's language to the phenomenology of lived experience. Das deals with the use of metaphors, images, symbols, code-switching along with the non-verbal mode of communication and narrative technique. Lawrence has evolved a semi-mystical language through employment of figures of speech to paint the picture human and environmental predicament as a result of a decadent industrialized society.

Asima Ranjan Parhi's essay deals with Lawrence's *Apocalypse*. "At the fag end of his literary career," Parhi writes, "D.H. Lawrence invests his mystical energy in unraveling human civilization through its cosmic, pagan, religious lense." He argues that *Apocalypse* contains this energy that questions the ascertained faith of the mass over institutionalized religion in general and Christianity in particular. Drawing his inspiration from the far south, especially the Hindu roots and its diverse spiritual and philosophical engagements, the author speculates and idealizes an ideal individual free from the miracle, from its dual trap of bondage and faith. Lawrence also believed that human beings are always in a state of flux as they are purely driven by their impulses deeper than they acquire in the form of knowledge.

In *Apocalypse*, Lawrence says that religion as such is not harmful but rather the rigid religious practices make it toxic.

These practices are static and hence dead in nature and open no gate for actual liberation. He expounds the nature of flux in human existence. He is very close to the Indian mythical, scriptural essence of life. The Hindu concept of liberation matches well with his search for the mystical self-negation and the surrender of ego in human relationship. Institutionalized religion ask for blind submission. Apocalypse on the other hand questioned such servile multitude by emphasizing on individual integrity and insight. Lawrence is utterly displeased by the way revelation is considered by the Christians. Rather there is an urgency of looking at religion and salvation from different philosophical and ethical points of view. The relevance of *Apocalypse* in a world poised with religious intolerance and political affiliations of religious sects is immense.

Sachidananda Mohanty's essay on exile, creativity and the First World War relates to Lawrence's response to the great war. British literary responses to the war, stretching from the trench poetry of Wilfred Owen and the work of non-canonical women poets like Vera Brittain to the writings of Eliot, Pound, Huxley, Ford and Lawrence, have been generally recognized. It is not so much the senseless savagery of the "total war" and what Clive Bloom describes as "totalized paranoia" ["there is no knowing who is the enemy, therefore presume *all* are the enemy"], the latter stemming from the seemingly tranquil but xenophobic Edwardian era, ["Britain's prospects as bleaker and its enemies as more monstrous"] that are new, although they are worth recalling on the Centenary of the war event. More importantly, a closer look needs to be taken regarding the precise manner in which the war impacted on the fundamental choices—personal, intuitional and literary—that writers made and the way exile and creativity were played out in literary-cultural and political terms. Revisiting authors, texts and life-writing in the context of the Great War thus becomes a useful exercise.

A closer look at war and creativity would show the manner in which biography and creativity were enmeshed in the vortex of war and exile. This intermingling gave new meaning to the concept of exile. It was no longer to be seen as an involuntary act of self-isolation in a foreign location. More fundamentally, thanks to the new role of mass media and organs of the State, the dissenting writer would remain exiled within one's own country and community. More significantly, he/she remained an embattled and divided self.

In his paper, Mohanty pays close attention to the war years of D.H. Lawrence with regard to his creativity while bringing in the examples of some of the notable contemporaries such as Ezra Pound, Ford Madox Ford, Richard Aldington and Aldous Huxley. Unlike Wilfred Owen and Ford Madox Ford, Lawrence did not see action on the battlefield. He was not gassed or shell-shocked like some others but his "nightmare" was no less traumatic and agonizing. Subjected to a relentless regime of surveillance, persecution and physical and emotional abuse, he stood out alone among many of his established contemporaries.

Lalit Kumar's paper, "Lawrence in Mexico: The Myth of Quetzalcoatl and Dangers of Americanization", examines Lawrence's ambivalent feelings towards Mexico through a close analysis of his two major works on Mexico—*The Plumed Serpent* and *Mornings in Mexico*. It seeks to answer two significant questions. One, what precisely drove the British novelist to become a ceaseless wanderer and explore Mexico, Sri Lanka, and other parts of the world? And two, what makes contemporary readers, especially Indian readers empathize with his Mexican experience? The essay foregrounds a large number of issues, including Lawrence's constant enchantment with the new places, threats of Americanization, cruelty to animals, and the uncanny similarities between Mexican gods and the Indian gods which readers in India and elsewhere may relate to. Lawrence was well aware of the apprehension of the Mexicans regarding Americanization and the overwhelming praises of foreigners. The male protagonist of *The Plumed Serpent*, Don Ramon, mixes politics with religion in order to free his land from foreign occupation. If exico breeds contempt in Kate Leslie, it also produces wonder; it is the land of violence, but it is also the land of mystery. This contradiction, writes Kumar, "lies not only at the heart of this novel but at the heart of colonialism and racism." Ramon wants the ancient gods to come back and save the decadent and degenerated soul of Mexicans.

Lawrence's writings on Mexico, therefore, must be revisited in contemporary times in the midst of the Americans regarding their "Mexicanization", which the current US administration is trying to counter.

Joyjit Ghosh re-reads Lawrence's letters in the context of the First World War. He begins with how Lawrence did not like cities in general, whether it was London or Paris. His references to London in his letters are often couched in negative terms. He wrote to Walter de la Mare, "One breathes so much freer out of London". A close reading of his letters reveals how his dislike of the city reached its peak during the First World War. The metropolis of his youthful dreams turned into an inferno as the war broke out. To Lady Ottoline Morrell he wrote, "London *does* strike a blow at the heart". The "persistent nothingness" of the war enraged him.

Lawrence was convinced that the war was a "colossal idiocy" and the warring nations were "Bloody false fools" to him. The war pained his sensitive soul, but it could not alter his "beliefs or visions". In his letter to Lady Cynthia Asquith in 1915, he writes that the War was a "disintegrating autumnal process" while love was "the great creative process, like Spring...". Lawrence glorifies the "principle of life" against degeneration and death. He firmly believed that only love and trust alone could subdue the unholy spirit of war.

Rajan Joseph Barrett looks at Lawrence's *Study of Thomas Hardy* and negates claims that it is not about Hardy but about Lawrence's own metaphysic. He looks at the positions that Lawrence uses to construct his argument: with regard to self-preservation, the male-female principles, as well as the aristocratic principles. Barrett has tried, though obliquely, to trace the influence of Nietzsche on Lawrence as a kind of philosopher and prototype. Here we perceive a pessimism that characterizes the style of Lawrence's prose. It is true that Lawrence has not kept his esoteric theory on the man-woman relationship out which, if he did, would not be truly Lawrencian. He is occupied with art history and analysis of great masters like Rembrandt, Michelangelo, Leonard Da Vinci and others;

it leads to a practice of how to analyze a work of art. It does anticipate what Lawrence does with Hardy in the penultimate chapter of *Study.* The unique style of taking on an author by another practitioner of the art is something really interesting; It is the way Lawrence combines art and aesthetics, poetry, political theory, notions of freedom, the Romantic and the Victorian, the mechanical and the natural, that he makes the reader aware of the stasis and dynamics of Hardy as a writer.

As Deeptha Achar writes, Lawrence's paintings have not attracted much critical attention compared with his fiction and poetry. The fact that they were confiscated from the gallery where they were on show and literally banished to the U.S.A. by law often appears as an addendum to his more skirmishes with censorship qua *Lady Chatterley's Lover* and *The Rainbow*, as well as *Pansies.*

Achar examines the manner in which Lawrence stages his critique of censorship and addresses the obscenity in his paintings. She works away from an approach that would make obscenity as an attribute of Lawrence's art. In that sense, obscenity would not be an attribute that inheres within the work itself but rather it will be seen as being produced by social and political contexts that articulate obscenity in relation to the work. Therefore, her concern is more to pursue the Lawrentian argument around censorship with his paintings as an entry point. In his seminal essay, "Pornography and Obscenity", he is not so much interested in castigating the "censor-morons"; he is rather interested in articulating the social lie of the land that engendered such a hostile response to the work.

As Santosh Dash says, critical reception of Lawrence is one of extremes. There are the apologists that defend him by arguing that the times are now not right for a reception of a fine mind like his. There are also critics who are bitter critics who deride him stridently, are of the opinion that times are *never* right for men of his temperament.

Dash's paper offers a reading of Lawrence's *Studies in Classic American Literature* (*SCAL*) in the context of his time without falling into the commonplace temptation in the background of his philosophy. Published in 1923, this book captures the mood of America at that point of time. Besides, the individual essays in the book, written during the First World War, I carry references to relationships between Europe and America. The book is perhaps the first to set up a canon of American Literature.

Lawrence's purpose in reading old American literature is both premeditated and strategic. In the 1920s, Lawrence had clearly visualized a new nation coming into being, wrestling against its European past, desperate in its bid to chart out its own routes to freedom and democracy. It is quite likely that Lawrence thought it historically urgent to understand the new America that was taking shape before his eyes.

Lawrence's readings appear to accomplish two things: one, they show the inevitable entanglement of the histories of America and Europe; and two, they demonstrate the way the ideas of freedom and democracy have been forged historically in America, independent of Europe. By systematically raising questions of class, race and gender in the context of the history of American literature, Lawrence seems to suggest that the contours of American democracy and freedom would depend on the way it engages with its own past.

Rabindra Pradhan's essay on Lawrence's poetry explores the relationship between man and the natural world. The natural world was a source of inspiration for Lawrence. Human responsibility for the fellow inhabitants of the planet is arrived at through anecdotal drama and meditation.

The originality and mystery in his poems represent the intuitive behaviour of the non-human creatures. It analyses the achievement of Lawrence's ecological interdependence of animals and plants. The essay also shows how Lawrence uses the idea of open form.

My essay on Lawrence's nonfiction prose attempts to illuminate unexplored aspects of key rhetorical strategies employed in Lawrence's nonfiction prose. Although Lawrence produced a substantial body of nonfiction prose in the form of letters, essays, literary criticism and travel narratives, his fiction has attracted wider critical attention. By focusing on neglected aspects of Lawrence's nonfiction prose and responding to F.R. Leavis' emphasis on the need to recognize Lawrence's ability to explore "complete fields of experience", the essay shows how his prose asserts the mystery of existence and records his feeling of wonder in the face of life's innumerable forms. Lawrence's prose is pervaded by "human metaphors" and draws its essential strength from its intimate concern with human relationships.

The urgency and the clean imaginative sweep of his prose; the passionately imitative rhythm, recreating, in verbal language, a flight that has something curiously "artistic" about it; the metaphoric exuberance; the continuous suggestion of the soul's liberation through the body: these are the essential Lawrence. They are a fulfilment in practice of his long-cherished aesthetic intentions. The essay undertakes a close study of the techniques, such as qualification and repetition, which Lawrence deploys to achieve the intended effects in his prose writings. It goes on to demonstrate how the act of reiteration helps Lawrence to bring clarity to his beliefs. The use of single-sentence paragraphs and aphorisms lends a hymnal quality to Lawrence's nonfiction prose and shapes it as a powerful vehicle for prophecy.

List of Contributors

Anita Bhela, formerly Associate Professor and Head, Department of English, DCA College, University of Delhi, is the recipient of the 2011 SEE Fellowship, awarded by the Society of Extension Education for outstanding contribution in the field of Knowledge Management, Promotion of Cultural Diversity and Work for the Underprivileged Section of the Society. She has authored the book *Aesthetics of Romance: An Intercultural Perspective* and has published research papers in national and international journals. Her areas of interest are Comparative Studies; Literature, Ethics, Religion, Culture; Shakespeare Studies; and English Language Teaching.

Bibhu Padhi took early retirement as Associate Professor from Dhenkanal College, Orissa. He has published a book on D.H. Lawrence (Whitston) and (with his wife, Minakshi Padhi) a reference book on Indian Philosophy and Religion (McFarland). His scholarly articles have been published, among others, in *D H Lawrence Review*, *Interpretations*, *Liberal and Fine Arts Review*, *Modern Fiction Studies*, *Modernist Studies*, and *Philological Quarterly*. A two times Pushcart nominee, he has published seventeen books of poetry. His poems have been published in distinguished magazines throughout the English-speaking world, such as *Contemporary Review*, *London Magazine*, *The Poetry Review*, *Poetry Wales*, *The American Scholar*, *Commonweal*, *The Manhattan Review*, *The New Criterion*, *Poetry*, *Southwest Review*, *TriQuarterly*, *The Antigonish Review*, *The Dalhousie Review*, and *Queen's Quarterly*. They have been included in numerous anthologies and textbooks. Five of the most recent are *The Bloodaxe Book of Contemporary Indian Poets, Language for a New Century* (Norton) *Journeys* (HarperCollins), *The HarperCollins Book of English Poetry,* and *The Penguin Book of Indian Poets.*

Gagan Behari Das taught English literature for more than three decades at Madhabdev College, Narayanpur in Lakhimpur District of Assam. He worked on the topic of *D.H. Lawrence and Dialectics of Spatial Form* for his Ph.D. degree. He is a staunch follower of Mahimadharma, a nineteen century religious path of life and has had a monk's life for over four decades of his life.

Nigamananda Das is Professor of English, and Dean, School of Humanities and Education at Nagaland University, Kohima. His interests include Commonwealth Literature, Saint Literature, Multiethnic literature, ELT and Contemporary Theories. He has written three books and edited five anthologies of critical essays on Contemporary Commonwealth Literature. He has co-edited two anthologies of English literature (Macmillan).

Sachidananda Mohanty is Professor and former Head, Department of English, University of Hyderabad. He is the recipient of several national and international awards including those from the British Council, the Salzburg, the Katha and the Fulbright. He has to his credit twenty-six books in English and in Oriya including *D.H. Lawrence Studies in India,* Writers' Workshop, 1990; *Lawrence's Leadership Politics and the Defeat of Fascism,* Academic Foundation, 1992; *Understanding Cultural Exchange,* Vision Books, 1997; *Literature and Culture,* Prestige, 2000; *Travel Writing and the Empire*, Katha, 2002, *Early Women's Writing in Orissa, 1898-1950: A Lost Tradition,* Sage Publications, 2005; *Gender and Cultural Identity in Colonial Orissa,* Orient Longman, 2008; *Sri Aurobindo: A Contemporary Reader,* Routledge India, 2008; rpt. 2009, 2010; *Sarala Devi*, Central Sahitya Akademi, 2011; and *Cosmopolitan Modernity in Early Twentieth Century India* (Routledge).

He has lectured at a number of leading universities in India and abroad, including the Jawaharlal Nehru University, Cornell University, University of Pittsburgh, City University of New York, University of New Mexico, Australian National University, and National University of Singapore.

Lalit Kumar teaches English at Deen Dayal Upadhyaya College, University of Delhi. His English translation of Harimohan Jha's Maithili classic *Kanyadan* (1933) will be published by Harper Perennial in 2022. He has co-translated the Hindi best seller, Anurag Pathak's *Twelfth Fail* (HarperCollins, 2021) into English. He has written articles for several national dailies, including *The Hindu, The Indian Express, The Times of India* and *Jansatta*. For his doctoral research he has worked on Maithili print and literary cultures in north Bihar at the department of English, University of Delhi. Currently, he is working on an edited volume on Amaranatha Jha for Sahitya Akademi.

Asima Ranjan Parhi is a Professor of English at Utkal University. Specialising in ELT, he has a book, *Indian English Through Newspapers* (New Delhi: Concept), and many research papers published in journals, like *Journal of English and Foreign Languages Studies in Humanities and Social Sciences* (Shimla: Indian Institute of Advanced Study), *Journal of Media and Communication Studies*, *International Journal of Multidisciplinary Thought,* and *Atlantic Review*. He did his postdoctoral research as an Associate at the Indian Institute of Advanced Studies, Shimla during 2005-2008.

Joyjit Ghosh is a Professor of English, Vidyasagar University, Midnapore, West Bengal, India. The areas of his interest include Animal Studies, Translation Studies and Indian English Literature. He has a book called *Imaging D.H. Lawrence: His Mind and Art in Letters* (New Delhi: Authorspress, 2012). His article entitled "The Last Poems of D.H. Lawrence: Poetry of the Eternal Present" was published in *Etudes Lawrenciennes*. Ghosh frequently attends national/international-level conferences.

Rajan Joseph Barrett teaches at M.S. University, Baroda. His book publications include, *The Self and the Sonnet* (Cambridge Scholars, 2010), He has co-edited (with J.V. Dave and Tapas Chakraborty), *The Life and Works of John Keats*. He has co-authored *English for Academic Purposes* (Gujarat Granth Nirman Board), and *Basics of Academic English* (Orient Black Swan). His research interests include Theatre, Liberation Theology, Cultural Studies, Identity Studies, and Music.

Deeptha Achar is a Professor of English at M.S. University, Baroda. She studied at Bangalore University and Central Institute of English and Foreign Languages, Hyderabad. She is on the editorial advisory board of the open-access journal, *Open Cultural Studies*. Her books include *The Age of Adventure: Childhood, Reading and British Boys' Fiction*. She has co-edited *Towards New Art History: Studies in Indian Art, Discourse, Democracy and Difference: Perspectives on Community, Politics and Culture*, and *Articulating Resistance: Art and Activism*. Her research interests include Visual Culture and Childhood Studies.

Santosh Dash teaches at an undergraduate college in Savli, Gujarat. He has degrees from Central Institute of English and Foreign Languages and M.S. University, Baroda. He has a book, called *English Education and the Question of Indian Nationalism: A Perspective on the Vernacular.* He has received the South Asia Regional Research Fellowship as well as the SARPF Collaborative Grant from SSRC, New York, for translation and comparative research. His area of research is Nineteenth and Twentieth Century Gujarat.

Rabindra Pradhan heads the English Department at Sashi Bhusan Rath Government Women's College. His critical books include *The Theme of Isolation in Anita Desai's Fiction, The Concept of Paranoia in Eugene O'Neill's Plays,* and *The Fiction of British Asian Authors: An Interpretative Study*. His research interests include Linguistics, Indian Literature, Comparative Literature and Diaspora Writings. He is a bilingual poet and translator.

1

The White Peacock: A Study in Realistic Symbolism

Anita Bhela

D.H. Lawrence's first novel *The White Peacock*[1] has a complicated history. It was re-written and retitled three times. Lawrence first started writing the novel in 1906 titled *Laetitia* while undergoing a teacher training course at Nottingham University College. He completed the first version nearly a year later in 1907. The story/plot of *Laetitia* differs from that of *The White Peacock*. In the first version, Lettie marries George and not Leslie. Also. George's family is called Worthington, which was later changed to Saxton. Additionally, for the final version Lawrence worked upon and developed in greater detail the character of Meg whom George marries after he is rejected by Lettie. Jessie Chambers critically evaluated and scrutinized the first version. She did not have a high opinion of it and it appeared to her "story-bookish and unreal", yet she felt that "in spite of its sentimentality, a thread of genuine romance ran through the story; something in the atmosphere was alive" (116). According to her "the poem *Love on the Farm* is a sort of epitome of the first version of the novel" (116-17). Valuing the comments of Jessie Chambers, Lawrence set out to rewrite the novel. He completed his revision of *Laetitia* in May 1908, in which, among other changes, Lawrence also introduced the character of Annable. In the Autumn of 1908, after completing his course at Nottingham University College. Lawrence took up the job of a school teacher at Davidson Road School, Croydon, Surrey, here in 1909, he started reworking on the novel giving it the title *Nethermere*. Lawrence sent the manuscript to Ford Madox Hueffer, who had earlier published some of his poems in the *English Review*, for approval. After Hueffer's approval in 1910 Lawrence sent the letter of approval from Hueffer to William Heinemann asking him if he could send him *Nethermere* for publication (Lawrence, *Letters*, 148-49). A.R. Atkins believes it was Hueffer who sent the manuscript to Heinemann, as he finds no evidence that the manuscript sent to Hueffer was returned to Lawrence. However, the manuscript got Heinemann's approval subject to certain changes being made (346-47). Lawrence then again reworked on the novel taking the assistance of three Croydon school teachers for suggestions and for copying out the manuscript. Heinemann accepted this version but was dissatisfied with the title and wanted Lawrence to find a new title. Lawrence thought of many titles: "Lapwings", "Pee-wits", "The Cry of the Peacock", "The White Peacock", "The Talent in the Napkin", "The Talent, the Beggar, and the Box" (*Letters*, 163). The first galley proofs reached Lawrence when his mother was battling cancer. The novel was finally published with the title *The White Peacock* in 1911, soon after the death of his mother. Although, *The White Peacock* was one of the titles suggested by Lawrence, Andrew Robertson says that "Lawrence had suggested withdrawing the final title, but the publisher must have decided to retain it" (Intro, xxx) as ten days after suggesting the title Lawrence wrote "That 'White Peacock' must be shot: it is a bird from the pen of Wilkie Collins or Ibsen" (quoted in Robertson, Intro xxx). The title change is similar to what was done with the title of *Sons and Lovers* which was earlier titled Paul Morel. The change of title from character name to a more generalized one in both novels shifts focus from the particular to the more universal aspects.

The novel received several reviews and though there was criticism about the meandering style and the use of the first-person narrator, it was greatly appreciated for its lyrical quality, complexity of characterization, truthfulness and hailed as a work that revealed Lawrence's potential as a genius. In contrast, the response of his family to the publication of the novel was not very encouraging. Lawrence's mother's reaction when he put the first copy of the book into her hands:

> She looked at the outside, and then at the title-page, and then at me, with darkening eyes. And though she loved so much. I think she doubted whether it could be much of a book, since no one more important than I had written it. Somewhere in the helpless privacies of her being, she had a wistful respect for me, but for me in the face of the world, not much. This David would never get a stone across at Goliath. And why try? Let Goliath alone! Anyway, she was beyond reading my immortal work. It was put aside, and I never wanted to see it again. She never saw it again. (Lawrence, *Phoenix*, 232)

Later, after his mother's funeral, his father looked curiously at the book and "struggled through half a page" and enquired how much Lawrence was paid for it. On learning that Lawrence had received 50 pounds for it, his father was astonished: "Fifty pounds! An' tha's niver done a day's hard work in thy life" (*Phoenix*, 232), was his father's reaction. His father could not appreciate his work and Lawrence states that even in later years his father "looked upon him as a sort of cleverish swindler, who gets money for nothing" (232). His sister's reaction to the book also surprised Lawrence as she simply said "You always were lucky!" (232).

Lawrence's genius as a writer is very much visible in the novel. Scenes of domesticity and nature are described with such minuteness and precision that they collate to form visual pictures that enchant like captured scenes in paintings. Scenes of extreme realism are splashed right through the novel. The various images weave themselves into stunning and enthralling vignettes. The interplay of shades of light and darkness in the descriptions gives a dramatic effect to his words that seem to dance and sing and come to life. In the descriptions, Lawrence's sensibility of the painter comes to the fore and the reader is presented with a series of visual images that blend the mundane with fantastic. However, these descriptions don't just capture the eye of the mind, they are both realistic and symbolic. The realism is in the nature of Zola but transcends it as it is combined with a symbolism that reflects intense emotions, creates mood, and depicts character and atmosphere. Lawrence is perhaps one of the few novelists who was also a painter. Besides, he was also a poet. So, a combination of the visual and lyrical elements in his portrayal of people, events and places creates extraordinary effects on the reader. An audio of the text strikes a deeply lyrical note that touches every nerve of the body and enhances meaning. Henry Savage, one of the first reviewers of *The White Peacock,* catches the spirit of the novel when he says that "Mr. D.H. Lawrence is one of those rare writers who intends only to tell the truth as he sees it, and nothing but the truth" (43). The novel abounds in the truthful and realistic creation of nature, of death, of man-man and man-woman relationships, however unpleasant or tragic. However, the realism is combined with an intense symbolism that strengthens and enhances the reality, giving it a deeper meaning.

In Lawrence's first novel, the symbolic scenes are sporadic while the later novels *The Rainbow* and *Women in Love* are characterized by "a continuous indefinable symbolism", which according to Yeats is "the substance of all style" (155). In *The White Peacock*, there is more telling than showing. This could be under the influence of Balzac. Lawrence read Balzac's *Eugenie Grander* and found the "book as perfect a novel as [he] had ever read. It is wonderfully concentrated; there is nothing superfluous, nothing out of place" (*Letters*, 91). He appreciated it for its "earnestness" and for "no touch of melodrama, or caricature, or flippancy" or sentimentality (91). In the same letter to Blanche Jennings, whom he had approached to review his novel, Lawrence writes that much of the dialogue could be replaced with narrative: "You can none of you find one essence of its failure; it is that I have dragged in conversation to explain matters that two lines of ordinary prose would have accomplished far better; I must cut out my pages of talk and replace them with a few paragraphs of plain description and narrative" (*Letters*, 92). But 'Plain description' is not Lawrence's style. Lawrence's forte is the richness of dialogue and presentation of dramatic scenes. Most characters do come out as life-like, but others like Frank Beardsall fall flat as we are only told what he was:

> He was a liar, without notion of honesty, and he had deceived my mother thoroughly. One after another she discovered his mean dishonesties and deceits, and her soul revolted from him, and because the illusion of him had broken into a thousand vulgar fragments. She turned away with scorn of a woman who finds her romance has been a trumpery tale. (40)

His mother "rejoiced bitterly" when he left her "for other pleasures" eighteen years ago, when Lettie was three and Cyril, the narrator five. In comparison, the character of the father Walter Morel in *Sons and Lovers*, whose behaviour parallels that of Frank, is revealed subtly in actual dramatic scenes powerfully charged with emotions, so that the reader can experience what is merely told in *The White Peacock*.

Other than Frank Beardsall, all other characters and in the novel are infused with the spirit of symbolic realism. Lawrence in *The White Peacock* presents scenes of death and funerals with a great deal of emotion and poignancy that resonate in the heart of the reader. Lawrence himself was satisfied with the "death scenes". He considered the death of the father a 'strong scene' and in response to Jennings criticism said that "the father scene is not ugly and superfluous" (92). Lawrence devotes a whole chapter "Father" to the death and funeral of Cyril and Lettie's father, Frank Beardsall. Cyril is "numbed" on reading the letter of his father and painfully tries to recall him but in vain (4). Lettie is not informed of this letter and is also kept in the dark about his and his mother's visit to where his father was. Frank is dead by the time Cyril and his mother reach him. Cyril touchingly describes his and his mother's feelings when they first see his father's corpse in the dim light of two tapers:

> She turned back the hem and began to make painful wailing sounds. My heart was beating heavily, and I felt choked. I did not want to look—but I must. It was the man I had seen in the woods—with the puffiness gone

> from his face. I felt the great empty space. I felt beyond myself as if I were a mere fleck drifting unconsciously through the dark. Then I felt my mother's arm round my shoulders, and she cried pitifully, "Oh, my son, my son!"
>
> I shivered, and came back to myself. There were no tears in my mother's face, only a great pleading. "Never mind, mother—never mind," I said incoherently. (45)

Confrontation with death is not only an extremely painful experience for Cyril but also an experience the truth of which he tries to deny: "Outside, in the fresh air of the fading afternoon, I could not believe it was true. It was not true, that sad, colorless face with grey beard, wavering in the yellow candle-light. It was a lie, that wooden bedstead, that deaf woman, they were fading phrases of the untruth" (49). Nature and its beauty offer escape, it also offers assurance and warmth: "That yellow blaze of little sunflowers was true, and the shadow from the sun-dial on the warm old almshouses—that was real. The heavy afternoon sunlight came around us warm and reviving; we shivered, and the untruth went out of our veins, and we were no longer chilled" (49).

Perception of death casts its shadows and changes human relations and human behaviour. Cyril is given the hard task of giving Lettie the news about the death of her father, and he conveys the news to her a week later. Although Cyril and Lettie have never known their father yet "The death of the man who was our father changed our lives. It was not that we suffered a great grief; the chief trouble was the unanswered crying of failure. But we were changed in our feelings and in our relations; there was a new consciousness, a new carefulness" (53). Lettie who always "seemed to hear the water laughing, and the leaves tittering and giggling like young girls:...now...began to notice the cruel pitiful crying of a hedgehog caught in a gin...the traps for the fierce little murderers, traps walled in with a small fence of fir, and baited with the guts of a killed rabbit" (53).

Later in the novel, the detailed description of the death of Annable is described movingly. The devastating impact of the death of Annable on his son Sam is described with great realism and feeling. Sam's agony and behavior on discovering that his father is dead is powerfully described through a focus on Sam's actions and emotions. Sam frantically pulls away the stones under which his father is buried and then puts "his face against his father's" and "sniffs" around him like a dog, "to feel the life in him". He then tries "to close the lips which were drawn with pain and death, leaving the teeth bare; then his fingers hovered round the eyes, which were wide open, glazed," in a trembling attempt "to touch them into life" followed by his cry of "Feyther! Feyther!" (173). The heart-breaking moment comes when Sam lifts "a corner of the handkerchief to peep and see if his father's eyes are closed in sleep" only to find "his father's face...unchanged in its horror, when the covering is removed" (173) and the look of pain, agony and despair in his eyes makes an unforgettable impression on Cyril. The description reminds the reader of the scene of Cyril and his mother sighting the corpse of Frank Beardsall.

The realism and the horror of death stun the reader. A similar uncompromising realism in characterization and delineation of the man-man and man-woman relationships in the novel prevails; be it the flirtatious Lettie, the slighted lover George, or the rich coal mine owner, Leslie. The focus is on the relationships and marriages of the protagonists. The marriages lead to frustration and degradations. Many critics see these as mismatched marriages based on erroneous choices. The view that the novel is about wrong choices that lead to tragic consequences may be questioned. The implication here is that marriage between George and Lettie would have been more successful than that between Lettie and Leslie. The novel does not state that both men and women are critically analysed by the narrator Cyril. He is able to make us see sympathetically the point of view of men as well as women characters. Cyril understands Lettie's point of view and presents it lucidly, although he is a little critical of her for not giving into her passionate sexual side. At the same time, he does not present either George or Lettie as the best choices for her. Rather, it is more a question of choices available, especially for Lettie and the first title *Laetitia* of the novel titled after Lettie points to that. The main story is of Lettie who must choose between two men who belong to different social classes but are similar in their attitude towards women. Both have a certain vision of woman which Lettie is expected to live up to. Neither George nor Leslie ever for a moment think that Lettie might have her own desires. Lettie experiences passion but tries not to acknowledge it because it comes from a man whom she does not respect and who fails to understand her. Sproles comments that "Lettie never frees herself from the conflict between what she wants and what she is told to be" (237). In fact, Lettie is very much aware of the rights of women as after her father's death she becomes very restless and contemplative and "she, who had always been so rippling in thoughtless life, sat down in the window sill to think, and her strong teeth bit at her handkerchief till it was torn in holes" and "read all things that dealt with modern women" (86). Yes, the conflict is there but she has no alternatives present to which she can turn. Cyril presents Leslie as an attractive young man and is not too critical of him. Nowhere is it implied that Lettie's marriage to George would have been better, rather as Sproles says it was "doomed" (251). In the end George is "Like a tree that is failing, going soft and pale and rotten, clammy with small fungi" (359). Cyril in fact presents Lettie's dilemma empathetically. It might be for this reason that Lawrence had to bring in Annable to present an opposing view of women—women who totally reject passion and are 'souly'.

Jeffery Myers in *Painting and the Novel* states that "while writing *The White Peacock* Lawrence trained himself as an artist by copying pictures of the Pre-Raphaelites and their followers" (46). Throughout *The White Peacock* we find references to many painters, especially the Pre-Raphaelities. In the chapter "A Vendor of Visions", Lettie brings some pictures for George to see, and when Cyril goes to leave Alice, George and Lettie continue watching them. George, we are told, is "a romanticist" as he likes Anthony Fielding (1787-1855), George Cattermole (1800-68), and Myles Birket Foster (1825-99); however, he sees "nothing whatsoever" in Thomas Girtin (1775-1802) or David

Cox (1783-1859). George and Lettie have an argument over the water color painting Hoeing by George Clausen (1852-1944). George Clausen, influenced by Naturalism painted landscapes and scenes of peasant of life. The painting they are viewing shows men and women working together on a farmhoeing turnips. Lettie likes the painting because she feels that Clausen is "a real realist" who makes "common things beautiful" and "sees the mystery and magnificence that envelopes us even when we work menially" (34). She even imagines herself hoeing in the fields beside George at sunset, but the very idea is shocking to George's romantic imagination. Lettie bemoans his inability to appreciate things, saying: "You are blind; you are only half-born; you are gross with good living and heavy sleeping. You are a piano which will *only* play a dozen common notes. Sunset is nothing to you—it merely happens anywhere" (35). George fails to understand her, and looks confused. She thinks she has been too harsh and comforts him. This love-hate-love-attitude of Lettie towards George continues through the novel. George is unable to appreciate the realistic painting by Clausen but Maurice Greiffenhagen's *An Idyll* fascinates him. Lawrence himself was fascinated with Greiffenhagen's 1891 painting *An Idyll.* It was as if the painting had cast a spell on him. He copied it several times and gifted copies to friends. Regarding its influence on him, he wrote; "As for Greiffenhagen's 'Idyll', it moves me almost as if I were in love myself. Under its intoxication, I have flirted madly this Christmas" (*Letters,* More, 44). Grieffenhagen's brightly colored painting shows a young couple in embrace, surrounded by red puppies and daisies on a pastoral landscape at sunset. The bare-chested man is dressed in leather skin garments, while the woman wears a purple robe. The man is dark-skinned with a weather-beaten face while the woman is white and pale. The man is kissing the woman passionately, but the woman appears to go limp in his arms, giving into him passively. Remarking on the passive figure of the woman in the strong man's muscular embrace, Lawrence remarked, "By the way, in love or at least in love-making, do you think the woman is always passive, like the girl in the 'Idyll'?" (*Letters*, 103). In fact, this painting served as an inspiration for the novel and Lawrence through the reaction of Lettie and George to the *Idyll* defines the Lettie-George relationship. The picture arouses George, as it did Lawrence himself, and he visualizes Lettie as the passive woman and himself as the strong muscular man. Though Lettie remembers her own enthusiasm about the picture, when she first saw it, she does not acknowledge it before George and asks him: "What of it?" He responds with glowing eyes by saying: "Would it be fine?".... "That—a girl like that—half afraid—and passion!" Lettie disagrees: "She may well be half afraid, when the barbarian comes out in his glory, skins and all" (35-36). However, George, all lost in his own approach to the painting fails to understand her desire not to be the passive, half-afraid, woman, and can only uncomprehendingly say: "'But don't you like it?'" She dismisses his question with a shrug of her shoulders, saying: "Make love to the next girl you meet, and by the time the poppies redden the fields, she'll hang in your arms. She'll have need to be more than half afraid, won't she?" George still unable to fathom reasons for Lettie's objections can only utter half-broken sentences in protest. Lettie "in a mock-caressing voice" calls him "Precious Sir Galahad" and tauntingly says that he "he ought to have been a monk—a martyr, a Carthusian" (36) but her taunts and remonstrations have no effect on George. He only laughs, "taking no notice" and smilingly looks with glowing eyes at Lettie and "breathlessly quivering under the new sensation of heavy, unappeased fire in his breast, and in the muscles of his arms. He glances at her bosom and shivers" (36). Lettie is afraid to acknowledge the passion and attempts to dampen his spirits by analysing the picture and putting off George who right from the beginning has been speaking in half-broken incomplete sentences, and can only utter "No-but". Lettie tries to continue the "make-belief conversation" but fails as George looks at her with a "declaration that made her shrink back as if flame had leaped towards her face" (36). She tries to deny her innermost responses and refuses to give into the moment by acknowledging her own passion.

> They gazed at each other for moment before they hid their faces again. It was a torture to each of them to look thus nakedly at the other, a dazzled, shrinking

> pain that they forced themselves to undergo for a moment, that they might the moment after tremble with a fierce sensation that filled their veins with fluid, fiery electricity. She sought almost in panic, for something to say.... Their eyes met in the briefest flash of a glance, then both turned their faces aside. Thus averted, one from the other, they made talk. (37)

Gathering the books Lettie prepares to leave but looks back "to steal another keen moment", and once again "they feel the blood beating madly in their necks. Then, suddenly breaking into a slight trembling, Lettie turns around and leaves the room" (37). When she returns, she talks to herself wildly in French; "She laughed at him, and at herself, and at men in general, and at love in particular" (37).

Lettie, unsure of herself and her feelings, tries to dismiss the wild passion she has experienced by analyzing it rationally and dismissing it as a kind of madness, necessary to keep them feeling youthful. This confused attitude of Lettie towards her lovers persists throughout the novel, because she is satisfied with neither of them. She continually vacillates between kindness and cruelty towards her lovers Leslie and George. George fails to understand her wild talk, and seeing his perplexity she feels an "insurgent kindness" towards him and involuntarily presses his fingers and holds them for a while, while wishing him good bye, but she is again ashamed at her own display of feeling and afraid to acknowledge it, resorts to mundane talk as a means of escape. She attempts to withhold her sensuous impulses. The incident reveals two aspects of Lettie's personality: one, her desire to be unlike the passive woman in the painting and the second, her refusal to acknowledge and respond to her sexual desires and impulses which she dismisses as moments of madness. The incident also reveals her sympathetic nature and desire to make up when she sees someone hurt. She ultimately chooses to marry Leslie, the bourgeois coal magnate, over the rustic, less educated farmer, George. In fact, Lettie is forced into an engagement through an appeal to her sympathy for the injured Leslie. Lettie has limited choice: George and Leslie though from different cultural backgrounds, are not much different in their attitude towards women; both praise her beauty but do not acknowledge her feelings and desires. In an incident, almost a replica of the one that takes place with George. Leslie kisses Lettie without her consent and as a matter of right. Leslie touched by the "appealing, half-pitiful girlishness" of Lettie as she sleeps with her head resting against the window with the sunshine falling on her innocent face, kisses her. Awakened from her sleep by "'Leslie!—oh!—Let me go!... You are mean!'" (54). Leslie cannot understand her resentment and feels justified in his action as he just couldn't help kissing her as she was looking pretty like the sleeping beauty. Lettie, however, "'frowning with irritation'" continues to protest "'It is not nice!'" but Leslie still unable to understand questions her, "'Why shouldn't I kiss you?'" and Lettie literally has to spell out the reason in black and white: "'Because it is a question of me, not of you alone'" (54). Leslie always wants Lettie to do things his way and is often angry when Lettie refuses to bow to his demands. She mocks and defies him when he is overbearing, but it only angers him and he never attempts to understand her point of view. Lettie's dissatisfaction with the position of women and women themselves is better understood in her analysis and comments on the painting *Hope* by George Frederick Watts (1807-1904). In the chapter "Lettie comes of age" Leslie proposes to Lettie by presenting her with a Sapphire and Diamond ring. In the conversation that follows the blue in the sapphires is associated with hope through a reference to Speranza in the *Faerie Queen* as there she is described dressed in blue[2] and accompanied by Faith, dressed in white. An extremely popular painting of the time, it depicts a suffering 'Hope' sitting bent and blindfolded on an orange globe playing desperately on a lyre which has only one string left and struggling to listen to the music, if any, with all her strength. Watts depiction was radically different from the traditional representations of 'Hope' as a religious virtue, holding either a flower or an anchor, and it is interesting that Lettie superimposes her own ideas of womanhood on the painting through her analysis of the painting. To her it represents women in general. She wonders why the woman did not drop her "silly harp with no string…over the edge of the globe, and take the handkerchief off her eyes" to take a look around and then answers the question herself saying that it was foolish to expect that, as she is not only "a woman" but "a man's woman". Her views reflect the restrictions within which women willingly live: "Do you know I believe most women can sneak a look down their noses from underneath the handkerchief of hope they've tied over their eyes. They could take the whole muffler off—but they don't do it, the dears." Her tone is indulgent towards women who blindly live on "hope". She herself seems to be in that situation. In the same scene, when Leslie tells her to wear the ring as it would hold her "faster than that fair damsel tried to a tree in Millais' picture" (122-23), she jokingly refers to Sir John Everett Millais's (1829-96) *The Knight Errant*, depicting a distressed nude maiden, stripped and tied to a tree, being rescued by a knight, clad in armor, who to preserve her modesty is cutting the string "discreetly from behind". While George, the Romanticist, thinks of himself in the role of a Sir Ghalad, Leslie says he is not the "souly sort" and can't stand Pre-Raphaelites referring to Millais painting. For him Lettie is the "Atlanta" he had won. He rejects her teasing proposal to be like two soul-lovers as in Rossetti's *The Blessed Damsel.* For him she is not a "Burne-Joneses" but an "Albert Moore" as "there more in the warm touch of a soft body than in a prayer" and he will "pray with kisses" (98). Emily K. Dalgarno states that "Leslie should be reminded by Moore's work of the warmth and softness of the body speaks of the insularity of his understanding of Lettie" because according to her the "self-reflective gaze of the woman in the painting...rebuff's the viewer's presence" and that the painting is a "a statement about female narcissism which suggests that a woman's intense contemplation of self makes her as remote from the viewer in time and space as a Greek statue" (8).

Both George and Leslie are alike as neither is wiling to understand Lettie's point of view. Cyril, the first-person omniscient narrator, presents both George and Leslie impartially. He presents Leslie as an attractive young man, full of pride in his wealth. George too has moments of attractiveness and appeal but his actions of cruelty are disturbing. The complex nature of the relationships in the novel makes it difficult to come to any conclusion about whom to blame for the failed marriages. "Lettie resists the sensuous aspect of George, or the sensuous aspect of her attraction to him, choosing to privilege her social rather than her sexual self" does not reveal the whole truth (Becket, 284). Virginia Woolf's character Clarissa in *Mrs. Dalloway* (1925) like Lettie, chooses status and economic stability over passion and insecurity. Both Lettie and Clarissa find something lacking in their passionate lovers; an element of unrealistic romanticism, which makes them fear the thought of marriage with them. Hence Lettie rejects George and Clarissa Peter Walsh. In choosing their partners both Lettie and Clarissa do lose some part of themselves and their marriage does hamper their self-development as Clarissa is reduced to Mrs. Richard Dalloway and Lettie to Leslie Tempest, but that marriages of passion would have worked out better is debatable.

Lawrence in *The White Peacock* exhibits an ambivalent emotional attitude towards women; mother and women are viewed as both nurturing and devouring. Cyril, the omniscient narrator, and a character in the novel, represents Lawrence himself. The association of Cyril with his mother becomes clearer as Cyril's surname is Beardsall, after Lydia Beardsall, the family name of Lawrence's mother. Lawrence was extremely close to his mother. He understood and sympathized with her for the suffering that she had to undergo at the hands of an alcoholic husband, but also felt that because of her dominance and control over him, he could not form healthy relationships and desired to free himself from this bondage, a theme he elaborated on in *Sons and Lovers*. The misogynistic view is presented through Annable. One day, while in search of Annable, Cyril perches on the "neck of an old bowed angel" (166). The second time the peacock cries, it lifts its crested head, opens it feathers to show "the full wealth of its tail glimmering like a stream of colored stars over the sunken face of the angel," Annable calls it "The proud fool! Perched on an angel as if it were the pedestal of vanity" and compares it to the soul of a woman: "That's the very soul of a lady" he said, "the very, very soul. Damn the thing, to perch on that old angel. I should like to wring its neck" (167) and when the peacock flies away after he throws pieces of sod at it, his anger doesn't subside and he disgustingly remarks "'Just look!'...'the miserable brute has dirtied that angel. A woman to the end, I tell you, all vanity and screech and defilement'" (167). These statements followed by the narration of his life story, Cyril brings out of reasons for his hatred for women. He talks of his initial infatuation and love for Lady Chrystabel, the 'cultured' woman he married and how he was deceived by her and her belief in an idealized world of romances and idealized Greek statues Croton and Hercules. The marriage turned sour after her refusal to have children. She rejected his pride of body and his remonstrations amazed her. She thought of herself as the distressed maiden of *Lady of Shallot* presented in Waterhouse's paintings (169). In a way, it was the end for him. This happened when he was twenty-six, yet while narrating his story he discovers that the wounds are raw even in middle age. Cyril, on learning that his lady love is dead, calls her Annable's 'poor peacock' and Annable pondering over his remark acknowledges that "'she was fair enough'". Annable's story again reveals the complexity of relationships where the full blame for a failed relationship cannot be placed completely on one person—man or woman. While Lawrence shows stress in the man-woman relationship, the scenes depicting male bonding are shown as perfect. It is in this context that two figures emerge in the novel highlighting the attraction of the male body. The special bonding created by the flesh between men is established in a special bonding that exists between Cyril and Annable and between Cyril and George. Annable and Cyril share a bond of sympathetic understanding where they can communicate emotion through tough: "It was this power to communicate his unhappiness that made me somewhat dear to him...he liked to put his hand on my shoulder or my knee as we talked; yet withal, he asked me questions, and saved his thoughts to tell me, and believed in my knowledge like any acolyte" (165). While narrating his story, Annable talks proudly of his good physique and pride of body. He asks Cyril to feel his muscle and Cyril holds out his hand to him in sympathy and Annable grips it, cleaves to it for a moment, and then leaves. Like Annable, George too is well proportioned, heavily limbed and of handsome physique and is conscious and proud of it. Cyril himself establishes a connection between the two as he watches George drying himself in the sun. Seeing him polish his arm he "watched the deep muscles of his shoulders, and the bands stand out in his neck as he held it firm; I remembered the story of Annable" (249). When George presses him against himself Cyril says:

> the sweetness of the touch of our naked bodies one against the other was superb. It satisfied in some measure the vague, indecipherable yearning of my soul; and it was the same with him. When he had rubbed me all warm, he let me go, and we looked at each other with eyes of still laughter, and our love was perfect for a moment, more perfect than any love I have known since, either for man or woman. (223)

This epiphanic moment between George and Cyril can be understood in various ways. Firstly, it is a perfect scene of male bonding where there is love but no fear which prevails in man-woman relationships. There is lack of conflict and the two complement each other. The parallel of this kind of bonding between the same sex individuals is replicated by Virginia Woolf in *Mrs. Dalloway* (1925). She creates a perfect scene of female bonding between Sally Seton and Clarissa. For Lawrence, opposites attract. Cyril is attracted to George because George is all that he himself is not. He is thin and has a slender frame like figures in Beardsley, as George remarks. Clarissa too is charmed by Sally because she is exactly the opposite of Clarissa; "Sally was everything that she wasn't; she was openminded, rebellious, and uninhibited". In her recklessness she "did the most idiotic things out of bravado; bicycle round the parapet on the terrace; smoked cigar. Absurd, she was—very absurd" (32). Clarissa nostalgically recalls with great happiness, the perfect moment of physical intimacy with Sally Seton when Sally, after picking a flower, had "kissed her on the lips". With the kiss it appeared to her that the "whole world may have turned upside down! The others disappeared; there she was alone with Sally". She feels as if "she had been given a present, wrapped up, and told just to keep it, not to look at it—a diamond, something infinitely precious, wrapped up, which, as they walked (up and down, up, and down), she uncovered, or the radiance brunt through, the revelation, the religious feeling!" (33). Clarissa, like Cyril, considers this kiss as the "most exquisite moment of her whole life", as it is an ecstatic religious feeling which she never experienced again. The epiphanic revelation gives her a memory she cherished for life and gains strength from by reviving and reliving it. However, her explanation and analysis of the emotions that she experienced are extremely significant as they explain the reason behind female perfect bonding, and explanation that helps us understand same sex bonding, be it male or female:

> The strange thing, on looking back, was the purity, the integrity, of her feeling for Sally. It was not like one's feeling for a man. It was completely disinterested, and besides, it had a quality which could only exist between women, between women just grown up. It was protective, on her side; sprang from a sense of being in league together a presentiment of something that was bound to part them. (32)

The White Peacock questions men's dependence on women for their happiness and their inability to create a balance and nurture themselves after failure in love. The conflicted images of women as nurturers and devourers also questions the legitimacy of men who depend totally on them for their happiness. Be it Annable or George, unhappiness in love turns them into monstrous men, the women on the other hand can create balance. Lettie, despite not having found the man who would be perfect for her, still manages to create a balance in her life and is not broken like George. The dependence of men on women for their happiness gives women a certain kind of power over them. The men play on their sympathy for understanding and support. Sensitive as women are they are quick to observe feelings and unable to see man hurt, try to console them with a nurturing instinct. Men on the other hand are blind to the feelings of the women. Cyril's mother harbors the guilt of having separated the father from the children and bemoans the fact that the children never had a father, although he abused and ill-treated her. She also pities him his fate and has a soft corner for him. The nurturing role of women and the satisfaction derived by them in this role is highlighted. In the end, Emily takes on the nurturing role for her brother George. Cyril observes that after her marriage Lettie looks a little older in a black dress at the mourning of one of Leslie's maternal aunts but "otherwise there seemed to be no change in her. A subtle observer might have noticed a little hardness about her mouth, and disillusion hanging slightly on her eyes" but she was in full control, overflowing "with clever speeches and rapid, brilliant observations" (313).

Lawrence, in this novel, on the one hand, presents Lettie as a victim, as her aspirations remain unfulfilled, but later he seems to be changing his perspective, presenting Lettie as a woman conscious of her beauty and aware of her power over men which she uses to her advantage. In the chapter "Puffs of Wind in the Sail" in part III of the novel, we see a changed Lettie in complete control of herself: "She had developed strangely in six months. She seemed to have discovered the wonderful charm of her womanhood" (282). One evening in Nethermere, after having dined with the Tempests and walking on the frost-bound road in the moonlight, we see Lettie flirting with George and Leslie bending down to tie Lettie's shoe laces and later at home taking off her shoes, and pressing her tired feet. This awareness of the charm of her womanhood is described by Lawrence with reference to Aurbrey Beardsley's painting for Oscar Wilde's *Salome*. Beardsley's painting breaks not only the Victorian ideas of sexuality but also cross the boundaries of fixed gender attributes. The paintings show the moon, peacock feathers, nude androgynous figures, phallic symbols, and Salome as a powerful woman who badly expresses her sexual desires, and uses her alluring seductive beauty to fulfil her desires and take revenge. Lettie is associated with Salome through references to peacock feathers, the moon, and the dance:

> Lettie dropped her draperies and rusted into the drawing-room. There the lamp was low-lit, shedding a yellow twilight from the window space. Lettie stood between the firelight and the dusky lamp glow, tall and

> warm between the lights. As she turned laughing to the two men, she let her cloak slide over her white shoulder and fall with silk splendour of a peacock's gorgeous blue over the arm of the large settee. There she stood, with her white hand upon the peacock of her cloak, where it tumbled against her dull orange dress. She knew her own splendour, and she drew up her throat laughing and brilliant with triumph. The she raised bother her head and remained for a moment delicately touching her hair into order, still fronting the two men. Then with a final little laugh she moved slowly and turned up the lamp, dispelling some of the witchcraft from the room.... As she leaned forward with her arm outstretched to the lamp, as she delicately adjusted the wicks with mysterious fingers, she seemed to be moving in some alluring figure of a dance, her hair like a nimbus clouding the light, her bosom lit with wonder. The soft outstretching of her hand was like the whispering of strange words into the blood, and as she fingered a book the heart watched silently for the meaning. (282)

The image of the peacock operates as a symbol with infinite possibilities of meaning. The peacock though a male bird has the qualities of beauty and power of attraction traditionally associated with the female. Unlike in many other species, there is no male show of strength or duel fought to win the female prize rather the right to choose the male rests with the peahen. So the peacock operates as a symbol of androgyny with a confusion of gender roles. Tradition of course associates the peacock with sin of pride. Is the description of Lettie's mesmerizing beauty, her self-admiring conscious gaze, and her seductive charm indicative of gender role reversals? Is Lettie now conscious of her own power and using it to her advantage like Salome? This enigma is difficult to resolve as there are no dogmatic answer in Lawrence: "Doubt and enquiry are far more typical of Lawrence's fiction than dogmatism" (Niven, *Intro*, 6). The reader has to be satisfied with a narrative where certain areas are clearer than the others and one can only wonder about what lies beyond.

Notes

1. D.H. Lawrence, *The White Peacock,* ed. David Bradshaw (Oxford: OUP, 1997). All references are to this edition and will henceforth be given in the text.
2. Her younger sister, that Speranza hight,
   Was clad in blue, that her beseemed well;
   Not all so cheerful seemed she of Sight,
   As was her Sister: whether Dread did dwell,
   Or Anguish in her Heart, is hard to tell.
   Upon her Arm a silver Anchor lay,
   Whereon she leaned ever, as befell;
   And ever up to Heav'n, as she did pray,
   Her stedfast Eyes were ne, and swerved other way.

   Faerie Queene, Book I, Canto X.

Works Cited

Atkins, A.R. "A Bibliographical Analysis of the Manuscript of D.H. Lawrence's *'The White Peacock'*", *Studies Bibliographical* 44 (1991), JSTOR.

Becket, Fiona. *The Complete Critical Guide to D.H. Lawrence.* Routledge: London, 2002.

Chambers, Jessie. *D.H. Lawrence: A Personal Record.* Cambridge University Press, 1980.

———. "D.H. Lawrence: Social ideology in Visual Art." *Mosaic: A Journal for the Interdisciplinary Study of Literature*, 22.3 (1989), JSTOR.

Lawrence, D.H. *The White Peacock.* ed. Andrew Robertson. Oxford University Press, 1983.

———. *The Letters of D.H. Lawrence,* Vol. 1 (September 1901-May 1913), ed. James T. Boulton, Cambridge University Press, 1979.

———. *The White Peacock.* ed. David Bradshaw, Oxford University Press, 1997.

———. *Phoenix: The Posthumous Papers of D.H. Lawrence.* Delphi Classics, 2017.

Meyers, Jeffery. *Painting and the Novel.* Manchester University Press, 1975.

Niven, Alastair. *D.H. Lawrence: The Novelist.* Cambridge University Press, 1978.

Savage, Henry. *Academy* (18 March 1911), LXXX, 328, 42-43, included in *D.H. Lawrence: The Critical Heritage*. Ed. R.P. Draper. London: Routledge, 1997.

Sproles, Karyn Z. "Shooting 'The White Peacock': Victorian Art and Feminine Sexuality in D.H. Lawrence's First Novel." *Criticism* 4.2 (1992): 237-59. JSTOR.

Woolf, Virginia. *Mrs Dalloway*. London: Granada Publishing, 1978.

Worthen, John. *D.H. Lawrence: The Early Years 1885-1912. The Cambridge Biography of D.H. Lawrence*. Cambridge University Press, 1991.

Yeats, W.B. *Essays and Introductions*. London: Macmillan, 1961.

2

Man, Nature and Motions of the Spirit: Symbolic Scenes in *Sons and Lovers*

Bibhu Padhi

In several essays, Lawrence shows his deep faith in the continuous interdependence of man and what he calls the "cosmos." He firmly states that a "perfected relation between man and his circumambient universe is life itself," and that the business of art is to reveal this relation "at the living moment" (*Phoenix*, 175-76). His own fictional technique unobtrusively unites motions of the spirit with the natural environment in a symbolic-ritualistic relationship. Scenes and episodes that bring man and nature intimately close to each other remain a prominent functional feature of Lawrence's fictional mode. In these scenes Lawrence does not merely provide evocative nature imagery (although such imagery is an essential feature of most of these scenes); he is concerned with larger conceptual issues. In this essay I shall discuss, with reference to *Sons and Lovers*, the symbolic nature and narrative significance of these scene and their relevance to problems of communication and expression.

Several scenes and episodes seem to be especially pertinent for such an inquiry: Mrs. Morel's night outside, after she is thrown out of the house by her husband; Paul and Miriam's long walk through the scent of ivory roses; Paul and Miriam, and later, Paul and Clara, seen against the infinite and impersonal landscape of the sea at Theddlethorpe; Paul, Miriam, and Clara's walk through the cowslips and bluebells; Paul's scattering of the flowers over Clara's face and his regathering of these as though from a sacred spot; the gathering of cherries by Paul and Edgar as Miriam watches the slow fading of the day's last lights; Paul's final decision during his walk in the garden to leave Miriam; Paul and Clara's walk along the vivacious Trent; the love-making of Paul and Clara among "the cry of the peewit, the wheel of the stars;" the long episode of Mrs. Morel's death.

In each of these scenes and episodes Lawrence delicately portrays the closeness of the human-personal and the natural-impersonal. As Mark Spilka pointed out several years ago, there is something ritualistic about these scenes and episodes, for "just as the essence of religious ritual is communion, so Lawrence saw all deeply significant contacts between human beings—or even between man and the living universe—as spontaneous forms of communion" (56). Lawrence's people participate in "ritualistic situations which fall within the larger flow of the novels. And so, as the novels move along, these figures rise up out of a raw marble base—still rooted in the vague unknown but nevertheless organic in themselves" (Spilka, 56). A balance is maintained between the hard actuality of the immediate situation and its remote and mysterious implications. It is during these moments that what appears to be a traditional realistic narrative seems to suggest a lot more than itself. The narrative flow pauses and begins to expand with meanings suggested by nature and natural things. A close examination of a few of these scenes shows several significant aspects of that conjunction of man and nature and the peculiar narrative force Lawrence achieves.

We know that Mrs. Morels nights outside are a result of the angry and drunken "displays" of her husband; however, by their repetition within the novel. They point not only to the domestic tension within which she is forced to live, but also to the loving generosity with which Nature seems to take care of her difficult moments. But at the same time it must not be forgotten that Nature also sends her back into the difficult but necessary condition of living with an impossible husband. During her first night outside, with the child Paul in her womb, Nature makes her realize that the child, whom she bears at this moment with as much intensity of passion as she bears everything *natural*, is also a result of her husband's love—however inconsistent or strange that love may have been—and therefore must be brought back to him. Her garden experience, apart from achieving other things for the narrator, helps suggest the lonely helplessness that haunts Walter Morel immediately after, or even during, his violet and noisy domestic demonstrations.

The desolation that Mrs. Morel experience in the "mysterious out-of-doors" is entirely different from (and probably much less cruel than) the fear of the "abstract"—of mysteries that visit the larger atmosphere of the night—which troubles her husband. Lawrence's indirect poetic technique carries home this crucial fact. The feeling of complete relaxation, of an almost total absorption of one's essential being into the impersonal and "open" beauty of the landscape that Mrs. Morel experience, refers back to the description of Walter Morel immediately before the garden episode, as well as forward to the description of him as he suffers his "peevish misery." It suggests the painful inarticulatenesses which the "indecent" and uneducated miner must endure:

> [Mrs. Morel] became aware of something about her.... The tall white lilies were reeling in the moonlight, and the air was charged with their perfume, as with a passion. Mrs. Morel gasped slightly in fear. She touched the big, pallid flowers on their petals, then shivered.... She bent down to look at the binful of yellow pollen; but it only appeared dusky. Then she drank a deep draught of the scent. It almost made her dizzy.
>
> Mrs. Morel leaned on the garden gate, looking out, and she lost herself awhile. She did not know what she thought. Except for a slight feeling of sickness, and her consciousness in the child, herself melted out like scent into shiny, pale air. After a time the child, too, melted with her in the mixing-pot of moonlight, and she rested with the hills and lilies and houses, all swum together in a kind of swoon.
>
> When she came to herself she was tired for sleep. Languidly she looked about here.... A few whiffs of the raw, strong scent of phlox invigorated her.... She

> touched the white ruffles of the roses. Their fresh scent and cool, soft leaves reminded her of the morning-time and sunshine. She was very fond of them. But she was tired, and wanted to sleep. In the mysterious out-of-doors she felt forlorn. (*SL*, 35)

The passage is not simply an example of Lawrence's lyrical prose. It has a mystical quality that would not have been there without a *human* presence. What we have here is not just a description of natural objects, but the evocation of the quality of an experience with Nature by a sensitive person with an instictive understanding of things. What at a different time would have been considered only a visual or olfactory response is now transformed into a medium of emotional identification and release.

Coming immediately after the angry demonstration of Walter Morel inside what *should* have been a peaceful domestic interior, the passage creates and ideal world of peace and fulfillment; it suggests a feeling of immensity commensurate with the infinite distances. The flowers and the moonlight have a quality of repose as well as of a slow but spontaneous "expansion." It is this quality which seems to seep into everything, including the child in the womb. As Lawrence explains later in the book, for Mrs. Morel "it was one of those still moments when small frets vanish, and the beauty of things stands out," and one has "the peace and strength to see [oneself]" (*SL*, 50). The unborn child, who is now in mystic communion with the moonlight and the night (even as he is within another "night"), is to become, in a later chapter, the infant Paul. He is offered to the "crimson, throbbing sun" by nervous Mrs. Morel in her desperate effort to explain to herself the justification for that infant's *being there*. Thus, every described object, retaining its substantiality, becomes also a quality. The various smells and sights move into one another in the "mixing-pot of moonlight"; "the hills and lilies and houses" swim together in "a kind of swoon"; the "tall white lilies...reeling in the moonlight" become a "perfume" and a "presence." For Mrs. Morel it is a moment of realization and illumination. She probably realizes, for the first time in her life, that the child she is carrying does not belong to the crampy interiors of which (so she thinks) her husband is the cause, but to a world of pure sensation in which every single sense-experience is invigorating—a revelation. She realizes that her having carried this child through all this fluent communion with the benevolent and tender aspect of nature, is also significant in that it makes both herself and her child partners in a ritual of new birth.

Lawrence repeats his performance in a slightly different context, when Paul and Clara make love. Nature remains, once again, a "presence through the entire sequence and is instrumental in making spontaneous communication possible":

> All the while the peewits were screaming in the field. When he came to, he wondered what was near his eyes, curving and strong with life in the dark, what voice it was speaking. Then he realized it was the grass, and the peewit was calling. The warmth was Clara's breathing heaving. He lifted his head, and looked into her eyes. They were dark and shinning and strange, life wild at the source staring into his life, stranger to him, yet meeting him; and he put his face down on her throat, afraid. What was she? A strong, strange wild life, that breathed with his in the darkness through this hour. It was all so much bigger than themselves that he was hushed. They had met, and included in their meeting the thrust of the manifold grass-stems, the cry of the peewit, the wheel of the stars. (*SL*, 430)

Lawrence achieves a similar effect when he uses the Theddlehorpe coast as a background for the Paul-Miriam friendship and later, for the Paul-Clara friendship. The contrast between the two episodes, however, is emphasized. Miriam's love for abstractions—her habit of sentimentalizing over commonplace events and everyday object—is contrasted with Clara's passionate enjoyment of the immediate moment. For Clara, every single moment is meant to be shared rather than stored away in some shadowy part of the mind in order to be brooded over, later. While Miriam lets herself be overwhelmed by the impersonality of the "great sweeping" landscape, Clara is strong enough—and willing enough—to take charge of the moment.

It is interesting to note how Lawrence's suggestive imagery handles the first moments of doubt in the long and hitherto safe-looking relationship between Paul and Miriam:

> Paul and Miriam walked in silence. Suddenly he started. The whole of his blood seemed to burst into flame, and he could scarcely breathe. An enormous orange moon was staring at them.... He stood still, looking at it.
>
> 'Ah!' cried Miriam, when she saw it.
>
> He remained perfectly still, staring at the immense and ruddy moon, the only thing in the far-reaching darkness of the level. His heart beat heavily, the muscles of his arms contracted.
>
> 'What is it?' murmured Miriam, waiting for him.
>
> He turned and looked at her. She stood beside him, for ever in shadow. Her face, covered with the darkness of her hat, was watching him unseen. But she was brooding. She was slightly afraid-deeply moved and religious. That was her best state. He was impotent against it. His blood was concentrated like a flame in his chest. But he could not get across to her. There were flashes in his blood. But somehow she ignored them. She was expecting some religious state in him.... The crisis was past.
>
> He did not know himself what was the matter. He was naturally so young, and their intimacy was so abstract, he did not know he wanted to crush her on to his breast to ease the ache there. He was afraid of her. The fact that he might want her as a man wants a woman had in him been suppressed into shame. When she shrank in her convulsed, coiled torture from the thought of such a thing, he had winced to the depths of his soul. And now this 'purity' prevented even their first love-kiss. It was as if she could scarcely stand the shock of physical love, even a passionate kiss, and then he was too shrinking and sensitive to give it. (*SL*, 220-21)

The "blackness" and the "stillness" of the landscape, mentioned in the passage, are significant. They not only suggest the state of a physical landscape, but also refer to the manner in which a character—cold to the point of seeming "religious"—reacts to it and forces another to react in a similar fashion. Miriam belongs to the "black and still" country and remains "for ever in shadow." She can respond to the "enormous orange moon" and to Paul's state of passion only by either ignoring them or asking a tame, "What is it?" Lawrence's mildly ironical insertions ("She was slightly afraid-deeply moved and religious. That was her best state."/ "She was curious about him. The crisis was past") are not only pointers to his own authorial sympathy for Paul's state of utter helplessness; they are also fairly conclusive comments on Miriam's limitations. In either case, however, Lawrence seems to refer to an inarticulateness, to the characters' inability to *show* and communicate their latent emotional states.

It is significant that Lawrence should have chosen the same natural background for the Paul-Clara episode. The differences, however, are obvious, and perhaps nowhere more so than in the metaphoric richness of the prose-something, we might even say, which the other relationship had never allowed Lawrence. If in the Paul-Miriam episodes, the theme is imprisonment and "suppression," here the themes are exposure and abundance. Both nature and the two human characters seem to be "filled strong with the sweeping relentlessness of life":

> A flush came into the sky, the wan moon, half-way down the west, sank into significance. On the shadowy land things began to take life.... The long waster of foreshore lay moaning under the dawn and the sea; the ocean was a flat dark strip with a white edge. Over the gloomy sea the sky was red. Quickly the fire spread among the clouds and scattered them. Crimson burned to orange, orange to dull gold, and in a golden glitter the sun came up, cribbling fierily over the waves in little splashes, as if someone had gone along and the light had spilled form her pail as she walked.
>
> The breakers ran down the shore in long, hoarse strokes. Tiny seagulls, likes specks of spray, wheeled above the line of surf. Their crying seemed larger than

> they. Far away the coast reached out, and melted into the morning, the tussocky sandhills seeming to sink to a level with the beach.... They had alone the space of all this level shore, the sea, and the upcoming sun, the faint noise of the waters, the sharp crying of the gulls. (*SL*, 433-34)

The entire landscape seems to be supernaturally alive, as though every natural thing was full of anxious, nervous activity. And although the ocean still remains "a flat dark strip" as in the earlier episode, value is not being located elsewhere—at those places where bright colors, like emotional moods, follow each other in a spontaneous, uninhibited fashion. Lawrence underscores the gay openness of the Paul-Clara relationship elsewhere in the passage. For instance, we are shown how the lovers move from the initial "cold" into the reassuring warmth of plain physical relationship, the intermediate movement having been suggested through words like "raced," "run," "quick," and "rush." In the same way, the "flush" that appears in the sky passes through several transitional colors-red, crimson, orange, dull gold—before the sun comes up in a "golden giltter." With the variety of moods and the elation of the spirit which Paul and Clara experience now (one may contrast this with the cold and abstract monotony suggested in the earlier beach episode involving Paul and Miriam) go the tiny but sharp-crying seagulls, the "faint noise of the waters." Everything seems to be filled with a mysterious activity. Physical and emotional landscapes overlap and influence each other and supplement each other's quality and intensity, even as the lovers wholeheartedly expose themselves to the beauty and grandeur of the moment. Every little object—both organic and inorganic—seems enjoy to a "common" life, a fact which Lawrence's prose clearly celebrates.

Elsewhere in the novel, important decisions are taken in a more symbolic mode. Paul's decision finally to leave Miriam, for instance, "is confirmed in an epiphanic moment of intense symbolism" (Fowler, 119). It comes at the end of a long and tortuous process of irresolution and conflict (during which Paul's language is uniformly evasive and restless), and it *stands for* his final realization of the nature of the destruction that

that process has caused in him. The "scent madonna lilies" that comes "stealthily" into his room is—as it was several chapters earlier—a "presence." But the "deep draught of the scent" which had made Mrs. Morel "dizzy" with passion, has now turned into an active instrument of perception and is bringing Paul to the verge of a difficult knowledge. To Mrs. Morel, the scent was basis of a permanent relation with Nature, with Paul as the product of that relationship; to Paul, it is the basis of his realization that he has a right to end a relationship that has been at best only haltingly meaningful.

The flowers, apparently innocent on their stalks, raise questions and answer doubts. There is a certain quality of luxuriance in the language in which Lawrence describes them; but they also make one conscious of an absence of activity. Flowers can be brutal, and Miriam stands at the other end of their free, luxuriant growth and, therefore, stands single and alone, vulnerable to every attack:

> Through the open door, stealthily, came the scent of madonna lilies, almost as if it were prowling abroad. Suddenly he got up and went out of doors.
>
> The beauty of the night made him want to shout. A half-moon dusky gold, was sinking.... Nearer, a dim white fence of lilies went across the garden, and the air all round seemed to stir with scent, as if it were alive. He went across the bed of pinks, whose keen perfume came sharply across the rocking, heavy scent of the lilies, and stood alongside the white barrier of flowers. They flagged all loose, as if they were painting. The scent made him drunk....
>
> A corncrake in the hay-close called insistently. The moon slid quite downwards, growing more flushed. Behind him the great flowers leaned as if they were calling. And then, like a shock, he caught another perfune, something raw coarse. Hunting round, he found the purple iris, touched their fleshy throats and their dark, grasping hand. At any rate, he had found something. They stood stiff in the darkness. Their scent was brutal.

> The moon was melting down upon the crest of the hill. It was gone; all was dark. The corncrake called still.
>
> Breaking off a pink, he suddenly went indoors.
>
> 'Come, my boy,' said his mother. 'I'm sure it's time you went to bed.'
>
> He stood with the pink against his lips.
>
> 'I shall break off with Miriam, mother,' he answered calmly. (*SL*, 358-59)

As Roger Fowler points out, although Paul is experiencing the scent of the flowers, he "does not respond to the surface of the situation"; the "brutal eroticism of the metaphors makes it clear that Paul is interpreting the flowers as symbols of his own sexual predicament—his simultaneous desire and revulsion." He also refers to Paul's "ability to symbolize," to appropriate "features of an immediate situation to stand for his feelings about himself and other people"—something which allows him to "objectify his problem, to realize what they are and treat them with relative detachment" (Fowler, 119-20). The flowers, apart from other functions (for instance, as agents of consolation and means of release during periods of emotional crisis), also offer Paul (and Lawrence the artist) an opportunity to appreciate the nature of his doubts. The passage echoes the use of flowers earlier in the story, when Paul throws the cowslips over Clara's hair and neck, and then gathers them up again. His act makes him understand the nature of the mysterious "sharp pang" that Clara's neck gives him; and thus, a subtle mode of communication is established between the lovers. But even while the little cowslips bring Paul and Clara closer to each other, they put Miriam at a distance. The pinks that Paul takes off their stalks some fifty pages later only confirm his "rejection" of her.

All these are spontaneous acts—"episodes of everyday life that...tell their own story." But there is something larger about them. During these acts, "narrative is transcended...without damage to the relation of acts and persons." For instance, the episode of Mrs. Morel's night outside is "so intensely realised... that the mind is satisfied without further interpretation, though interpretation, if offered, will be absorbed" (Kermode, 17). Even the long and painful episode of Mrs. Morels' slow death seems to rise out of the narrative to become a symbolic enactment of Paul's disturbed consciousness. But it also records the slow disintegration of a family. Thus, it enacts a dual disintegration—that of a personal consciousness as well as of a domestic and familial consciousness.

The prose throughout the episode shows a cruel, unfailing attention to detail; it weighs heavily upon the reader's mind. But, at the same time, it is an extremely subdued prose that is without any sign of excitement or passion—a prose that smacks too much of the here-and-now. Nowhere do we encounter a reference to anything other than the terrible fascination that death can have for the sensitive inmates of a dying house. And yet, there seems to be something that does not belong to the immediate situation, something rather too familiar and too real to have a simple effect. What is evoked is not a "physical" landscape (although such a landscape is vividly rendered), but an emotional landscape, in which familiar objects and conversations refuse to remain themselves and dissolve, as it were—as do, perhaps, the "scenes of a stained-glass window" (Delavenay, 356) into a condition of muteness. The feeling of distance is present through all the little activities, the sense of loneliness is alive through all the efforts of Paul and his sister towards keeping their house warm and livable.

Their activities, including their adding an overdose of morphine to their dying mother's cup of milk, only suggest the total suspension of all activity, the end of a particular mode of life; they suggest what might be called a consciousness of winter. The words (and the activities they describe) seem to close in from all sides, as they do upon the Morel household; it looks as though the characters are trying to avoid this invasion from the region of inaction and death, while conscious that there is no escape. There is something solid and immovable about the manner in which the fact of death and all that is associated with it—a feeling of restlessness, of loss, isolation and defeat—come down upon us. The long episode, more than being a symbolic enactment of the state of Paul's consciousness—a falling, crumbling consciousness—is also a realization, in fiction, of those very feelings and moods that are generally avoided in real life. Lawrence seems to reflect on the possibility of communicating the actuality of concepts as well as of formulating a language by which he could deny the merely "objective" nature of death. His style here is the opposite of what might be called, "philosophical." It does not discuss the nature of death as an idea, not does it discuss the social implications of death; rather, it sinks into the fact of a death, lets it usurp an entire action.

The episode involves a death in a household, in a "close" dwelling-place; and death is clearly another order of fact. It is terminal experience—an experience of nothingness and desolation—and appropriately, there is a certain minimal quality about the entire episode. Nature may still figure as artistic device, but it is Nature in its bare, diminished form. Every description seems to suggest the "end" as well as the characters' conscious efforts to avoid it. Early in the episode, the ailing Mrs. Morel is carried into that garden where she had earlier spent an entire night among flowers which were then alive and whole. But now

> The gold wedding-ring shone on her white hand, her hair was carefully brushed. And she watched the tangled sunflowers dying, the chrysanthemums coming out, and the dahlias.
>
> Paul and she were afraid of each other. He knew, and she knew, that she was dying. But they kept up a pretence of cheerfulness. (*SL*, 467)

Death and new life, order and destruction, appear together—the "gold wedding-ring" shining on anemic-white fingers, the new-sprung chrysanthemums and dahlias teasing the fading sunflowers. There are also repeated references to the snow interspersed with quick glances at Christmas preparations, at the characters' nervous efforts to keep life somehow going. The "snow," like death, seems to be everywhere, within the household as outside it, as if Nature had shed all its colors and all its variety and hence, can only be described in terms of its most diminutive aspects. And, in the midst of this "consciousness of failure," Mrs. Morel, a miserable "child," lack any defences and is vulnerable to winter, waste, and death:

> It was nearing Christmas; there was more snow.... A bud of gas was burning in the sick chamber.... Annie huddled into the dressing-gown, Paul wrapped himself in a brown blanket. It was three o'clock. He minded the fire.... He looked out of the window, and could faintly discern the snow in the garden.... Paul heard his father's heavy steps go thudding over the deadening snow. Far away over the snow sounded the hooters of the fireworks.... Then there was silence. He mended the fire.... Still it was dark. Perhaps there was a lighter tinge. Perhaps the snow was bluer. He drew up the blinds got dressed. Then, shuddering, he drank brandy.... The snow *was* growing blue.... A grey, deathly dawn crept over the snow. (*SL*, 477-83)

Even after the death, the family activities remain commonplace, with Paul leaving his "warm, dead mother" in order to visit a friend's house. The house is "empty," the room of the dead is "cold": "Flowers, bottles, plates, all sick-room litter was taken away; everything was harsh and austere" (*SL*, 485). What is important to note here is the richness of empirical material, through the artistic manipulation of which is conveyed a nuance of death's profound actuality in a manner no circumstantial realism can approach.

The richness of empirical material does not, however, obscure the complexities. It does not neglect the "real tragedy" that preceded the death and will follow it. It is a tragedy that does not so much involve a single fact of death as entire ways of dying and wasting oneself. It extends in all directions, and it includes Paul—who does not know how to deal with a lingering life or with a lingering death—as well as his "insensitive" father. The death is even greeted with a certain kind of ecstasy: a final event has taken place, and with it end the painful efforts to understand it. The episode of Mrs. Morel's death might be said to function as the climax of a tragedy of non-communication, symbolised so well in Walter Morel's activities immediately after his receiving the news of her death. But it is also clear that nothing could better describe the "real tragedy" that went on in "Morel in spite of himself" than these seemingly ordinary acts of everyday existence:

> The father came home from work at about four o'clock. He dragged silently into the house and sat down. Minnie bustled to give him his dinner. Tired, he laid his black arms on the table. There were swede turnips for his dinner, which he liked Paul wondered if he knew. It was some time, and nobody had spoken. At last the son said:
>
> 'You noticed the blinds were down?'
>
> Morel looked up.
>
> 'No,' he said. 'Why has she gone?'
>
> 'Yes.'
>
> 'When wor that?'
>
> 'About twelve this morning.'
>
> 'H'm!'
>
> The miner sat still for a moment, then began his dinner. It was as if nothing had happened. He ate his turnips in silence. Afterwards he washed and went upstairs to dress. The door of her room was shut. (*SL*, 485)

The miner's lonely grief is apparent everywhere—in his son's half-ironical question, in the tired way he lays his black arms on the table, in the turnips that he eats, in the "silences" in which he imprisons himself. No single object becomes a complete symbol of his loneliness and inarticulateness; rather, all the objects around him together exude a symbolic aura, but all the while keeping their materiality intact. After all the uneducated miner is *capable* of being as intimately close to death, destruction, and waster as anyone else. Lawrence's style, with its close and sympathetic attention to the details of everyday life, is an example of the habitual extension of his sympathy to these miserable human beings, who do not even know the language through which they might have *known* the nature and extent of their lonely misery.

Works Cited

Delavenay, Emile. *D.H. Lawrence: The Man and His World.* London: William Hanemann, 1972.

Fowler, Roger. *Linguistics and the Novel*. London: Methuen, 1977.

Kermode, Frank. *Lawrence* (Fontana Modern Masters Series). London: Fontana/Collins, 1973.

Lawrence, D.H. "Morality and the Novel", *A Selection From Phoenix*. Ed. A.A.H. Inglis. Harmondsworth, Eng.: Penguin Books, 1971.

———. *Sons and Lovers*. Harmondsworth: Penguin Books, 1967.

Spilka, Mark. "Was D.H. Lawrence a Symbolist?". *Accent,* Vol. 15, 1955.

3

Circular Repetition: A Reading of Lawrence's *The Rainbow*

Gagan Behari Das

1

The pattern of repetition in *The Rainbow* has been intimately worked out in the structure of *The Rainbow* and one's reading of that structure leads to the problem of spatial form. Lawrence presents a polar opposition of "Mind consciousness" and "blood consciousness" of the Brangwen female and male which has been developed in this three-generation story of *The Rainbow.* A repetitive image pattern connects this polar opposition with character's search for fulfilment. The play of opposition between the two consciousnesses gradually accentuates, reducing the whole structure of the novel into repetitive patterns. For example, Ursula's final reflection on the rainbow is an anticipation, a looking towards the futuristic world that also resembles the initial "looking beyond" of the Brangwen women. If this initial "looking beyond" is taken into account, what progress does one notice in the novel's action? In Patricia D. Tobin's words, "the Brangwens neither rise nor decline, succeed nor fail; structurally they lack the initial and the final terminals that make such assessment possible" (84). All action, motif, experience of character convert movement into a static state, undeveloped, as a circular pattern of repetition, in which time seems to be ever present, and interwoven with myth, it recreates the same pattern over and again.

2

In temporal progress one can observe that Will and Anna's search is a repetition of the traditional search, and at the same time, it seems to be different, like Hans Gadamer's "celebration" image. Each celebration should be correct, conforming to the norms, yet it is expected to be different from the past, which looks like both a circle and a spiral constructed by line. Of linearity and circularity, which one Gadamer wants to emphasize, is a question of ambiguity. Discussing Gadamer's problem, W.W. Holdheim remarks that the former has worked out a concealed synthesis between temporality and atemporality in the celebration image (156-57). But viewed spatially, repetition of the same image, experienced by each generation, in the story of our concern, is a kind of celebration, recreating the original archetype; which breaks linearity, reverting past to the present. The problem is more determined by how one looks at it than what a theory explains. Let us see what Murray Krieger has to state about the issue: "Through all sorts of repetitions, echoes, complexes of internal relations it converts its chronological progressions into simultaneity, its temporally unrepeatable flow into eternal recurrence; through a metaphorical bending under the pressure of aesthetic tension converts its linear movement into circle" (105). Gadamer's phenomenological position determines his attempted compromise between history and myth, while Krieger's attempt connects the function of literature with that of plastic art.

In "Ariadne's thread: Repetition and the Narrative Line", J.H. Miller states, "Without line, there is no repetition, but repetition is what disturbs, suspends or destroys the linearity of the line" (70). He defines repetition as "anything which happens to the line to trouble, or even to confound its straight forward linearity: returnings, knottings, crinklings to and fro, suspensions, interruptions, fictionalizings" (68). According to Miller, realistic novel subverts itself by becoming complex—"knotted, repetitive, doubled, broken, phantasmal" (69). What one observes as "repetitive pattern" in *The Rainbow,* according to the critical observations, is a subversion of its chronological progress due to intricate internal relations between characters, incidents and images. But the reader needs to rise above theoretical conflict in order to experience what the work itself has to offer. If a logical connection between repetition and simultaneity is established, then what one perceives as meaning will be exclusively spatial and total at a certain point of time. This central problem will be the thrust area of the whole discussion, for *The Rainbow* gradually emerges as a metaphor of such repetition in every character, image, parallel and episode. For example, textual consciousness, that moves back and forth, perceives both Tom's frustration during Lydia's pregnancy and Will's during Anna's pregnancy simultaneously. Similarly, the reader perceives simultaneous juxtaposition of paired lovers when Ursula and Skrebensky: "Continued to walk on, quivering like shadows under the ash-trees of the hill, where her grandfather had walked with his daffodils to make his proposal, and where her mother had gone with her young husband, walking close upon him as Ursula was now walking upon Skrebensky" (251). This repetitive pattern, yoking past and present together into simultaneous experience, happens to be the characteristic technique of Lawrence.

Tobin states that Lawrence converts the historical distinction between generations into a repetitive pattern of self-discovery appropriating his thought with the structure of *The Rainbow.* He argues that the structure of the novel is not sequentially wrought, rather perceived spatially across temporal barriers. Explaining the scene of Tom's meeting with Lydia in the Vicar's kitchen, he observes: "Within the unifying stasis...tension dancing in space of tension suspended. The scene is thus liberated by its time and space from a narrative that would call the time" (90). Ursula's dance with Skrebensky is described like this: "The scene is enacted in space and need have no temporal index.... In Lawrence's hands the scene functions as an abrogation of historical time, blurring the crisp outline" (96). Tobin, in this essay, tries to established how Lawrence successfully subverts the boundaries of "linear economy" of traditional fictional style to "circular economy" of his own. Tom's experience outside the window and Ursula's dance with Skrebensky are not closed incidents in time, rather they are repeated as a "cycle of dance", "theme, context, structure, scene and sentence all coincide in their cyclic efforts". In the "cycle economy", the critic states, "a different system of preservation and storage that always gets back what it uses up, that preserves what it spends, that returns to the self all that is other" (99). In such an accounting the critic, like a psychoanalyst, seeks to turn away from the descriptive statements in order to ask the crucial question of "motivation".

Exploring the same scenes, Marianna Torgovnick argues that the pictorial quality of the images moving along light and darkness likens the painting; and Ursula-Shrebensky's union in the setting amid the hay stack recalls the earlier encounter of Will and Anna among gathering sheaves, drawing an analogy based upon the visual memory of setting and place (146). She comments on Tom's waiting outside the Vicar's kitchen: "Much of the "picture's" point now rests in the contrast between the quiet and stillness of the scene inside the window and turbulence of the scene outside it—the "frame" has now broadened to include not just Tom outside the window but the awareness of nature "framed" by his consciousness" (145).

When the narrative turns out to be a picture, the flow of time is eliminated; in other words, the reader experiences a static state of the image presented, which is what Torgovnick aims to drive at. Her position seems to be unrelated with the problem of this discussion, but beneath the inconsistency, "visual rhyme" parallels Tobin's "repetitive pattern", and both work against linearity, or horizontal progress of the narrative. Let her comment on the function of pictorial images in the novel be examined. She remarks that such uses "unfold overtime, with the process of understanding", and involves the characters' "piecing together" data from various points in the novel, so that the characters freeze various objects or moments as "pictures" in the visual imagination and, at will, have all the pictures simultaneously present (191). In her analysis, "piecing together data from various points" clearly suggests that "visual rhyme" moves to-and-fro recalling Miller's definition of repetition—"returning, knotting, re-crossing. The connection between images across temporal progress also involves a metonymic digression: shifting attention from the object or image named/

described to the object/image meant branching in different and even opposite direction simultaneously. What follows from this connection between "repetitive pattern" and "visual rhyme", then, diverts attention to the novel's action that is subverted into a circular motion through interlinking of images. In analysis of *The Rainbow,* Tobin's purpose is to show a "cycle of dance" has been enacted within its structure, and in so doing he draws attention to the latent issue-reduction of sequentiality producing spatial effect. But Torgovnick does that exactly from a different angle, i.e., visual images and pictorialism. However, both of their concerns synergically make easy for the present discussion to establish the dialectics of spatial from. In the patterned repetition, Tobin argues, the narrative event seems to be a temporal action that never progresses, and the novel does "hang together" (97), which implies circular repetition and simultaneity at once.

3

The term, "repetition" has been designed as "recurrence" in the critique of Northrop Frye, who has developed spatial dialectic in *Fables of Identity,* that also forwards a poetics of reading similar to Joseph Frank's concept in "Spatial Form". In both cases of temporal and spatial arts "the organizing principle is recurrence, which is called rhythm when it is temporal and pattern when it is spatial" (14). Thus, Frye distinguishes "rhythm" and "pattern" with difference between temporal form and spatial meaning. He explains: "We may call the rhythm of literature the narrative, and the pattern, the simultaneous mental grasp of the verbal structure, the meaning or significance. We may hear or listen a narrative, but when we grasp a writer's total pattern we 'see' what he means" (14). Both Frye and Frank, following Lessing's distinction of temporal and spatial art, analyse literary texts with different purposes, but the former pushes forward critical interest to spatial act in the following:

> In direct experience of fiction, continuity is the centre of our attention; our later memory, or what I call the possession of it, tends to become discontinuous. Our attention shifts from the sequence of incidents to

> another focus; a sense of what the work of fiction was all about...the incidents themselves tend to remain... discontinuous, detached from one another and regrouped in a new way. (23)

Frye provides a psychology of reading that moves sequentially from line to line, sentence to sentence, but gradually the sequential incidents tend to be discontinuous in order to be regrouped for relationship and significance. In the second part of the quotation emphasis is put on "image patterns", which, according to Frye, "derives from the epiphanic moment, the flash of instantaneous comprehension with no direct reference to time" (15). The point that Frye brings to focus is that meaning is constructed not by sequential unfolding of the text but by interrelationship of images. Therefore, he argues, when the critic encounters the text, "the most natural thing for him to do is to freeze it, to ignore its movement in time and look at it as a complete pattern of words, with all its parts existing simultaneously" (21). It seems that Frye does Frank's problem surprisingly with a different purpose and develops spatial dialectic in a more convincing manner. One can observe from the analysis that interrelationship also serves for a trope of "repetition" or "recurrence".

4

It will be helpful to pause here and consider what Lawrence himself has to say about interlinking via repetition and circularity of imagination. He states: "For the relatedness and interrelatedness of all things flows and changes and trembles like a stream, and like a fish in the stream the characters in the novel swim and drift and float and turn belly-up when they're dead" ("The Novel", 185). This concept of structural dependence in the novel appears similar to the views of Frye and Frank discussed. In his typical linguistic diction Lawrence rules out any rigid form for the novel in the first place, and then he suggests the meaning inside the structure is indeterminate and flexible. His character concept radically departs from the conventional notion of development for they "Swim and drift and float" within the structure. The critical Jargons of his time have undergone reorientation and development to a great extent in the history. However, he articulates the concept of circular movement and repetition more clearly in the *Apocalypse:*

> To get at the Apocalypse we have to appreciate the mental working of the pagan thinker or poet—pagan thinker were necessarily poets—who starts with an image, sets the image in motion, allows it to achieve a certain course of circuit of its own, and then takes up another image...image thinking often followed no plan whatever, not even the sequence of action. We can see it in some of the Psalms, the flitting from image to image with no essential connection at all, but just the curious image association. The oriental loved that.
>
> To appreciate the pagan manner of thought we have to drop our own manner of on-and-on-and-on, from a start to finish, and allow the mind to move in cycles, or to flit here and there over a cluster of images. Our idea of time as a continuity in an eternal straight line has crippled our consciousness cruelly. The pagan concept of time as moving in cycles is much freer, it allows movements upwards and downwards and allows for a complete change of the state of mind, at any moment. (47-48)

This critique on literary composition is a radical departure from the conventional practice, in that one can mark a dichotomy drawn on time and space logic, Aristotelian and the pagan manner of thought, the structure of western philosophy and the *Bible.* Lawrence, in this dichotomy, seems to be on the side of the pagan and the *Bible.* What Frye and Frank have argued for interlinking images, ignoring the sequentiality of the novel, has been clearly explained in the quotation with "curious image-association", "allow the mind to move in cycle", "a complete change of the state of mind" and so on besides, Lawrence forwards a psychology of reading, surprisingly identical with that Frye has discussed. Lawrence's observation of the working of the pagan mind anticipates late modern and post-modern discovery of aesthetic form in poetry and fiction, which is of definite interest. This is because Frank's recognition of similar aesthetic form existing in modern poetry and modern fiction has led him to the conception of spatial form. It seems that Lawrence has recognized the literary composition that reveal the philosophy of spatial dialectics much earlier Frank's seminal essay. This is not, of course, the whole story, for the above quotation also high lights the specific point of the present analysis, i.e. interlinking of images presupposes circular repetition, which will be explored precisely in the following part.

5

Ursula's search for an "unknown reality" interlinks all the threads of *The Rainbow* with two epiphanic images like "wild horses" and "the rainbow". The symbolic horse-chasing scene before the final rainbow image is the culmination of her experience and knowledge as a "traveller on the face of the earth". Her plan to marry Skrebensky before the wild horses-scene has been reversed after it. Why does the author do this? The enigma addressed by Julian Moyanahan reads: "Why do some of the characters succeed in saving themselves while others fails? This question is virtually impossible to answer" (47). G.H. Ford remarked: "It is also one of the most difficult passages he has ever composed. The complexity derives in part from the narrative method,...and in part from the complexity of antecedent relationship itself" (152). When the reading process is conventional seeking the meaning of individual word/word-group with one correspondence, one fails to see the total view of the work that appears like Ariadne's thread. In order to overcome this constraint, one needs a different kind of reading, a reading that Lawrence recommends in the *Apocalypse*—"to drop our own manner of on-and-on-and-on, form start to a finish, and allow the mind to move in cycle" (47-48). Lawrence's suggestion corresponds to what Frank observes in "Spatial Form": suspension of immediate referentiality of verbal signs until the whole images and symbols are held together simultaneously in the mind (12). Ford's reference to "narrative method" must look to Lawrentian notion of pagan images that don't move in sequential straight line, but in "cycle". The horses in the context are interpreted in different, and even opposite ways by critics. For example, Leavis and Moyanahan interpret the stallions as representatives of Skrebensky, while Ford shows that they are the dark force and negate what Skrebensky, while Ford shows that they are dark force and negate what Skrebensky stands for. In this polemical conflict, the objective of the present discussion is not to pass a judgment regarding the validity of either interpretation, but to show how interrelationship for a pattern turns out from image association.

What then is the true mission of Ursula's search for the "unknown reality"? Is it a drive towards the world of civilization, education and science, or something else? The reader is informed that from her early adulthood she has a yearning for "the Sons of God", which is seemingly connected with the wild horses. This is how Lawrence presents the whole thing: "There were giants in the earth in those days; and also after that, when the Sons of God came in unto the daughters of men, and they bore children onto them, the same became mighty men which were of old, men of renown" (*TR*, 231). The giants described in these lines are, in fact, horses, which are more clearly pronounced in the *Apocalypse:* "Far back in our dark soul the horse prances.... He stamps and threshes in the dark field of your soul the horse prances. He stamps and threshes in the dark fields of your soul and mine. The Sons of God who came down and knew the daughters of men and begot the great titans, they had "the members of horses", says Enoch. Within the last fifty years man has lost the horse. Now he is Lost" (97-98).

In both the quotations mighty men, giants, great Titans stand for the idea of "the Son of God". This image, which is how the narrative presents: "Raging destructive lovers, seeking the moment when fear is greatest, and triumph is greatest, the fear is not greater than the triumph, the triumph is not greater than fear, these were not lambs nor doves. She stretched her limbs like a lion or a wild horse" (*TR*, 288). The lines describe a violent exercise in love, and the last two words signify her musing on Moloch in the previous paragraph of the work. Thus, lion, eagle, Moloch, wild horse are metonymical, replaced by fierce, violent love signified by the image "the Sons of God".

The novel provides a number of clues directly or indirectly that construct this connection between "wild horses" and "the Sons of God". Explaining the aims of symbolic writing Mallarme formulates the principle—"...describing not the object itself, but the effect it produces" (83). Lawrence, in the world horse image contrives to do both—the horses in the scene are clearly before us, we hear their "thudding hoofs" and at the same time, we recognize the feelings they arouse. Ursula's fear gets intensified by the typical Lawrentian touch of her sensing that "something" is there before she sees anything "like living seed of fear."

In *The Rainbow* and *Apocalypse,* the horse reveals another side—the darkness which connects Ursula's essential being and "the Sons of God". In her essential being a dichotomy of light and darkness interplay, sustaining the action of the novel. When she is drawn into the wider circle, the world of light represented by education, science, civilization—parallel swing also draws her to the mystic vision of the *Bible.* Her experience of relative value of light and darkness leads her to the discovery that all education, science, and civilization are only a "side-show" that epiphanically awakens her latent connection with darkness. Her intimacy with her father and grandfather accounts for the blood consciousness, and it is the same consciousness that turns the bedroom stories of her grandmother into the story of the *Bible,* connecting her with the Sons of God. Organic connection with the cosmic being beneath critical consciousness of man seems to be the implication of darkness and the Sons of God, while the other consciousness is explicated as a "side-show", or the world of light. In "Bitterness of Ecstasy", Ursula reflects this dichotomy:

> The world in which she lived was like a circle lighted by a lamp. This lighted area, lit up by man's most complete consciousness, she thought was all the world: that here is all disclosed forever. Yet all the time, within the darkness she had been aware of light like the eyes of wild beasts, gleaming, penetrating, vanishing. And her soul had acknowledged in a great heave of terror only the outer darkness. This inner circle of light in which she lived and moved, wherein the train rushed

> and factories ground out their machine produce and the plants and animals worked by light of science and knowledge suddenly it seemed like an area under an arc lamp, wherein the moths and children played in security of blinding light, not even knowing there was darkness, because they stayed in the light.
>
> But she could see the glimmer of dark movement just out of range, she saw the eyes of wild beasts gleaming from darkness, watching the vanity of the camp, which said 'Beyond our light and our order there is nothing' turning their faces always inward towards the sinking fire of illuminating consciousness, which comprised sun and stars and the creator, and the system, of righteousness, ignoring always the vast darkness that wheeled roundabout with half revealed shapes lurking on the edge. (368-69)

This epiphanic passage marks a division in Ursula's consciousness and connects her with the cosmic being. When Lawrence selects Skrebensky the reader ironically foresees the subsequent fallout, the doomed separation. Skrebensky is the type that never comes near Ursula's soul, her knowledge and understanding; and whom, in a series of events, she has negated and rejected, but continued only for exploration and adventure. In her final turn down she reflects: "He seems added up, finished. She knew him all round, not on any side did he lead into the unknown" (400). Her knowledge of the Sons of God and Skrebensky's character are mutually exclusive; if Ursula decides to marry him, the decision is nothing but a simulation and self-deceit, which swing is quite natural to her. When one comes back to the question of her attempted escape from the wild horses, the enigma can be interpreted in different ways. The escape may be deciphered as her escape from the darkness since she has borne the mark of Skrebensky in her womb that she has failed to obey her essential bond with that force. If Skrebensky is assumed as symbolic of the horses and tempts in final strike to win her, she also makes her last exercise to reject him, to remain true to her real self. This, in further reference to her falling sick and miscarriage after the scene, makes her release from the past association with Skrebensky. It seems, the enigma has not been solved by the author, like Gudrun's rejection of Gerald, but the purpose of this formulation is not to provide any particular interpretation, but to show how interlinking of images scramble the temporal movement for a simultaneity of narrative unit.

6

Interrelationship of images is a matter of perception and recognition of significance, unlike intentional signification. This exercise will be undertaken to notice the associative value of the two images analyzed, with "the rainbow". The word "darkness" has been used as a trope for unity with cosmic life beyond, in the fragmented, temporal existence. Secondly, it implies uncreated Adam-faculty that undermines any exercise of critical intelligence. Man-Cosmos relationship, according to Lawrence, is one totality of human relationship that reveals a deeper sense of his existence. "I do set my bow in the cloud, and it shall be a token of covenant between me and the earth" (273), which mythic image is a symbol that Lawrence describes: "They do not mean something. They stand for unity of human feeling, human experience...and the power of the symbol is to arouse the deep emotional self, and the dynamic self beyond comprehension" (*SCW*, 318). The rainbow image as a symbol stands for resolving conflict, anticipation and syntheses of conflicting forces with significance of deep emotional self.

When Tom Brangwen feels, "like a broken arch thrust sickeningly out from support", following a separation from his wife, the image implies a loss of emotional connection, but as they reunited like a "baptism to another life", the union radiates with colour of the rainbow. Then their child plays "between the pillar of fire and the pillar of cloud in confidence.... Her father and mother now met to span the heavens, she, the child was free to play in the space beneath, between" (79). Here, the rainbow connects heaven and earth, like God's covenant, with the implication of resolving conflict and perfect male-female relationship. Its two feet, being light and darkness; dawn and dusk, are inclusive of all time, the timeless whole. One can see in the image a juxtaposition of temporal fragmentation and timeless whole—the light and darkness compromised, synthesized. In Chapter 6, Anna's experience has been epitomized in the image, "like a door half opened", an archway faintly coloured coping above; the half realized, obscured and shadowy image is left for Ursula to pursue. In Ursula's vision, the image serves two function—it stamps out corruption/disintegration of old houses, factories, and heralds a new architecture of the earth with a new generation. There is then, always a tendency to go beyond to the greater like from its immediate referents, like recognition of movement and figures beyond the lighted circle. Uniting force that identifies individuals with the cosmic being seems to have figurative role in "the rainbow", "the Sons of God" and "the wild horses". The same signified returns regularly with different verbal signs that do not refer to sensible objects of the real world but to the vision like dream-objects. Seen through Ursula's bedroom window the rainbow is described:

> There was a faint vast rainbow. The arch bended strengthened itself till it arched indomitable, making great architecture of light and colour and the space of heaven, its pedestals luminous in the corruption of new houses on the low hill, its arch the top of heaven... the rainbow was arched in their blood and would quiver to life in their spirit, that they would cast off their horny covering of disintegration, that new, clean, naked bodies would issue to a new germination, to a new growth, rising to the light and the wind and the clean rain of heaven. She saw in the rainbow the earth's new architecture, the old, brittle corruption of houses and factories swept away, the world built up a living fabric of truth, fitting to the over-arching heaven. (418)

The picture, presented from Ursula's point of view, unlike the previous ones, refers to the subjective vision and has relevance to her transformation in the wake of the horse scene. The first part of the image denotes its physicality—position, expanse, colour and stature connecting heaven and earth, man and God, light and darkness. In its second part, the image becomes a symbol, being dislodged from its physical context in order to make its presence in our blood and spirit, thus compelling the organic relation with cosmic being in physical and spiritual level.

In describing the wild horses as fierce, powerful, and massive, the adjectives also describe the rainbow and the Sons of God. "Large, large seemed the bluish incandescent flash of the hoof-iron, large as a halo of lightning round the knotted darkness of the flanks" and "Like circles of lightning came the flash of hoofs from out of the powerful flanks," describe the horses (412). In mythic images, the Sons of God, the covenant bow, and the horses are implicative of the dichotomy of light and darkness and the organic connection between them. A released Ursula rhetorically questions—"Who was she to have a man according to her own desire? It was not for her to create, but to recognize a man created by God...the man would come out of Eternity to which she herself belonged" (417). This means to her the Sons of God, and the Son of God, and the antithesis of Skrebensky. The language that describes the horses and the Sons of God is also the language that describes the rainbow. The objects are not referred to the language. The reader is simply puzzled to find that the verbal signs and their signifiers are not connected, because the objects described are neither real nor are they referred to our in the kind of language of absence the narrative repeats the same signified connecting with different signifiers. This reductionism interlinks all images and symbols together.

The structure of the novel's thought emerges like a body of binary opposition of images and symbols, a taxonomic reading of Adam/Eve, blood conscious/mind conscious, darkness/light, preconscious/conscious. When one signifier-image replaces another, the metonymic/metaphoric act can be defined as repetition that, in a circular motion substitutes the notion of sequentiality. In the Marsh Farm, characters figure out as Adam and Eve, which, in second generation resume the category of blood conscious and mind conscious, and extended forward in the category of light and darkness. If Ursula dislikes to make love in a house, runs with her man in the dark, like soft a wind under the open sky and stands on earth mound, like a stone age man watching for light, what does one read from the development, if not the Edenic state? This circular motion of the work's action recalls Tobin's remark as "cyclic economy" and missing terminals of Brangwen family's beginning and end. This discussion, however, is engaged to ignore individual value judgement and interpretation of images, in order to discover the way they are reduced to repetitive pattern.

7

Lawrence's use of myth reorients a linearity of the work to circular repetition. Reading *The Rainbow* one can experience, as if the work were a plaster over the *Bible,* the undercurrent of which surfaces in every incident, character and action of the story (Ford, 134). In the opening part, a picture of Eden comes to view in presentation of Marsh Farm, with abundance and surfeit of landscape and life: "They lived full and surcharged, their senses full fed" (4). Here, Tom and Lydia are described "Like two children camping in the plain" (112). This picture comes to our full experience due to—first, the Brangwen couple is shut out from the crowding world making for them a remote psychic land of primitive form. Secondly, the male is endowed with a fecundity of blood intimacy, with the mystic creative force, and to the religious service of darkness. Thirdly, the female, with a desire to know the unknown, looks beyond "to see the far off world of cities...where secrets were made known and desires fulfilled" (5) reminding of the Eve figure. In the fourth place, tension between the couple seems to be the cause behind the transformation and industrialization of the Farm. Besides this, the picture of flood, Noah's ark, Genesis of the *Bible,* dominate the narrative tone. The symbolic events develop within the work's structure in close resemblance to the *Bible.* Though the word "Eden" is not mentioned in the description of Marsh Farm, the imagery, symbol, parallel are closely worked out as allegorical like the *Bible.* After 165 pages a key reference draws the notice on Will's reflection—"Serpent in his garden"—that impresses the reader, as if he were reading Adam and Eve in place of Will and Anna.

When the Eden world metaphorically falls in the wake of education, science and industrialization; when Eve revolts against the commandments, we don't know what mutation they were to pass through. But in *The Rainbow* we notice the quarrel between the couple, their alternate breaking away and reunion, the desire to search for meaning outside their relationship may guide our imagination to see the transformation working in Adam and Eve after the Fall. For information, one example of "wine in Cana" shall confirm our knowledge of the splitting of unified being of Edenic world:

> Did he believe the water turned to wine at Cana? She would drive him to things as a historical fact: so much rain water—look at it—can it become grape-juice, wine? For an instant, he was with the clear eyes of the mind and said no, his clear mind answering her for a moment, rejected the idea. And immediately his whole soul was crying in a mad, inchoate hatred against this violation of himself. It was true for him. His mind was extinguished again at once, his blood was up. In his blood and bones, he wanted the scene, the wedding, the water brought forward from the firkins as red wine.... Brangwen loved it, with his bones and blood he loved it, he could not let it go. Yet she forced him to let it go. She hated his blood attachment. (142-43)

The quotation works for their own critique of the play of tension on two levels of existence. What is a "historical fact" in case of Anna, proves to be a "violence of self" for Will, drawing a parallel with mind and blood consciousness. Like balloon prickers, Anna deflates the mythical sense of her husband, forcing him to examine the evidence "with clear eyes of the mind". This tension, in fact, is the tension between temporal and atemporal character of the work that, in extension, also denotes the order of presentation and the total meaning. Between the couple, one's refusal means the other's acceptance of the two modes of consciousness, juxtaposed in the same instance—"the water brought from firkins". This paradox is instructive to read time and space as interdependent necessary condition in art and literature. Neither of these can be totally ruled out, and the suppression of one alters the aesthetic quality of the work with the other.

8

In the concluding part of this discussion, once again, attention is called back to the problem raised earlier of this discourse—linking circularity with simultaneity, which has been done all along the course. With the vignette of the cathedral, the problem will be specifically reiterated. Like Ursula's self critiquing the juxtaposition of relative world and absolute world, Lawrence in this image suggests a change of system from one level to another for interpretation of meaning. As a "great, involved seed", church united all "before" and "after at one point, in the "circle of silence", and holds the "secrets of all between its parts"; this experience is described in a language at once mythical and personal, not to be translated in any other term than its own:

> Away from time, always outside of time! Between east and west, between dawn and sunset, the church lay like a seed in silence, dark before germination, silenced after death. Containing birth and death, potential with all the noise and transition of life, the cathedral remained hushed, a great, involved seed, whereof flower would be radiant life inconceivable, but whose beginning and whose end were the circle of silence. Spanned round with the rainbow, the jewelled gloom folded music upon silence, light upon darkness, fecundity upon death, as a seed folds leaf upon leaf and silence up on the root and the flower, hushing up the secret of all between its parts, the death out of which it fell, the life into which it has dropped, the immortality it involves, and the deaths it will embrace again.
>
> Here in the church, 'before' and 'after' were folded together, all was contained in oneness. Brangwen came to his consummation.... Then between—while he had pushed open the doors of the cathedral, and entered the twilight of both darkness, the hush the two-fold silence,

> where dawn was sunset, and the beginning and the end were one. (168-69)

This quotation seems like a piece of poem celebrating a single image. The language and the idea it communicates are equally mystic and ambiguous. However, the concept exemplifies a stasis of presence in the form of cathedral, eliminating sense of duration and progress. Will's consummation with the mystery of the church likens his consummation in the honeymoon scene, for both sexual union and religious consummation involve blotting out of the subject's mind as much as the sense of duration, so that the pilgrimage may be celebrated. The church is a symbol, a unit of mythic archetype that tells the story of genesis, and regenerates the sacred time, uniting man with divine creation every moment. In conception of this structure that has only one time—the timeless present, historical categories of duration and movement are suspended. Transition, immutability, silence and music are placed in one and the same image—"circle of silence". Henri Charles Puech, in *Man and the Time*, argues that "circular movement that assures the survival of the same things by repeating them, by bringing about their continuous return, is the perfect expression of the absolute immobility. The same sum of being is preserved, nothing is created and nothing is lost, indicating that circular time is also still time" (40-41). Puech refers to the Greeks saying that they considered movement and change as inferior reality. Citing the platonic definition of time, he states that the time, that is determined and measured by revolution of celestial spheres, is the mobile image of immobile eternity that it imitates by moving in circle. Thus, both the cosmic process and the time of our world develop in a circle, or an indefinite succession of cycles, so that the same reality appears to have been made, unmade and remade for ever (40-41). This is what Lawrence does to convey time in the cathedral image.

He compares the church with a "great involved seed", which implicitly contains a potential presence of the whole creation that is folded, refolded in a complex. The beginning, the end, and threads of all connections in the created, uncreated world are held together in a knotted centre, the "circle of silence". He explains the flower that develops into a radiant life, is potentially contained in the seed, and also the end of the flower connects to the seed through maturity/death. It can be expressed that if life ends in death, it also begins from it; the "before" and "after" of the flower is thus contained at one point, whichever creates its type. Seen in both temporal and atemporal categories, all transformations, movements, duration of phenomenal and sacred things co-exist in the cathedral image. To reduce the whole creation/work into the figure of a circle is to state that the cathedral that tells eternal repetition also tells simultaneous presence of all in binary opposition.

Circular repetition is an important dimension of literary work that, like a genre, recreates itself by imitation (which is unlike the act of invention in the field of science), yet no telling can exhaust the mystery of the work. If "Eikphrastic Principle" reduces a narrative complex to a picture held fix, the consciousness of phenomenology compels one to understand the narrative in sequence of time; yet how close they seem to be with spatial from is their basic objective.

Works Cited

Ford, D.H. *Double Measure: A Study of the Novels and Stories of D.H. Lawrence.* New York: Norton Library, 1969.

Frank, Joseph. "Spatial Form in Modern Literature," in *The Widening Gyre.* New Brunswick: Rutgers University Press, 1963.

Frye, Northrop. *Fables of Identity: Studies in Poetic Mythology.* New York: Harcourt Brace, 1963.

Holdheim, W.W. *The Hermeneutic Mode.* Ithaca: Cornell University Press, 1984.

Krieger, Murray. *The Play and Place of Criticism.* Baltimore: John Hopkins University Press, 1967.

Lawrence, D.H. *The Rainbow* (1915). "Introduction", Lionel Kelly. Hertfordshire: Wordsworth Classics, 2001.

———. *Apocalypse.* New York: Penguin, 1932.

———. "The Novel" in *Selected Critical Writings.* Ed. Michael Herbert, New York: Oxford University Press, 1998.

———. "Introduction" to *The Dragon of the Apocalypse in Selected Critical Writings*. Ed. Michael Herbert, New York: Oxford University Press, 1998.

Mallarme, Stephen. *Selected Prose*. Trans. Bradford Cook. Baltimore: Johns Hopkins University Press, 1956.

Miller, J.H. "Ariadne's Thread: Repetition and the Narrative Line", *Critical Inquiry*, 2.1 (1976): 58-77.

Moynahan, Julian. *The Deed of Life: The Novel and Tales of D.H. Lawrence*. New Jersey: Princeton University Press, 1963.

Puech, Henri-Charles. "Gnosis and Time" in *Man and Time*. Ed. Joseph Campbell. New York and London: Princeton Legacy Library, 1957.

Tobin, P.D. *Time and the Novel*. New Jersey: Princeton University Press, 1978.

Torgovnick, M. *The Visual Arts: Pictorialism and the Novel*. New Jersey: Princeton University Press, 1985.

4

The Language of *Women in Love*

Nigamananda Das

1

D.H. Lawrence uses a unique language in his narratives. His fictional narratives have several repetitions, smiles, metaphors, symbols, paradoxes and other figures of speech. Though in prose, the novels have more of poetic verve; essentially by stimulating the spirit, moving minds mystically into unknown zones of realities that make one forget the 'self', freeze into the unconscious. Many passages present the monologues depicting the exterior silence where the conflicts are garrulous in the aggrieved souls. *Women in Love* is replete with several such instances, which have been tangential to the minds of Ursula, Birkin, Hermione, Gudrun, and Gerald.

The repetition in different chapters assume different dimensions. Diana Neill considers the repetitions 'inartistic' and comments on the style of the book as "...singularly fluid and unrestrained by inartistic repetitions of words and phrases. Much of the writing is even amateurish by any literary standard" (322-23). But she again considers *Women in Love* a "visionary book" (323). She continues to comment, "Running through the book is a vein of exciting kinaesthetic imagery that can turn the simple gesture of throwing a stone at the moon mirrored in a pond into a cosmic art" (323). Repetitions in dialogues are usual with people with several obsessions; these are sometimes as word-twisting, continuing in different meanings with different intentions. These repetitions emphasize the issue and draw attention of listeners/readers, and these are components of educative/informative missions. But Lawrence in his "Foreword" to the book explains the cause of this 'fault' terming it as 'natural':

> In the point of style, fault is often found with the continual, slightly modified repetition. The only answer is that it is natural to the author: and that every crisis in emotion or passion or understanding comes from this pulsing, frictional to-and-fro, which works up to culmination. (Lawrence, 486)

Repetition is a significant element of Lawrence's language. Sometimes repetitions are there on the same page, continuously occurring and sometimes they come up after many pages in different contexts. Though modern perversions were disturbing him, he juxtaposed scenes of modern degenerations with natural scene-painting. His language is unique in its own way of unravelling his philosophy of life. A close reading of Lawrence's *Women in Love* makes one realize his spiritual height and his language of divinity even though he is charged with the language of perverse sexuality and obscenity. His fictional style is poetic and significantly impressive with an intense visual attitude. It is said that he fails in exact depiction when the situation is alien to him and beyond his experience (Dataller, 56). Very often he is misunderstood by the readers; hence one has to be very enlightened reader to understand the philosophy of Lawrence. "His idea of language can be examined by exploring the elements of the language which is central to an understanding of the exploratory processes at work in his fiction" (Padhi, 65). Lawrence is an inventor of a different kind of language, it is esoteric, fluid, divine, electric, magical, and "of passionate vehemence, wave after wave of turgid, exasperated writing impelled towards some distant and invisible end" (Murray, 21). In his foreward to the novel, Lawrence denies of the charges of obscenity and explains the ways of reading and comprehending his writing:

> In England, I would never try to justify myself any accusation. But to the Americans, perhaps I may speak for myself. I am accused, in England, of uncleanness

> and pornography. I deny the charge, and take no further notice. In America the chief accusation seems to be one of "Eroticism." This is odd, rather, puzzling to my mind. Which Eros? Eros of the jaunty "amours," or Eros of the sacred mysteries? And if the latter, why accuse, why not respect, even venerate? (Lawrence, 485)

He clarifies the differences between sexuality, passion, spirituality and obscenity. Human passion, spontaneity of human feelings and naturalness should be respected. Hence the reader must be enlightened of the truth and realities and must also be honest and truthful to his/her own self. Hence he declares:

> Let us not hesitate to announce that the sensual passions and mysteries are equally sacred with the spiritual mysteries and passions. Who would deny it anymore? The only thing unbearable is the degradation, the prostitution of the living mysteries in us. Let man only approach his own self with a deep respect, even reverence for all that the creative soul, the God-mystery within us, puts forth. Then we shall all be sound and free. Lewdness is hateful because it impairs our integrity and our proud being.
>
> The creative, spontaneous soul sends forth its promptings of desire and aspiration in us. These promptings are our true fate, which it is our business to fulfil. A fate dictated from outside, from theory or from circumstance, is a false fate. (Lawrence, 485)

Lawrence was very badly obsessed with modernism. He was an anti-modernist. His obsessions are reflected in the characters in *Women in Love*. Hence the novel presents a panorama of destruction:

> *Women in Love* is indeed "purely destructive"; it is grimly apocalyptic and misanthropic. There is little sense of the presence of nature this time; the novel moves entirely within the conscious and (more importantly) subconscious minds of its four main characters. And the backdrop is ugly, human-built mechanicalness of the industrialized Midlands. (Hawthorne: http://www.

> counter-currents.com/2011/01/d-h-lawrence-women-in-love-part-1)

The author also hints at the turmoil of time and prompts his readers to arouse their conscience to tackle the problems concerning us and ponder over the solutions, of the ways to escape the crises, sharpen our senses to understand the reality and bring out healthy ambience:

> We are now in a period of crisis. Every man who is acutely alive acutely wrestling with his soul. The people that can bring forth the new passion, the new idea, this people will endure. Those others, that fix themselves in the old idea, will perish with the new life strangled unborn within them. Men must speak out to one another. (486)

Birkin, who is an extension of Lawrence himself, outpours the venom against the humanity and modern world, though he finds some fulfilment in his love life. His life is a paradox as in spite of the fulfilment in love he exposes his frustration in speaking a language of frustration and fulfilment of human ambitions, calling "humanity a huge aggregate lie" (126). Gerald was a strong man, nothing was impossible for him but he was not happy and his love life ended in turmoil. For Lawrence,

> submission to a male is depicted as the means of woman's salvation.... It is much more difficult for woman than for man to 'accept the universe,' for man submits to the cosmic order autonomously, whereas woman needs the mediation of the male.... Lawrence sees woman as the unconscious repository of truth, passive fleshly object who is intermediary between man and the gods simply through her existence, not by any choice. (Siegel, 13)

Lawrence's treatment of Ursula is anti-modernist as "she kneels in homage to the phallus" (*ibid*., 17), i.e., she emotionally accepts the love-making of the Birkin by surrendering herself to himself, whereas Gudrun is modern as she does not bow down before Gerald. Hence Lawrence creates a semi-mystical language to describe the man-woman relationships in degenerated world where this relationship has assumed devastative dimensions and has brought in turmoil and perversions.

2

As in his poetry, Lawrence's sentences in *Women in Love* are replete with alliterations, assonance, consonance, and similes, experienced mostly in the sentences of the omniscient author-narrator. Along with the dialogues of the characters these give the readers the feel of poetry, the melody, and the asphyxiated and sad strains in the tragic moments of life. With the repetition of words, there are repetitions of same consonants or vowels in several of words in the sentences. The authorial voices are pronounced in the dialogues of the characters as well as in the narrations of the plot development about modern perversion, decadence, degradation and degenerations. These ideas are depicted diversely in different episodes of different chapters.

There are many repetitions in fictional discourse of *Women in Love*. The repetitions are seen in the words, phrases, punctuations, etc. though these repetitions seem inartistic sometimes, these are organic to the plot, relevant and are ornamental. These bring in a strong sense of reality in the narrative. The following dialogues of Ursula in 'Excurse' exemplify some repetitions like the many dispersed in other chapters:

> "I *assure* you I don't, I don't mind in the least. Go where you belong—it's what I want you to do,"... (305)
>
> I jealous! I—jealous!... It is what Hermione *stands for* that I *hate,* I hate it, it is lies, it is false, it is death.—But you want it, you can't help it, you can't help yourself.... (306)
>
> "And *I, I'm* not spiritual enough, *I'm* not as spiritual as that Hermione—!..."
>
> "Then *go* to her, That's all I say, *go* to her, *go,*—Ha, she spiritual—*spiritual,* she! A dirty materialist as she is. *She* spiritual?—What does she care for, what is her spirituality? What *is* it?"
>
> I tell you it's *dirt,* and nothing *but* dirt—And it's dirt you want, you crave for it—Spiritual! Is *that* spiritual, her bullying, her conceit, her sordid materialism? She's fishwife, a fishwife, she is such a materialist. And all so sordid. (307)

The vocabulary of the novel as a whole is the vocabulary of thought, passion and belief. The vocabulary though largely from English, there are code-switching maximum to French, then to German, Italian, Latin, Greek, Indian, Uzbekistan, Japanese and to dialects of Tyrol, Cockney, Icelandic, etc. Lawrence has his novel coinages in this novel like 'word-bag' (188: 6), 'devolution' (204: 27), 'Excurse' (302), 'Elvin' (317: 31) and (426: 24), 'contributed' (358: 11), which assume different meanings or are rarely used by others. 'Word-bag' created in the manner of "wind-bag" means an empty-talker, whereas 'contributed' means 'given up' which is totally different in meaning from the original meaning of the word. There are colloquial usages and several Biblical allusions and to several other literary works. Though it is fictional narrative, it seems to be a thorough research document depicting human destiny, love affairs and their consequences, modern degeneration, the author's deliberate depiction of natural scenery and inevitability of man's association with nature and his inner urge to go out and get solace in the bosom of nature. Though there are fixed collections of words, yet Lawrence has designed his own collections of words befitting to his themes. In chapter called 'Gladiatorial,' when Gerald was suffering from boredom in "an agony of inertia" (266), he was thinking of drinking or smoking hashish or to be soothed by Birkin and the third was woman. Thereafter as Birkin came to his place, both of them discussed on the misery of nothingness. Birkin suggested Gerald to wait and mentioned "sleep, drink, travel" as cures for ennui (267). But Gerald in disagreement pointed out 'work and love' are the two as cures for boredom to which Birkin added 'fighting' as the third and thus new collection of cures to get rid of boredom was 'work, love and fighting' (267). Similarly, there are several new collections coined by Lawrence in different chapters like 'death-annihilation' (43), 'worship of perfect possession' (200), 'broken fragments of one whole' (200-01), 'mindless Godhead of humanity' (215), 'darkness and shame' (304), 'life-source, mystically-physically satisfying, dark fire of electricity, new current of passional electric energy' (314), 'suave perfect loins, and thighs of darkness, Egyptian concentration in darkness'

(318), 'movement of dream liberation' (343), 'additional perfect relationship between man and man,' and 'permanent union between a man and a woman' (352). There are several aphoristic lines which seem to be adages framed by Lawrence in the context of narrating the episodes in the plot: "A man can live by accident, and die by accident" (26), "Ursula wondered if the trees and the flowers could feel the vibration, and what they thought of it, this strange motion in the air" (22), "Anybody who is anything can just be himself and do as he likes" (32), "Anybody who is anything can just be himself and do as he likes" (32), "But your passion is a lie, It isn't passion at all, it is your *will*" (42), "We are sensual enough, without making ourselves so" (44), "We are too full of ourselves" (44), "You haven't the thousand obstacles a woman has in front of her" (48), "You mean if there isn't the woman, there's nothing?" (58). "What is mankind but just one expression of the incomprehensible" (59), "Humanity is a dead letter" (59), "There can be no reason, no excuse for education, except for the joy and beauty of knowledge in itself" (85), "Vocational education *isn't* education, it is the close of education" (85), "There is no flowering, no dignity of human life now", "humanity itself is dry-rotten really" (126), "mankind is a dead tree, covered with fine brilliant galls of people", "humanity is a huge aggregate lie", "a huge lie is less than a small truth," "humanity is less, far less than the individual", "humanity is a tree of lies" (126), "Man is mistake" (128), "Humanity never gets beyond the caterpillar stage—it rots in the chrysalis, it never will have wings. It is anti-creation, like monkeys and baboons" (128), "Love is one of the emotions like all others" (129), "Love isn't a desideratum" (129), "A man has very little need for a woman now", "the world is only held together by the mystic conjunction, the ultimate unison between people", "Love is a direction which excludes all other directions. It's freedom *together*" (152), "Some people are pure flowers of dark corruption" (173), "A dry soul is best" (173), "Reaction was a greater bore than action" (199), "It was sex that tuned a man into a broken half of a couple, the woman into other broken half" (199), "Everything must be referred back to her, to Woman, the Great Mother of everything, out of whom proceeded everything and to whom everything must finally be rendered up" (200), "All men are equal in spirit, they are all sons of God" (225), "Production or work is worship" (225), "A child is the child of the mystery" (225), "The nuisance is…that one would find almost any man intolerable after a fortnight" (263), "She believed that love was *everything*. Man must render himself up to her: he must be quaffed to the dregs by her. Let him be *her man* utterly, and she in return would be his humble slave—whether he wanted it or not" (265), "I don't know why one should have to justify oneself" (272), "Her passion and her complete indecision almost made her ill" (278), "This slight sense of romance stirred her like an intoxicant" (279), "One can preserve the decencies, even to one's enemies: for one's own sake" (308), "The only hopeless thing is a fool" (308), "Marriage is a *pis aller*" (351), "Marriage was a doom to him" (353) and so on.

In spite of its reaction to the modern mechanized and industrial world, the text of *Women in Love* contains many Biblical allusions and allusions to several other literary works. Lawrence holds an apocalyptic vision. He compares Birkin and Gerald to Jesus Christ in contrastive ways. In chapter 'Excurse' Ursula experiences the divine knowledge about Birkin being deeply enticed to him and was reminded of the Book of Genesis:

> She recalled again the old magic of the Book of Genesis, where the Sons of God saw the daughters of men, that they were fair. And he was one of these, one of these strange creatures from the beyond, looking down at her, and seeing she was fair... (312). It was here she discovered him one of the Sons of God such as were in the beginning of the world, not a man, something other, something more... (313). She had had lovers, she had known passion. But this was neither love nor passion. It was the daughters of men coming back to the Sons of God, the strange inhuman Sons of God who are in the beginning.... It was all achieved for her. She had found one of the Sons of God from the Beginning, and he had found one of the first luminous daughters of men. (313)

Birkin's attitude to love-life and life in general is regenerative whereas Gerald's degenerative. As mentioned in the Book of Genesis about the Son of God and the daughters of men, her Birkin is the Son of God whereas Ursula is the daughter of men. Birkin also wants to save Gerald from the ruin. He saves him from the agony of inertia by engaging him in wrestling to promote the life-force in him. But Gerald's own obsession betrays him. The way Jesus was murdered by his betrayer, Gerald was betrayed by his wrong attitude to life. "His idealism, his belief in will-power, his mechanism and his industrialism, all betray him in the long run.... Gerald is a Jesus-like figure...his death should be taken as a resurrection and rebirth in spirit" (Zheng, 127). Besides the Book of Genesis, there are allusion from *Book of Ruth, Matthew, John, Corinthians, the Ten Commandments, Romans, Book of Common Prayer, Exodus, Psalm,* Montaigne's *Essays.* S.T. Coleridge's "Kubla Khan" (1798), Sir James Frazer's *Totem and Taboo,* E.B. Tylor's *Primitive Culture,* George Meredith's *The Tragic Comedians* (1892), John Keats' sonnet, "On First Looking into Chapman's Homer" (1817), Gilbert Murray's translation of *The Bacchae* by Euripdes, Bernardin de St Pierre's *Romance* (1787), Charles Baudelaire's *Les Fleurs du mal* (1857), John Burnet's *Early Greek Philosophy* (1980), Shakespeare's *Much Ado About Nothing, King Lear, Hamlet,* and *Macbeth,* Plato's *Symposium* and *Republic*, William Dunbar's "Lament for the Makaris", Wagner's *Rheingold* and *Gotterdammerung* (1876), Robert Burton's *The Anatomy of Melancholy,* William Wordsworth's *The World is too Much with Us* (1807), J.M. Pryse's *The Apocalypse Unsealed* (1910), Francis Bacon's essay "Or Marriage and Single Life", Chaucer's *Nun's Priest Tale*, Alexander Pope's *Essay on Criticism* (1711), Milton's *Samson Agonistes*, Shelley's "The Skylark" (1820), Rousseau's *Confessions* (1782-90), Tennyson's *Lady of Shalott* and *In Memoriam* (1850), George Eliot's *Adam Bede* (1859) and her translation of Ludwig Feuerbach's *The Essence of Christianity* (1854). All these allusions create a mosaic of references and offer a mystic knowledge of human experience and metaphysic of reality which has obsessed and disillusioned the modern man.

3

Lawrence has displayed the height of his imagination in using a variety of novel images. Chiefly his imagery may be categorized as images indicating life, vitality, hopefulness and prosperity, images depicting hopelessness, coldness, decadence and death, nature imagery, abstractions and, complex imagery. These five groups are associated with Birkin and Ursula, and Gerald and Gudrun, other minor characters, scene-painting and thematic deliberations. There are similes comparing various states of life and activities. The images very often have symbolic overtones. *Women in Love* introduces a new kind of image:

> The new image is the ebb and flow of sea-cycles of creation and decay which are indifferent to human life. Yet humanity is somehow responsible for what is happening to it.... The animals and plants are integrated with nature in a way man is not. Man should, then, be swept away until some new evolutionary cycle is ready to begin. (Sagar 78)

The Novel disseminates this prophecy. The modern world has been eco-cidal and man is frustrated with tormenting decay and degeneration. Hence there is a necessity to revolutionize the concept of love as the concept of love has been made debased, immoral and inimical. Hence man has to establish intimacy with the natural surroundings to ameliorate man's healthy living and healthy thinking. Nature in its different aspects has been painted with metaphors, images and similes. There are long passages of painting natural surroundings. There are also single lines containing similes and metaphors and terms or phrases depicting sensual and sensuous impressions. The whole text is an excellent fabric of images, metaphors and similes representing diverse sense perceptions. The maximum of visual images are available in the text of *Women in Love.* Lawrence holds a strong visual attitude in his narrative technique. Even other sense perceptions are mostly associated with the visual attitude. Several paragraphs present epic simile-like descriptions of scenes, situations, feelings and experiences. The following are some of the examples of images culled from different chapters:

"[S]he felt like a beetle toiling in the dust" (visual image) (11), "They turned off the main road, past a black patch of common garden, where sooty cabbage stumps stood shameless.... It is like, a country in an underworld" (visual image) (11), "For the moment, the sunshine fell brightly into the churchyard, there was a vague scent of sap and of spring, perhaps of violets from off the graves. Some white daisies were out, bright as angels. In the air, the unfolding leaves of a copper-beech were blood-red" (visual and olfactory image) (13-14), "The carriage rattled down the hill, and drew near. There was a shout from the people" (visual and auditory image) (19), "The waters were loud on the shore" (auditory image) (247), and the like.

The following passage paints a picture of the landscape juxtaposing natural surrounding with modern industrial coal-fields of dirt in a manner maintaining equilibrium, but exposing the pollution:

> This sisters were crossing a black path through a dark, soiled field. On the left was a large landscape, a valley with colliers, and opposite hills with cornfields and woods, all blackened with distance, as seen through a veil of crape. White and black smoke rose up in steady columns, magic within the dark air. Near at hand came the long rows of dwellings, approaching curved up the hill slope, in straight line along the brow of the hill. They were of darkened red brick, brittle, with dark slate roofs. (11)

This passage above describes the human habitation, hills, cornfields—all darkened due to the black dust rising from the coal-fields and blackening roofs, roads, cornfields and surrounding as a whole and degenerating the fresh natural scene and surrounding. The narration gives a picture of the surroundings like an epic smile. There are so many passages like this painting natural surrounding exemplifying both the fresh nature imagery along with natural scenery beside the residential environment and artificial defacing of nature due to industrial expansions.

There are several abstractions which give mystical perceptions and express the inexpressible ideas, feelings, sensualities:

"Gudrun watched them closely, with objective curiosity" (14), "he looked so new, unbroached, pure as an arctic thing", "then she experienced a keen paroxysm, a transport, as if she had made some incredible discovery, known to nobody else on earth" (15), "And he was expressionless, neutralized, possessed by her as if it were his fate, without question" (22), "Hermione aroused herself as from a death-annihilation" (43), "God, what it is to be a man!... The freedom, the liberty, the mobility!". "He was very quick and slippery and full of electric fire" (268).

There are some complex images contrived of blending of sensual perceptions, abstractions, mystical ideas, and the like which are available in this fictional narrative of Lawrence; e.g., "She sat convulsed with fury and violation, speechless, like a stricken pythoness of the Greek oracle" (42), "If one cracked your skull perhaps one might get a spontaneous, passionate woman out of you, with real sensuality—As it is, what you want is pornography—looking at yourself in mirrors, watching your naked animal actions in mirrors, so that you can have it all in your consciousness, make it all mental" (42), "Then a sort of tension came over her, she raised her face like the pythoness inspired with oracles, and went on, in rhapsodic manner" (299), "He knew her verily, with subconscious, sinister knowledge, devoid of illusions and hopes" (427).

Women in Love is replete with symbols. Lawrence used three major kinds of symbol. He uses a number of private symbols in addition to the conventional ones. Images and similes also many times serve the role of symbols. In *Women in Love* the three layers of symbols may be; characters as symbols; symbolic themes and episodes and; symbolic words and images. Gerald-Gudrun relationship is destructive in nature whereas Birkin-Ursula relationship is a quiet, healthy relationship. Birkin and Ursula stand for the life-force. Hermione stands for intellectualism, ego, power and ultimate frustration. Loerke is symbolic of degeneration, corruption and sexual perversion. Dianna who drowned along with young doctor who jumped into the lake to save her, symbolizes accident and the fragility of human life. The colliers stand for modern degenerative life due to industrialization.

Gerald's cruelty to the mare and the colliers expose his true character. He fights with the rabbit Bismarck and gets scratches. He gives near-fatal blows to Loerke in his frustration and catches hold of Gudrun by her throat and leaves her finally and is found dead in snow the next day. In his boyhood days he killed his brother. He presents a strong will for chaos. He is a symbol destruction, spiritual degeneration and perversion. He was sexually attracted towards other women like Minette. But was really appreciated by both Minette and Gudrun as Napoleon and Bismarck. Gudrun is a smart woman. She spent several years in London, working at an art-school, as a student and lived a studio life. She is a mismatch with Gerald and hence is destructive. She is also a symbol of vulgarity, and is not decent like Ursula. In the chapter, "Coal-Dust" Gudrun's 'degenerative will' has been highlighted:

> Now she realised that this was the world of powerful, underworld men who spent most of their time in the darkness. In their voices she could hear the voluptuous resonance of darkness, the strong, dangerous underworld, mindless, inhuman. They sounded like the strange machines, heavy oiled. The voluptuousness was like that of machinery, cold and iron... (115). And it was these voices which affected Gudrun almost to swooning. They aroused a strange nostalgic ache of desire, something almost demonical, never to be fulfilled. She knew it was a vulgar thing to do; her father and mother could not bear it; but the nostalgia came over her, she must be among the people. (117)

In the "Water-party" chapter also she displayed voluptuous ecstasy in dancing towards the wild bullocks and daring the bullocks and afterwards striking Gerald on his face with the back of her hand. In the chapter 'Rabbit', Gudrun's symbolic character is revealed again. "She revealed again the mocking white-cruel recognition.... They were implicated with each other in abhorrent mysteries" (242). This is a prophetic statement and her cruelty was reflected when she deceived Gerald and got fascinated to Loerke. In "Snowed Up" chapter that matters and she finds Loerke superior to Gerald. This 'abhorrent mystery' stands for the discord in the love relationship, where the couple are not in harmonious relationship and they are not subdued to each other. Lawrence depicts the possessiveness of all women and their desire to dominate their men. But in case of Ursula, though she wanted to dominate Birkin, she was subdued to him. Hermione, being a symbol of intellectualism was also destructive like Gudrun. She also attacked Birkin on back of his head with a paper-weight in trying to kill him, but Birkin escaped and thereafter avoids Hermione. She symbolizes ego, tyranny, aggressiveness, possessiveness and frustration. The fourth woman character, Minette stands for perversity, whom Birkin calls a harlot and she was unfaithful to Halliday whom she wanted to marry. She represents rottenness of the Bohemian world, its casualness and aimlessness. Her attack on a young man and negligence of Halliday is Like Hermione's attack on Birkin and Gudrun's negligence of Gerald.

Birkin stoning the moon-image in the lake symbolizes attacking the woman's dominance, possessiveness and insistence on controlling their men. He throws stones at the moon-image in the lake recurrently to annihilate the woman's possessiveness, tyranny and constant suppression of their men. Finally, Ursula stops him from further stoning of the moon-image. Hence, it is difficult for a man to get rid of the dominance of women.

The wrestling bout between Birkin and Gerald in the "Gladiatorial" chapter stands for passionate brotherhood and loyalty which is essential for Birkin. Though Gerald wants it to escape boredom in life, Birkin considers this a very important way of feeling life itself. He says, "But to make it complete, really happy, I wanted eternal union with a man too: another kind of love" (481) to the query of Ursula, "You are enough for me. I don't want anybody else but you. Why isn't the same with you?", which again Ursula considers, "It's obstinacy, a theory, a perversity" which Birkin does not believe in. The language used in describing the wrestling bears a stamp of the homoerotic tendency of the author. Women in their dominating instinct do not allow their men any intimate relationship with anybody. Here Ursula suspects Birkin's intimacy with even Gerald or others and disapproves it which is evident in the dialogues quoted above. The African statuette of about two feet high woman which Birkin saw at Halliday's flat assumes significant symbolic value. Birkin pondered over it for some time and in 'Moony' its importance is described:

> It was a woman, with hair dressed high, like a melon-shaped dome. He remembered her vividly: she was one of his soul's intimates. Her body was long and elegant, her face was crushed tiny like a beetle's she had rows of round heavy collars, like a column of quoits, on her neck. He remembered her; her astonishing cultured elegance, her diminished, beetle face, the astounding long elegant body, on her short, ugly legs, with such protuberant buttocks, so weighty and unexpected below her slim long loins. She knew what he himself did not know. She had thousands of years of purely sensual, purely unspiritual knowledge behind her. It must have been thousand of years since her race had died, mystically: that is, since the relation between the senses and the outspoken mind had broken, leaving the experience all in one sort, mystically sensual. Thousand of years ago, that which was imminent in himself must have taken place in these Africans: the goodness, the holiness, the desire for creation and productive happiness must have lapsed, leaving the single impulse for knowledge in one sort, mindless progressive knowledge through the senses, knowledge arrested and ending in the senses, mystic knowledge through the senses, knowledge arrested and ending in the senses, mystic knowledge in disintegration and dissolution, knowledge such as the beetles have, which live purely within the world of corruption and cold dissolution.... He realised that there were great mysteries to be unsealed, sensual, mindless, dreadful mysteries, far beyond the phallic cult. How far, in their inverted culture, had these West Africans gone beyond phallic knowledge? Very, very far. Birkin recalled again the female figure: the elongated, long body, the curious, unexpected heavy buttocks,... This was far beyond any phallic knowledge, sensual subtle realities far beyond the scope of phallic investigation. (253-54)

Birkin initially reacted positively to the African statuette, but finally rejected their inverted culture. He is a leader, a creator, and recognises himself as a little Jesus (Sagar 91). He distinguishes the contrast between the white races and the Africans. He is inquisitive of the happy creative being and questions; "Is our day of creative life finished?" (254). He gives reasons about the contrastive life of the white races and says:

> The white races, having the arctic north behind them, the vast abstraction of ice and snow, would fulfil a mystery of ice-destructive knowledge, snow-abstract annihilation. Whereas the West Africans, controlled by the burning death-abstraction of the Sahara, had been fulfilled in sun-destruction, the putrescent mystery of sun-rays. (254)

The discourse Lawrence created in his writing narrating the act of love and physical union which has been termed as obscene by his critics/readers bears a holy significance and represents a symbolic phallic language that is mystic, mythical and significant in Hindu Shaivism. Lawrence considers sex divine and life-fulfilling:

> [H]e saw sex as a means to awaken the true self, and to discover not only our own inner being but inner being of all things.... Lawrence...saw the inner essence of things as having religious significance. He felt that the "life mystery" at the core of all was the only thing that he could honestly call God. (Hawthorne 2)

The London Bohemia represents the failure of meaningful life in the modern world of perversion. Café Pompadour stands for the world of disintegration and dissolution. Similarly the resident area of the colliers symbolizes the dirty and degenerative surrounding.

There are several images in different chapters which depict decay, destruction, conflict, love, sex, death, corruption, various roles and components of nature, which represent a deep significance. Some words like fire, white, darkness, dark, flame, coldness, snow, ice, light, water, electric, electricity, power, motion are used as both conventional and private symbols. As private symbols they are used with different meanings in different contexts. The sun as source of warmth, energy, freshness and life is a male symbol whereas the moon as feminine symbol stands for virginity, whiteness, beauty, coldness, ghostliness, possessiveness, selfishness and negation of spontaneous love and life.

4

There are also several words from other languages used in the dialogues and descriptive sentences of *Women in Love.* In *Women in Love*, there are instances of use of words/phrases of several other languages like French, German, Italian, Latin, Greek, Japanese, Indian and dialects of Tyrol, Uzbekistan and so on. The highest number of French words and phrases are used in this novel. German and Italian assume the second and third positions in terms of the number of words/allusions used. Even in the chapter 'Rabbit' the little French Governess speaks in French about the rabbit Bismarck and Gudrun and Winifred speaks in French about Bismarck that it is a mystery and wonder (237). This is very important about the novel and its author, D.H. Lawrence that so many code-switchings are used and these are organically mixed with English narrations.

Women in Love, in its several chapters presents a mode of symbolic and non-verbal communication, which is mystical, and significantly meaningful, expressing the inexpressible and pacifying the torment and turbulence in the souls of his characters. These kinds of communication are available in chapters like 'Water-party', 'Rabbit', 'Mooney', 'Gladiatorial' and 'Excurse'. In "Water-party" Ursula and Gudrun take off their clothes and jump into water for a swim and after swimming a few minutes they run into the grove and dance. The swimming, running and dance and intermittent silences expose their obsessions in love, their passion and the movements symbolize their electric energy. Even the drowning accident does not affect them. Gudrun becomes impatient to visit Gerald to comfort him whereas Ursula keeps pondering over Birkin. In 'Rabbit', Gudrun's concerns and passion for Gerald are exposed. When Gudrun was not able to control the rabbit and the rabbit scratched Gudrun's wrist, it is Gerald who came to her rescue.

> Gudrun looked at Gerald with strange, darkened eyes, strained with underworld knowledge, almost supplicating, like those of a creature which is at his mercy, yet which is his ultimate victor. He did not know what to say to her. He felt the mutual hellish recognition. And he felt he ought to say something, to cover it. He had the power of lightning in his nerves, she seemed like a soft recipient of his magical, hideous white fire. He was unconfident, he had qualms of fear.... She looked up at him, and a slight sinister smile contracted her white face.... The vindictive mockery in her voice made his brain quiver. Glancing up at him, into his eyes, she revealed again the mocking, white cruel recognition. There was a league between them, abhorrent to them both. They were implicated with each other in abhorrent mysteries. (241-42)

In "Moony," Ursula finds Birkin throw stones at the reflection of the moon in the pond water at Willey Green in trying to destroy its roundness. Without knowing his presence there Ursula also comes there. She hears Birkin speaking to himself and then becomes silent. He was steadfast in throwing stones in his obsession and absence of mind and "was not satisfied" (247).

> Like a madness, he must go on. He got large stones, and threw them, one after the other, at the white-burning centre of the moon, till there was nothing but a rocking of hollow noise, and a pond surged up, no moon any more, only a few broken flakes tangled and glittering broadcast in the darkness, without aim or meaning, a darkened confusion, like a black and white kaleidoscope tossed at random. (247-48)

As he was throwing stones at the moon in the pond, Ursula was looking at him dazed. Temporarily he stopped throwing stones and stood listening to other sounds. Silence followed, but Birkin lingered by the water. Being afraid that he would throw stones again at the moon, Ursula went to him to ask him not to throw stones again. He did not know that Ursula was watching him all along. The act of throwing stones at the reflection of the moon is a non-verbal communication of one's obsession and anguish of non-fulfilment of one or many desires. And that desire got fulfilled when they conversed and silenced and again began on topics of England and France and life and love, like "My life is so unfulfilled"…. "And I feel as nobody would ever really love me" (249)…said Ursula to which Birkin replied about her female ego and asks her to drop her ego and says: "I want you to drop your assertive *Will,* your frightened apprehensive self-insistence, that is what I want—I want you to trust yourself so implicitly, that you can let yourself go," (250-51) and he finally says: "Yes, I do, I love you, and I know it's final, so why say any more about it" (251).

In the chapter "Gladiatorial", Birkin and Gerald wrestle where their silent wrestling unites their white flesh into one. Gerald was extremely bored suffering from "this misery of nothingness" (266). When he saw Birkin, he was happy and relaxed. Birkin proposed the third one to Gerald's two cures for *ennui,* i.e. work and love. They prepared for fighting where automatically their *electric* energy got united: "we are mentally, spiritually intimate, therefore we should be more or less physically intimate too—it is more whole" (272). In 'Excurse' the sweet union of Ursula and Birkin at the little parlour of the inn at Southwest Minister expresses the unspeakable. The physical union of the couple was extremely silent and nonverbal whereas both were inwardly violently active:

> She was beautiful as a marvellous flower opened at his knees, a paradisal flower as she was, beyond womanhood, such a flower of luminousness…. It was a dark flood of electric passion she released from him, drew into herself. She had established a rich new circuit, a new current of passional electric energy, between the two of them, released from the darkest poles of the body and established in perfect circuit. It was a dark fire of electricity that rushed from him to her, and flooded them both with rich peace, satisfaction. (313-14)

Again in the same chapter, in the darkness of the Sherwood Forest where they spent the night, "a night of unbroken sleep"…, "the body of mysterious night upon the body of mysterious night, the night masculine and feminine, never to be seen with the eye, or known with the mind, only known as palpable revelation of living otherness" (320), the first perfect union of their souls, where Birkin "found the pure lambent reality of her forever invisible flesh" the non-verbal physical activity reveals the essence in silence:

> She had her desire of him, she touched, she received the maximums of unspeakable communication in touch, dark, subtle, positively silent, a magnificent gift and give again, a perfect acceptance and yielding, a mystery, the reality of that which can never be known, vital, sensual reality that can never be transmuted into mind content, but remains outside, living body of darkness and silence and subtlety, the mystic body of reality. She had her desire fulfilled. For she was to him what he was to her, the immemorial magnificence of mystic, palpable, real otherness. (320)

Lawrence's uses both expressionist and impressionist techniques. So many symbols, metaphors and similes used in depicting the physical activities which stand for non-verbal communication are very much alluring. Lawrence is deft in employing this mode of "clash of contradictory languages" which depict non-verbal exposition of relationship between the characters. *Women in Love* encodes a mystery which holds an inexplicable symbolic significance. There is a strong positivity in the seemingly negative role of Gerald:

> ...One has immediately to admit that the closing scene of Gerald's life is dominated by a quite electrifying sense of emptiness and loss...but for all the criticisms the novel itself makes of Gerald and Gerald's way of life—or ways stabilising force. He is a centre against which Birkin's free inquiry is played off: until Gerald's death, when the prospect that faces Birkin is rendered. I think with absolute frankness on Lawrence's part, as dismayingly problematical...its relevance to the modern world is of an active and positive kind. (Tomlinson 65-66)

Depicted in Lawrence's own image, Birkin holds more negative views on the modern world than Gerald. Gerald is a dynamic personality, symbolic of the adventures of modern times, and of progressive industrialism, whereas Birkin is full of despair and deliberates elaborately on the evils of modernity and modernism. Hence he is more negative one of the two. Pertinently Langman comments: "Faced with the death of the old ideals, how minimal, Birkin's positive is: how close to sheer negation. All that he has is a tentative willingness insistent rather than confident, to let life make a claim on him" (85). Birkin constantly speaks a language of difference, despair, uncertainty and nihilism. He stresses on friendship with a man like Gerald who is his strength whereas in spite of her successful marriage with Birkin, Ursula questions: "Why aren't I enough?" (481). The four women in love symbolize the four states of affairs with the random realities experienced as explored by Lawrence within the fictional boundaries.

Lawrence is both a romanticist and a modernist. He created a new idiom for his fictional narratives. As an original thinker, he was an innovator of the fictional forms of writing, and did not believe in the traditional norms. With his myriad allusions he has developed a montage technique for giving order to the disorderly disillusionment of the modern, decadent, industrial and mechanical world. Personal life has been a source of material for his fictional writings, which is mostly common with several fictionists. To objectivise the subjective is a significant role of every artist. But Lawrence has evolved ideals for his characters and made them symbolize those ideals. He has juxtaposed opposites to balance the values/idealisms to be followed in life. Hence readers find paradoxes in his narratives. Integrity and tenacity to follow the ideals are noticed in his characters who speak his mystical idioms pondering deep on situations of life, accepting the inevitable and not believing in the predetermined destiny.

Works Cited

Dataller, Roger. "Elements of D.H. Lawrence's Prose Style", *Critics on D.H. Lawrence*. Edited. W.T. Andrews. New Delhi: Universal Book Stall, 1995. 52-57. Print.

Hawthorne, Derek. "D.H. Lawrence's *Women in Love:* Anti-modernism in Literature", Part-1, Counter-Currents Publishing. https://www.counter-currents.com/2011/01/d-h-lawrence-women-in-love-part-1/ accessed on 24th March 2019. Web.

———. "D.H. Lawrence on the Meaning of Sex", Counter-Currents Publishing. https://www.counter-currents.com/2013/08/d-h-lawrence-on-the-meaning-of-sex/ accessed on 24th March 2019. Web.

HRITCU, Oana Ruxandra. "Non-Verbal Communication in D.H. Lawrence's *Women in Love.*" www.ijer.eu/articole/55_pdfsam_IJCR/204-2011.pdf. accessed on 24th March 2019. Web.

Langman, F.H. *"Women in Love", Critics on D.H. Lawrence.* Edited. W.T. Andrews. New Delhi: Universal Book Stall, 1995. 81-86. Print.

Lawrence, D.H. *Women in Love.* London: Penguin Classics (1920), 2007, edn. Print.

Murry, J. Middleton. "The Nostalgia of Mr. D.H. Lawrence", *Critics on D.H. Lawrence.* Edited. W.T. Andrews. New Delhi: Universal Book Stall, 1995. 20-24. Print.

Neill, S. Diana. *A Short History of the English Novel.* New Delhi: Kalyani Publishers (1971), 1979. Print.

Padhi, Bibhu. "Lawrence's Idea of Language". *Modernist Studies,* Vol. IV. 1985, 65-76. Print.

Sagar, Keith. *The Art of D.H. Lawrence.* Cambridge: Cambridge University Press, 1967. Print.

Tomilinson, T.B. "Lawrence and Modern Life: *Sons and Lovers, Women in Love*". *Critics on D.H. Lawrence.* Edited. W.T. Andrews. New Delhi: Universal Book Stall, 1995. 58-66. Print.

Zheng, Jianjun. "The Reinvention of Love in D.H. Lawrence's *Women in Love*". *Asian Social Science.* www.ecsenet.org/ Vol. 6, No. 3, March 2010, accessed on 24th March 2019. 125-27. Web.

5

Zeppelin Nights: Exile, Creativity, and the Great War (1914-1918)

Sachidananda Mohanty

> And the war will go on for a very long time. I knew it when I watched the Zeppelin the other evening, gleaming like a new sign in the heavens, a new supreme celestial body...which had assumed the heavens as its own.

As symbols go, it would not be easily identified with the Great War (1914-1918). Other icons, more ominous and monstrous, such as the trench or the gas mask, would be more recognizable as a metaphor and a memory. And yet, the image of a giant airship floating in the start-laden sky of London, hanging in mid-air, must have presented an eerie spectacle to those below. Immobile and ethereal, the Zeppelin, as a weapon of war, was evocative more of peace on earth than the deadly warfare engulfing entire nations. It is only the poet who could sense the essential paradox of the image, latent in 'a new celestial body', as he wrote to his sympathetic correspondent in America.

D.H. Lawrence was not the only one who saw the image as a paradox. The image of the Zeppelin seems to inform the classic Zeppelin Nights by his contemporaries, Ford Madox Hueffer (Ford) and his companion, Violet Hunt. Ford himself was a product of mixed German-British parentage, anathema to the all-pervasive war-mongering and hysteria raging then in England and the continent. The dropping of the more Germanic Hueffer in favour of the acceptable surname 'Ford' is a commentary on the time, just as the presence of the British-born David Herbert

Lawrence and his Germanic wife Frieda Von Richthofen (1879-1956) posed a threat to the overzealous patriots of Cornwall in England who ransacked their cabin as part of 'patriotic' duty.

The return of the Zeppelin image with its double-blinding message in recent times may not be entirely coincidental. *Zeppelin Nights: London in the First World War* is contemporary historian's account of the 'saga of futility and wasted human lives'. It provides a superbly detached account of everyday life in London from 1914 to the conflict's end in 1948. It is this paradox of war as a site of both destruction and creativity through acts of exile that will constitution the substance of this paper.

***

British Literary responses to the Great War, stretching from the trench poetry of Wilfred Owen (1893-1918) and non-canonical women poets like Vera Brittain (1893-1970), to the writings of Eliot, Pound, Huxley, Ford and Lawrence have been generally recognised. It is not so much the senseless savagery of the 'total war' and what Clive Bloom describes as 'totalized paranoia' (there is no knowing who is the enemy, therefore presume all are the enemy) (1990: 4), the latter stemming from the seemingly tranquil but xenophobic Edwardian era (Britain's prospects as bleaker and its enemies as more monstrous) (Hitchner, 2010: 413; Denning, 1987: 41) that are new, although they are worth recalling on the occasion of the centenary of the world event. More importantly, a closer look is required regarding the precise manner in which the war impacted the fundamental choices—personal, institutional and literary—that writers made, and the manner in which exile and creativity were played out in literary-cultural and political terms. Revisiting authors, texts and life-writing in the context of the Great War thus becomes a useful exercise.

A simple approach to the study would call for the traditional line-up of heroic resistance versus opportunistic acquiescence/alliance of intellectuals and artists. That is a surface narrative/reading very much there for everyone to see, a polarisation in Manichean terms, although it must be admitted that the response to wars has never been bereft of moral issues or considerations. After all, the Oxbridge culture, the elite world of Bloomsburry parties and publications continued blithely under the shadow of the war, even as, Janus—like sanctimonious patriotic slogans were mouthed by the newspapers and politicians of the day.

A closer look at war and creativity would show the manner in which biography and creativity were enmeshed in the vortex of war and exile. This intermingling gave new meaning to the concept of exile. It was no longer to be seen as an involuntary act of self-isolation in a foreign location. More fundamentally, thanks to the new role of the mass media and organs of the State, the dissenting writer would remain exiled within one's own country and community. More significantly, he/she remained an embattled and divided self thanks to the forces of containment.

In this essay, I shall pay close attention to the war years of D.H. Lawrence with regard to his creativity, while bringing in the examples of sine notable contemporaries such as Ezra Pound, Ford Madox Ford, Richard Aldington and Aldous Huxley. Unlike others, such as Wilfred Owen and Ford Madox Ford, Lawrence did not see action on the battlefield. He was not gassed or shell-shocked, but his 'nightmare' was no less traumatic and agonising. Subjected to a relentless regime of surveillance, persecution, moral and physical abuse, he stood out alone among many of his established contemporaries.

There are two literary texts by Lawrence that lend themselves to fruitful study in this respect: the story 'England, My England' (1922), and 'Nightmare' in the novel *Kangaroo* (1923) that he wrote at Thirroul in Australia. It must be stated at the outset that the war does not serve as a mere setting or backdrop to Lawrence's Literary works; it is integral to his overall artistic vision. Secondly, and more crucially, war does not occupy only a passing phase in his writing career. It encompasses the entire corpus of his writings, including his creative works towards the very end of his life. Thus, while Lawrence leaves the war and England, the war does not leave him. The opening paragraph in *Lady Chatterley's Lover*, his last novel, is a clear throwback to the Great War. The narrator stands poised as a witness to an era and reviews the essential paradox of the modern tragedy:

both human and civilised Lawrence wrote the novel as he was fighting his terminal illness. The novel opens evocatively and combines despair with a sense of hope:

> Ours is essentially a tragic age, so we refuse to take it tragically. The cataclysm has happened; we are among the ruins; we start to build up new habitats, to have new hopes. It is rather hard work: there is now no smooth road into the future: but we go round, or scramble over the obstacles. We've got to live, no matter how many skies have fallen.

This was more or less Constance Chatterley's position. The war had brought the roof down over her head. And she had realized that one must live and learn (1928: 1).

Indeed the central motif in Lawrence's last novel was the way war, or the unbridled quest for absolute power (British brand of capitalism or German brand of militarism), led to the crippling of human of life and civilisation, emblematic in the tragedy of Constance and Clifford Chatterley. The 'ruins' must give way to 'new hopes'.

It is easier to see that war is a recurrent motif in Lawrence's works than to see how his novels like. *The Rainbow* (1915) had varying fortunes on account of the war. Two specific arguments may be advanced in this context which go against much of critical opinion and received wisdom. The conventional view is that the novel was proscribed and persecuted on account of its alleged obscenity. On the other hand, there is evidence to suggest that the real reason for its banning, or the major contributory factor, was Lawrence's anti-war stand/sentiment. Again, following from the first, it is argued that hostile treatment Lawrence received at the hands of those he called 'the censor morons' led to his decision to leave the shores of England for Australia and the New World, just as some observers see his opposition to war as responsible for his exile.

The irony was that while he left England, and the war, the motifs of war and violence were increasingly manifest in his 'leadership fiction', including *Aaron's Rod* (1922), *Kangaroo* (1932), *The Plumed Serpent* (1926), and the disturbing novella, set in New Mexico, called *The Woman Who Rode Away* (1928). While the disillusionments with Western democracy led to the European anarchism of Emma Goldman and Peter Kropotkin, in Lawrence and others such as T.S. Eliot, Wyndham Lewis and Ezra Pound, it resulted, as Harrison argues cogently in "The Reactionaries: A Study of the Anti-democratic Intelligentsia", in an ideology of political orthodoxy, a viewpoint endorsed by Lawrence-biographer Jeffrey Meyers: "The war impelled Lawrence not only to advocate and autocratic dictator who would control and transform corrupt society, but also to plan an idealistic community that would escape this corruption and the nucleus of a new society" (1993: 172).

In any event, Lawrence's dream project, Rananim, based on literary models like the Brook farm of Nathaniel Hawthorne and Margaret Fuller in the 1840s and to the pantisocracy of Coleridge and Southey, would wait, for Lawrence had "conflicting desires for the stimulation of society and the solitude he needed for his work" (*ibid.*, 173). The Lawrences took up residence from late January until late July, 1915, in a portion of the house belonging to the poet novelist Viola Meynell situated at Greatham, Sussex. The Meynell family was the inspiration for one of his most moving stories—'England, my England'.

The tale employs and ironical title after W.E. Henley's patriotic poem "Pro Rigo Nostro" from *For England's Sake: Verses and Songs in Times of War*. Essentially, three motifs underline the narrative: first, placid agricultural England overtaken by the frenzy of war, second, Egbert's brand of individualism and aloofness vis-à-vis the domineering Godfrey Marshall; and, finally, the conflict between Egbert and Winfired, his wife, partly a fallout of the Egbert-Marshall imbroglio. The family get sucked into the mire of war, drowning response to war is characteristically detached. He sees the rivalry between British and German militarism as "between blue water-flowers and red or white bush-blossoms" or between the "wild boar and the wild bear" (*ibid.*, 252). For him, nationalism, militarism and industrialism are all sides of the same coin. He refuses to 'reckon with the world', for he sees war as the triumph of the ugly mob spirit and realises that "his feelings were his own, his understanding was man become inferior to his own true knowledge and self, just because the mob expects it of him?"

Nothing degrades Egbert as the mechanical uniformity of barrack life. Being ordered about by the 'pretty canaille of non-commissioned officers' destroys his soul. "In the thick, gritty, hideous khaki, his subtle physique was extinguished as if he had been killed.

In the ugly intimacy of the camp, his thoroughbred sensibilities were just degraded" (*ibid.*, 254). When he returns home, he finds no love but duty from his wife, she 'serves the soldier' but 'repudiates the man'. He was governed not by conscious will but only by the 'mechanism' of command and obedience. There was no attraction of the family and the children, only an overwhelming sense of emptiness. As he muses: "No, no! No Winifred, no children. No world, no people. Better the agony of dissolution ahead than the nausea of the effort backwards" (258).

England, My England is thus a meditation on the scourge of war. The automatism of war spares none. Even the stoical Egbert must pay the price and succumb to dissolution. Along with his death, there is the annihilation of an organic life/world that would be irrevocably gone.

Egbert's indifferent approach to dying may be carefully compared with the protagonist of Richard Aldington's later novel, *Death of a Hero* (1929). He wrote a fine biography of Lawrence published in 1950. It is interesting to see the affinities between Lawrence and Aldington in terms of novelistic techniques, characterization and their responses to war. Like Lawrence's Egbert, who dies in the battlefield, George Winterbourne of Aldington, too, perishes before his time, his life savagely cut down by the machine gun just before the end of the war, as an utterly meaningless act. David Ayers writers: "Like *Parade's End, Death of a Hero* sees the war not as the cause of change, but as a further blow to English society" (1998: 89). There is thus an affinity between Lawrence and Aldington in this regard. The major difference is that while in Lawrence there is the authorial voice that comments on the narrative action, Aldington employs narrator for serving his ideological ends.

Few works of art of the period can surpass Lawrence's depiction of tyranny and absolutism of war. The entire chapter is punctuated by the imagery of violence and cruelty. There is an ominous refrain of the word 'criminal' that stands for the civilian government (Lawrence, 1922: 235). The anger and rebellion are not so much against the actual combatants as the 'stay-at-home bullies'. Somers is no pacifist or conscientious objector. There are situations, he knows, that warrant defence and a judicious use of violence. But he aligns himself with no group because with the spirit of collapse, practically every man "lost his own centrality, his own manly isolation in his own integrity, which alone keeps life real". Those who went to war, did so in a vainglorious manner, 'with outward glory but inward shame', their vitality and inward spirit gone. It is a colossal tragedy, as Richard Somers sees it, leading to what he terms as 'Bottomleyism' (240).

Somers does not give in to this collective insanity. For, the greater the crisis, the more intensive should be 'the isolated reckoning with his own soul'. Summoned to a medical test prior to conscription, he feels like a 'condemned man', but is determined not to serve: "I will never obey another order if they kill me" (*ibid.*, 238).

It is indeed the ethics of every 'gentleman' to 'torture any single independent man as a mob tortures the isolated and the independent. Somers cannot go beyond a stipulated area and is periodically served with eviction orders. His private domestic life is violated with impunity. He is spied upon and the smallest words and deeds of the couple are monitored by overzealous patriots. A block of common salt or a diary comprising botanical notes is viewed as a subversive tool in the eyes of the custodians of State.

The loss of individuality is further reinforced by the impersonal numerals typical of military culture—C1, C2, and C3. At the camp, men are thrown together and jeered at by the perverse elements. At the site of inspection, they are stripped naked. They become jackals and "bay like some horrible unclean hound, bay with a loud sound, from slavering, unclean jaws" (236). When the individual suffers from the ultimate isolation, he becomes a spy (241). For the spy is an outcaste, outside the pale of law, with no access to legal or constitutional remedy. Somers refuses to give in. He learns to stand by the strength of his individual conscience: "He discovered the great secret: to stand alone as his own judge himself, absolutely. He took his stand absolutely on his own judgment of himself. Then, the mongrel-mouthed world would say and do what it liked. This is the greatest secret of behaviour: to stand alone, and judge oneself from the deep's of one's own soul" (278).

***

Following the armistice and the formal end of war by November 1919, Lawrence was finally permitted to leave England for Italy. Disillusioned by the war and psychic damage it caused, he sought out the free atmosphere of Italy and was determined to live there with his wife as expatriates (Meyers, 1993: 231).

We may see a somewhat different response in the case of the America poet and imagist Ezra Pound (1885-1972) who made London his home in the first decade of the 20th century. By the early summer of 1912, he, along with Richard Aldington and Hilda Doolittle, had begun a Movement in poetry called Imagism. The Movement did well and, in March 1914, Harriet Monroe produced the impressive anthology *Des Imagistes*. Friendship with Yeats in November 1913 and marriage to Dorothy on 20 April 1914 were further advances on the personal and professional fronts, and in all this England was hospitable.

Unlike Lawrence, who firmly opposed the war and sought out the life of an exile, Pound stayed on in England as an expatriate poet despite serious political reservations regarding the war, and continued his literary life in England until he left for Paris. Others like Ford Madox Ford and Aldous Huxley made more complex responses to the war. Huxley (1894-1963) volunteered to join the army when war broke out. However, he was turned down owing to partial blindness. Undeterred, he read English Literature at Balliol College, Oxford University, and taught French for a year at Eton. During the war he worked as a farm labourer at Garsington Manor, the property owned by Lady Ottoline Morrell. Here, he befriended some of the leading members of the Bloomsburry Group such as the well-known pacifist Bertrand Russell, and Clive Bell. He worked briefly for the Air Ministry in 1918. By the 1920s, Huxley and his wife Maria Nys (1899-1955) had left for Italy. They spent time with the Lawrence when there, and after a sojourn in Europe, travelled to New Mexico, Taos, in the 1920s, where they met the Lawrences in the company of Mabel Dodge Luhan, who attempted to create American counterculture in the south-west United States for which we may refer to Lois P. Rudnick's fascinating book, *Utopian Vistas: The Mabel Dodge Luhan House and the American Counterculture* (1998).

In 1937, Huxley moved to California with his wife Maria and son Mathew, where he died in 1963. It is worth nothing that unlike Lawrence, Russell and Pound, Huxley's attitude to violence and war was largely shaped by the post-World War I scenario. The experience he underwent in the New World, especially in Taos, and the cataclysmic events such as the Spanish Civil war, in addition to his attraction to Eastern philosophy, would make him a conscientious objector during World War II. He spoke out against war and nationalism in Eyeless in Gaza, and expressed deep disillusionment with violence and war in *Ends and Means: An Enquiry into the Nature of Ideals and into the Methods Employed for their Realization.*

While Huxley could not join the army during the Great War (1914-1918), Ford Madox Ford (1873-1939) did. Born in Surrey, England, of a British mother and German father, he founded *The English Review* in 1908 and published the works of some of the best writers of his times. During the war, he worked for the War Propaganda Bureau and wrote two propaganda books, *When Blood in their Argument: An Analysis of Prussian Culture* (1915) and with Richard Aldington, *Between St. Dennis and St. George: A Sketch of Three Civilisation* (1915). He enlisted at the age of 41 and fought on the Western front. His war experience led to *Parade's End* (1924-28). Other works he produced during the War include *The Good Soldier* (1915), and, as earlier cited, *Zeppelin Nights*.

Like Pound, Ford found the English literary scene no longer propitious in the 1920s and left for Paris. In 1924, with the help of an English patron, he founded the *Transatlantic Review* which published the works of James Joyce, Ernest Hemingway, Gertrude Stein, Ezra Pound and Jean Rhys. Today, he is known for the support he gave to American writer such as Allan Tate, Katherine Anne Porter, and Robert Lowell. He alternated between France and America and died in Deanville, France.

***

Of the four major figures discussed here—Ford, Huxley, Pound, and Lawrence—Lawrence clearly stands out for the manner in which he steadfastly opposed the war and paid the price for his dissent. The other notable, T.S. Eliot, stayed on, steered the course of Faber and Faber and dismissed Lawrence as 'rotten and rotting others'.

Biographical and critical opinion differs regarding Ford's role in the persecution of Lawrence and the reasons for Lawrence's exile Speaking on the issue, Meyers says:

> Ford's secret, semi-official report to Masterman on the Lawrences' opposition to the war and supposedly suspicious behaviour in Greatham combined with Lawrence's damaging association with Russell's pacifist activities and his powerful anti-war story, 'England, My England', encouraged the authorities to suppress *The Rainbow* in November 1915, and because Lawrence remained under government surveillance to expel him from Cornwall in October 1917.

Others, including Ford's biographer, Max Saunders, question Meyers' conclusion and argue that Meyers seems to base his assessment entirely on two sources: those of Richard Aldington and David Garnett. While Lawrence Biographers Meyers and Paul Delany (1978) come to similar conclusions regarding the role of Ford and Lawrence's exile because of the war, others like Max Saunders and Paul Skinner of the Ford Madox Ford Society think otherwise. They differ from the account provided by Meyers of what transpired at Alice Meynell's house. According to Saunders:

Terms like "testimony", "conformation" and "evidence" try to give the illusion of the biographer as an impartial judge. But when on flimsy basis, Meyers writes as if his wild allegation was a fact, saying that later "Ford justified his treachery by claiming he had go to Greatham to help Lawrence instead of to betray him, it is the biographer who is inventing the evidence (the 'secret semi-official report') and being opportunistically and cavalierly indifferent to obligation to find proof before libeling the dead" (1996: 476-78).

According to Paul Skinner, Lawrence's anti-war views created some hostility but it was largely the reviews by James Douglas and Clement short that prompted the authorities to act: many of the main libraries and bookseller had already rejected it. The book was published at the end of September and by 5 November the police were making their second visit to Methuen, confiscating all unsold copies. Methuen, of course, showed a very dispiriting lack of courage.

While there will always remain legitimate doubts based on differing perceptions of different biographer, there is no denial of the fact that it was a combination of anti-war sentiments as well as the charge of obscenity that led to the banning of *The Rainbow* and Lawrence's final decision to leave the country. His publisher Methuen showed a singular lack of courage; it was equally true that Lawrence did not receive any support from political quarters, thanks largely to his strong opposition to the war. As Meyers correctly concludes:

> The suppression of the novel made Lawrence desperately poor. He remained trapped in England (when subsequent requests for Passports were denied) and persecuted during the rest of the war. He was determined to leave the country as soon as the war was over and to live as an expatriate for the rest of his life. He abandoned all hope of achieving popular success in England and turned to America as his potential audience.

***

British literary response to the Great War varied in literary-cultural and political terms, and took myriad shapes.

As examples of four of the leading writers reveal, each was psychically affected by the war, and each learnt to deal with it in his own way. All four eventually left England. It was Lawrence who was the first to become an exile. He offered the strongest opposition to war, and, consequently, faced the greatest persecution at home. The experience caused a profound disillusionment in him of liberal democracy, and queered the pitch for writing his 'leadership fiction' with proto-fascist heroes until the very late stage of his career. Moving away from the dominant 'leader-follower' theme, he would, in the final stage, try and established leadership on alternate foundations.

Notes

D.H. Lawrence to Harriet Monroe, Editor, Poetry. See Monroe (1930)

http://www.theguardian.com/books/2014/apr/23/zeppelin-nights-london-first-world-war-jerry-w. Accessed on 3 August 2014.

Michael Denning writes that were popular literature had once been dominated by 'an assertive, confident, and expansionist genre' that is the imperial adventure story, this gave way to 'an increasingly insular, even paranoid, genre-stressing vigilance and protection against invasion'. Quoted in Hitchner (2010: 413-30). Also see Denning (1987).

For a detailed analysis of the text, see Mohanty (1993) www.egs.edu/library/aldous-huxley/biography. Accessed on August 2014.

Paul Skinner in an email dated 22 July 2014 to Sachidananda Mohanty.

Meyers' account may be compared with an early biography of Lawrence by Richard Aldington (1950). See Meyers (1990). Also see Paul Poplawski (1996: 38-43).

Works Cited

Aldington, Richard. *Death of a Hero*. London: Chatto & Windus, 1929 & Covisi Friede (USA), 1936.

———. *D.H. Lawrence: Portrait of a Genius But....* New York: Duell, Sloan and Pearce, 1950.

Ayers, David. "Richard Aldington's Death of a Hero: A Proto-Fascist Novel", English, Vol. 47, Summer, 1998.

Bloom, Clive (ed.). *Spy Thrillers: From Buchan to Le Carre*. New York: St. Martin's Press, 1978.

Delany, Paul. *D.H. Lawrence's Nightmare: The Writer and His Circle in the Years of the Great War*. New York: Basic Books, 1978.

Denning, Michael. *Cover Stories: Narrative and Ideology in the British Spy Thriller*. London: Routledge.

Ford Madox Ford and Violet Hunt. *Zeppelin Nights*. London: Lane, 1915.

Ford Madox Ford, *Good Soldier.* London: Lane, 1915.

———. *When Blood is Their Argument: An Analysis of Prussian Culture.* London and New York: Hodder and Stoughton, 1924.

———. *Parade's End*. London: Duckworth and Co.

Harrison, John R. *The Reactionaries: A Study of the Anti-democratic Intelligentsia*. New York: Schocken Publishing, 1917.

Henley, W.E. *'Pro Rigo Nostro', For England's Sake: Verses and Songs in Times of War*. London: D. Nutt, 1900.

Hitchner, Thomas. "Edwardian Spy Literature and the Ethos of Sportsmanship: The Sport of Spying", *English Literature in Transition*, 1880, Vol. 53, No. 4.

Huxley, Aldous. *Eyeless in Gaza*. London: Chatto and Windus, *Ends and Means: An Enquiry into the Nature of Ideals and Into the Methods Employed for their Realization*. London: Chatto and Windus, 1936.

Lawrence, D.H. *England, My England*. Reprint, 1985. London: Penguin Books.

———. *Kangaroo*. Reprint, 1985. London: Penguin Books, 1923.

———. *Lady Chatterley's Lover*. New York: Bantam Books, Reprint, 1983.

Meyers, Jeffrey. *D.H. Lawrence: A Biography*. London: Macmillan, 1993. First published in America by Alfred A. Knopf in 1990.

Monroe, Harriet. *Poetry: A Magazine in Verse*, Vol. 36, No. 2, May, 90-96. 1930.

Mohanty, Sachidananda. *Lawrence's Leadership Politics and the Defeat of Fascism*. New Delhi: Academic Foundation, 1993.

Poplawski, Paul. *D.H. Lawrence: A Reference Companion*. Westport, London: Greenwood Press, 1996.

Rudnick, Lois P. *Utopian Vistas: The Mabel Dodge Luhan House and the American Counter Culture*. Albuquerque: University of New Mexico Press, 1998.

Saunder, Max and Ford Madox Ford. *A Dual Life*. Two volumes. Oxford: Oxford University Press, 1996.

White, Jerry. *Zeppelin Nights: London in the First World War*. London: The Bodley Head, 2014.

6

Lawrence in Mexico: The Myth of Quetzalcoatl and Dangers of Americanization

Lalit Kumar

> It is dull! It is all dull! This Life here is one vast complex of dullness! I am dull. I am being dulled. My spirit is being dulled! My life is dulling down to London dullness.
>
> "Why I don't Like Living in London," D.H. Lawrence
>
> Who are these strange faces in Mexico?
>
> Pale faces, yellow faces, black faces? These are no Mexicans!
>
> Where do they come from, and why?
>
> Hymn of Quetzalcoatl, *The Plumed Serpent*

Introduction

The paper proposes to examine D.H. Lawrence's ambivalent feelings towards Mexico through a close analysis of his two major works on Mexico—*The Plumed Serpent* and *Mornings in Mexico*. It seeks to answer two significant questions. One, what precisely drove the British novelist to become a ceaseless wanderer and explore Mexico, Sri Lanka, and other parts of the world? And two, what makes contemporary readers, especially Indian readers, empathise with his Mexican experience? The essay foregrounds a large number of issues—including Lawrence's constant enchantment and disenchantment with the new places, threats of Americanization, cruelty to animals, and the uncanny similarities between the old Mexican Gods and the Indian Gods—which readers in India and elsewhere may relate to. Lawrence was well aware of the apprehension of the Mexicans regarding Americanization and the overwhelming presence of foreigners in Mexico. The male protagonist of *The Plumed Serpent*, Don Ramón, mixes politics with religion in order to free his land from foreign occupation. Lawrence's writings on Mexico, therefore, must be revisited in contemporary times amidst the anxieties of Americans regarding their "Mexicanization", which the current US administration is trying to counter.

Bull Fighting and Jallikattu Ban

In 2014, The Supreme Court of India banned Jallikattu, a two-thousand-year-old bull taming sport of Tamil Nadu. The sport was held during Pongal, a harvesting festival dedicated to the Sun God. The ban led to massive protests and pitted cultural traditionalists against animal rights activists. Save Jallikattu campaign was launched at an unprecedented scale, which overrode the concerns of cruelty to animals and loss of human lives. The popular sentiment eventually forced the government to bring an Ordinance nullifying the Supreme Court ban.

What Jallikattu is to Tamils, bull fighting is to Mexicans as a sport. It would be easier, therefore, for the animal rights activists of India and elsewhere, especially those who find the violence against bulls loathsome, to empathise with Kate Leslie, the protagonist of D.H. Lawrence's (1885-1930) novel *The Plumed Serpent* (1926). In the opening scene of the novel Leslie, an Irish widow, goes to see bull-fight in Mexico City, along with Owen, an American socialist and Villiers, another young American. Her expectations of a thrilling experience and fun are changed into disgust soon when she encounters an unruly crowd of locals. All that she finds is chaos, smell of blood, human cowardice and beastliness.

Leslie is so disillusioned with the gruesome violence perpetrated against bulls and horses that she begins to find the human species repugnant. Here, she seems to echo the sentiments of her compatriot Jonathan Swift's eponymous hero Gulliver in *Gulliver's Travels* (1726). Swift's protagonist Gulliver had found horses superior to men whereas she finds bulls nicer: "Ugh, how I detest them! The longer I live the more loathsome the human species becomes to me. How much nicer the bulls are!" (20). She rejects a game treated with reverence in Mexico as nothing but "just a performance of human beings torturing animals". "To leave the bull-fight is a national insult," says the omniscient narrator of the novel (14). Leslie, however, not only leaves the sport in the middle but also finds a suitable metaphor in "dirty little boys maiming flies" to express her anger against the slaughter. While her American friend Owen is mesmerized with it, she finds no "glamour, no charm in it", and calls the gallant toreadors "as gallant as assistants in a butcher's shop" (10).

Owen's socialist self, however, makes him more tolerant, sensitive and kind, not towards bulls but the masses. What he calls "Life", beauty and some skilful work in the bull-fight, Leslie calls "the insidious modern disease of tolerance" (21). Despite their differences over the cruelty to animals, they share the same distrust towards Mexico and Mexicans. Their personal experience becomes the foundation of political and cultural disdain in general for the entire Mexican population. Leslie finds "an underlying ugliness", "a sort of squalid evil" in Mexico and cannot conceal her sentiments from General Viedma, who rescues her from the euphoric spectators and helps her get back safely to the hotel in an automobile. "I do think Mexico City is evil, underneath," says Leslie. The General, also known as Don Cipriano, counters this accusation courteously: "It is unfortunate, but the foreigners seem to make the Mexicans worse than they are naturally. And Mexico, or something in it, certainly makes the foreigners worse than they are at home" (18). While Cipriano's first statement may sound musical to the ears of readers with experiences of colonialism, the second utterance ambiguously captures the dissatisfaction of a powerful Mexican General with the existing state of affairs in Mexico. The embittered experience that Kate Leslie had initially amidst the violence and bull fighting continues in the novel. But if Mexico breeds resentment to her, it also produces wonder; if it is the land of violence, it is also the land of mystery, if the bleak Mexican world generates pessimism, it also evokes hope and magic. This ambivalence lies not only at the heart of this novel but also at the heart of colonialism and racism.

The Myth of Quetzalcoatl and Sheshnag

The biggest source of fascination and wonder for Leslie is the old Aztec God called Quetzalcoatl. The God was precious to the Aztecs before Spain defeated them and conquered Mexico in 1521. The mysterious name Quetzalcoatl came from the name of a bird and a serpent. Quetzal is a bird that lived high up in the mists of tropical mountains. It had beautiful feathers. Coatl is the name of a serpent. Quetzalcoatl is the Plumed Serpent, the local Mexican God, who had been forgotten by the Mexicans ever since the coming of Christianity. Two powerful Mexicans—General Cipriano and Don Ramon, a judicious thinker and nationalist—are planning to revive the old God. Don Ramon describes the serpent before Leslie:

> At the heart of this earth sleeps a great serpent, in the midst of fire. Those that go down in mines feel the heat and the sweat of him, they feel him move. It is the living fire of the earth, for the earth is alive. The snake of the world is huge, and the rocks are his scales, trees grow between them. I tell you the earth you dig is alive as a snake that sleeps. (178)

The earth, as the Mexican legend says, rests on a large snake. Moreover, the earth is not dead but a living entity. While going through the above-mentioned description of the earth and the serpent, an Indian reader, if not informed about the context, may easily read it not as an excerpt from *The Plumed Serpent* but as an extract from the *Bhagavata Purana,* a Hindu mythological text. In Hinduism, it is believed that the earth, which is alive, rests on a huge snake called Sheshnag. In the *Ramayana*, Rama's younger brother Lakshmana is said to be an incarnation of Sheshnag whereas in the *Mahabharata,* Krishna's elder brother Balarama is an avatar of the celestial serpent. According to the Puranic beliefs, the divine serpent carries the burden of the earth on its hood, and whenever it moves its body, an earthquake strikes the earth. Similarly, in Hinduism, the equivalent to the Mexican bird Quetzal is the mythical bird Garuda, which is worshipped as the vehicle of the Hindu God Vishnu. Incidentally, due to its association with Lord Vishnu, Garuda Indonesia, the national airline of Indonesia, borrowed its name from the sacred bird.

The ancient Mexican God Quetzalcoatl, therefore, is as captivating and a source of wonder for Indian readers as it turns out to be for the Irish lady Kate Leslie. In her meeting with Don Ramon, Leslie confesses that she loves the word Quetzalcoatl. Ramon wants the Gods of antiquity to come back and save the decadent and degenerated soul of Mexicans. But Lawrence did not have a favourable opinion of Aztec Gods and Goddesses. They are, he wrote in his travel narrative *Mornings in Mexico* (1927), "unlovely and unlovable lot". Unlike Don Ramon, he finds no "grace or charm, no poetry" in these Gods. He found a perpetual grudge in them; one God grudges another, Gods grudge men whereas men grudge the animals. He even calls the Aztec Goddess of love the "goddess of dirt and prostitution".[1] Snakes and eagles are also used in more than one way by several local tribes. Lawrence describes various rituals of the Hopi tribe in *Mornings in Mexico,* including the annual sacrifice of eagle and snake dance. He saw the withered beaks, claws and bones of sacrificed eagles in the Hopi country, which lay in Arizona. He witnessed a crowd of three thousand people who came to see the Hopi snake dance in which men held live venomous snakes in their mouth (138). He argues that the lives of American aborigines are innately and radically religious. Lawrence finds the religion of Indians and the surviving Aztec "animistic". For him, they are "involved at every moment, in their old, struggling religion" (168).

For Don Ramon, however, the pursuit of a new cult is not only a religious endeavour but also a political project, for he is well aware of the increasing dangers of Americanization. The revival of old Gods is an instance of cultural and religious nationalism that Ramon subscribes to with a view to protecting the essence of Mexico. When Kate Leslie wants to know whether Mexico might die out Don Ramon says: "It might. Die out and become Americanized" (55). Another young Mexican points out the increasing number of foreigners and the dwindling population of Mexicans:

> But the last census of Porfirio Diaz[2] gave seventeen million people in Mexico, and the census of last year gave only thirteen millions. Maybe the count was not quite right. But you count four million people fewer, in twenty years, then in sixty years there will be no Mexicans: only foreigners, who don't die. (54)

Lawrence, during his visit to the Mexico City, had found it rather "ramshackle and Americanized".[3] The apprehension regarding the cultural invasion of Mexico by foreigners is portrayed in several hymns composed by Don Ramon in praise of the God Quetzalcoatl. Americans staying in Mexico have their own anxieties and apprehensions, too, which is a hallmark of an encounter between the colonizer and the colonized. Kate Leslie is in a dilemma, whether "to stay or not to stay in Mexico," as she had heard an old American, who had spent forty years in Mexico, say that a man without a strong moral backbone should not try to settle down in Mexico. If he does he will be broken into pieces, both morally and physically (63). But for Ramon, Mexico is another Ireland where no one can be his own master. Leslie decides eventually not only to stay on but is incorporated into the pantheon as a Goddess. A middle class white Irish lady is deified as an indigenous Mexican Goddess. This is, perhaps, the biggest irony of the cultural nationalism that Ramon meticulously plans and proposes in order to save the Mexicans from foreigners in general and Americans in particular. The irony would have been greater and even more perspicuous had the lady been an American. But since Ramon equates Ireland with Mexico, and Leslie had saved his life from bandits, her Irish identity becomes an enabling factor in her deification.

Kate Leslie is equally critical of both Mexico and America. Mexico gives her a strange feeling of "hopelessness" and "dauntlessness". In her opinion, Mexicans lived without hope, without care. On the other hand, she often wonders whether America was "the great death continent, the continent that destroyed again what the other continents had built up" (68)?

She was impelled to leave America behind, as the flow of life had broken there. Here, one is reminded of T.S. Eliot, who had left America behind and found a cultural home for himself in England? But Lawrence was equally disillusioned and bored with both the countries and found solace only in hitherto unexplored countries and territories. England brought much needed comfort and cultural stability to Eliot but Lawrence's protagonist cannot restart her broken life even in Europe. She says, "White men had a soul, and lost it" (69). As America and Europe pull her down and break her spirit, Mexico pulls down Don Ramon. White men have lost their soul; black men have lost their soul too. Don Ramon and the President of the Republic, Montes, both are committed to save the country but their ways are different. The President wants to save the country from poverty and "unelightenment" whereas Ramon wants to save its soul. To build a country, Montes believes, it becomes imperative to address the concerns of both an empty belly as well as an empty mind. Don Ramon, on the other hand, says, "if a man has no soul, it does not matter whether he is hungry or ignorant" (173). For Indian readers, it would be easier to empathise with this debate, as they are familiar with a somewhat similar line of argument between Nehru and Gandhi in the act of nation-building. When India got independence in 1947, Nehru wanted to use science, technology and rationality to extricate the masses from abject poverty and hunger whereas Gandhi emphasized the purity of soul and moral force. A combination of both Nehruvian and Gandhian model began the process of development in India. Montes and Don Ramon similarly are staunch nationalists who wish to find a panacea to an impoverished country. Lawrence, it seems, like the characters he creates, finds himself stuck in a world which has lost it soul, its purpose; hence he becomes a ceaseless wanderer exploring ancient cultures.

His rejection of conventional western values was carried to an extreme during 1925-27 in his "Mexican writings", which mainly included *The Plumed Serpent* and *Mornings in Mexico*. His objective in these books was to express the "uniqueness of the religious experience which he had encountered among the Indians [Mexicans]".[4] Being "unbearably tired of Europe," Lawrence wrote in 1921, "We really want to sail away to New Mexico."[5] He was also simultaneously contemplating to withdraw from the world, travel east and seek peace in Buddhism. Lawrence's friend had gone to Kandy, Sri Lanka to study Buddhism and Pali at the Buddhist monastery. "I am tired of the world, and want peace like a river," wrote Lawrence in 1922. He did not believe in "Buddhistic inaction and meditation" but the Buddhist notion of peace.[6] Lawrence eventually went to Kandy to seek peace but found it too hot and "enervating" and left it after spending a month there. The restless Lawrence captured his disenchantment with the east in a letter:

> I didn't like Ceylon—at least I liked looking at it—but not to live in. The East is not for me—the sensuous, spiritual voluptuousness, the curious sensitiveness of the naked people, their black bottomless, hopeless eyes—and the heads of elephants and buffaloes poking out of primeval mud—the queer noise of tall metallic palm trees—altogether the tropics have something of the world before the flood—hot dark mud and the life inherent in it makes me feel rather sick.[7]

After his disillusionment with the Buddhist conception of peace, Lawrence eventually reached Mexico in September 1922. He admitted in a letter written to E.M. Forster from Taos, New Mexico that he felt like a stranger there. But he had got used to that feeling and "preferred it to feeling homely". "After all, one is a stranger, nowhere so hopelessly as at home," Lawrence wrote in the same letter.[8] Soon, he regrets Mexico as well and continues his never-ending odyssey of enchantment and disenchantment.

The three antidotes for dullness or boredom in the ancient world, writes Lawrence, were sleep, drink and travel. He questions the ancient wisdom in his attempts to overcome "London dullness" and proposes his own theory: "From Sleep you wake up, from drink you become sober, and from travel you come home again. And then where are you?"[9] Lawrence, it seems, wished for a permanent solution to boredom, for he feels more alien in his hometown the Midlands than anywhere else in the world. As a perpetual wanderer he feels at ease in New Orleans, Mexico City, Sydney, or "in Rome or Paris or Munich or even London". But in Nottingham Road, Bestwood, he feels "at once a devouring nostalgia and an infinite repulsion".[10] He comes up with two remedies in order to dispel the monotony of a materialistic western civilization and industrialized England: love and crusade.[11] But in praxis he uses love and travel to overcome the dullness of life.

Lawrence and his wife Frieda, ever since they met in 1912, spent most of their married life travelling. During the First World War, he got exemption from the military service due to his deteriorating health but he had to face the consequences of war. Since his wife Frieda was German, they both were "persecuted by stay-at-home patriots and driven from place to place".[12] Once he escaped from this persecution, he never settled down in England again and spent rest of his life travelling from country to country, including Germany, Italy, Australia and Mexico.

"Monkey Tricks and Monkey Virtues"

The Plumed Serpent, wrote Katherine Anne Porter, "is a confession of faith, a summing up of the mystical philosophy of D.H. Lawrence". Porter, a novelist and short-story writer, wrote further in her review of the novel: "Lawrence went to Mexico in the hope of finding there, among alien people and their mysterious cult, what he had failed to find in his own race or within himself: a centre and a meaning to life."[13] For Porter, the author merely uses Mexico, the Indians[14] and the cult of the Aztec God Quetzalcoatl—the Plumed Serpent—as pretexts and symbols to express his preoccupations and anxieties.

The novel focuses on the theme of struggle between Catholicism and the ancient Mexican religion. Kate Leslie, like Lawrence, is utterly dissatisfied with the mechanical ways of western civilization and craves for new experiences in Mexico. She comes under the spell of Don Cipriano and Don Ramon, the two imposing male characters. They dress up like ancient Mexican Gods and pretend that the ancient Gods of Mexico have returned to earth. Leslie eventually marries the General and is persuaded by Don Ramon to stay on and join the new cult in the capacity of a Goddess.

"The heroes, Ramon and Cipriano," writes Kate Millett, are "Lawrentian men and mouthpieces, intellectual and earthy respectively. Together with the heroine, they form a characteristic Lawrentian triangle" (Millett, 1969, p. 284). Kate Leslie's ambivalence towards Mexico, her rejection of the established systems, beliefs, religion and revolution and her disillusionment with her native country brings her closer to the author's persona. Though Millet calls her a "female impersonator", Leslie exhibits both feminine as well as feminist traits throughout the novel. Through his female protagonist, Lawrence finds a "vehicle to fantasize what seems to be his own surrender to the dark and imperious male in Cipriano" (284). Kate Millett, who praised *Sons and Lovers,* was appalled by *The Plumed Serpent.* Its sexist as well as racist overtones may have flummoxed Millett. Mexicans as a mass are repeatedly denigrated by Leslie, the "female impersonator". They are denounced as "'mongrels', 'monkeys'; they are 'beastly' and 'malevolent', with 'black souls'; they desire death and 'foulness'; they nurture 'reptile-like evil'; the Indians are 'rabbits';...the 'dark races' (Kate believes) are 'born to be slaves'; while she herself, of course, 'belonged to the ruling races, the clever ones'".[15] "Savages are a burden," wrote D.H. Lawrence to Catherine Carswell from New Mexico after falling ill with "malaria, flue and tropical fever".[16] He maintained that the Indian way of consciousness is totally different from and fatal to the consciousness of the west. "It is almost impossible for the white people to approach the Indian [Mexican] without either sentimentality or dislike," Lawrence argued in *Mornings in Mexico* (101). Following his compatriot Rudyard Kipling, he calls them "two ways", "two streams", which are "never to be united". He writes: "They are not even to be reconciled. There is no bridge, no canal of connection" (102). For Lawrence it was the eternal paradox of human consciousness, for Europe can understand the consciousness of Mexicans only at the cost of death of its own consciousness.

Don Ramon is the representative of Mexican consciousness in the novel. Perhaps, he is a fictional representation of Lawrencian worldview that America and Mexico represent two diametrically opposite streams, which can never meet. However, Ramon's new cult does not face resistance either from the masses or the government but he has two major adversaries—the Catholic priests and his wife. Dona Karlota is a staunch Catholic, a true believer in Jesus. She thinks her husband has gone insane; she rejects old Gods as "dead illusions" (148). It is hard for her to imagine that an educated man may have such beliefs but she assumes that her husband is after power; he wants to be worshipped. For him the pursuit of religion is the pursuit of power. This revelation turns out to be partially true as the story progresses. Her husband's apotheosis into a God unsettles her completely and she dies in a state of delirium. But it's not the political power Ramon is after. He shows no interest when Montes, the President of the Republic, seeks his moral support and offers him the post of Secretary. His friend and staunch supporter General Cipriano brings the message and tells him that he could be even President when Montes' term is up. But Don Ramon remains unmoved. His wife finds his initiative to banish Christ from Mexico "monstrous" but he rejects Christ, for the Christian God has not been able to save Mexico. Don Ramon is equally suspicious of other factors such as charity, socialism, politics, reform and all other benevolent gestures. All these forces turn out to be inadequate in making Mexicans realize their true potential. Consequently, men "are not yet men in full, and women are not yet women". They all have become "half and half, incoherent, part horrible, part pathetic, part good creatures" (190).

Ramon composes the hymns of Quetzalcoatl in order to connect with the masses. These hymns tell the story of advent of Christ in Mexico through a fictional dialogue between the Christian God and the old Mexican God. In the conversation the local God uses words such as "stranger" and "strange words" for Christ, who claims to bring peace and prosperity: "I will bring peace into Mexico. And on the naked I will put clothes, and food between the lips of the hungry, and gifts in all men's hands, and peace and love in their hearts" (202). Here Lawrence seems to have put the claims of missionaries in the narrative form of a hymn. The old had to make way for the young God Jesus and say farewell to the people of Mexico. But now the time has come for the departure of the foreign God and return of the indigenous God Quetzalcoatl, which becomes a tool to counter the increasing influence of foreigners on Mexico. Ramon writes in his fourth hymn:

> How nice if we could take all these things away from the foreigners, and possess them!
>
> Take back our lands and silver and oil, take the trains and the factories and the automobiles. (233)

He is an astute landlord, and knows that people cannot understand the "high Christianity". The desire to free Mexico from the cultural and political occupation of foreigners accounts for his revivalist project, which his wife misses out completely. She is unable to perceive that the political, the religious, and the cultural are closely intertwined in the circulation of the myth of homecoming of old Gods. "Now, Father, we must speak to the Mexicans in their own language, and give them the clue-word to their own souls," addresses Don Ramon to the local Christian priest (239). The Italian archbishop forbids the people from listening to these hymns and orders his supporters to destroy them. But the President, too, perceives this as a nationalist project. Montes not only gives orders to the police and the military to give protection to the supporters of the new sect, he also contemplates the expulsion of all foreign priests. And eventually he does it. All churches were shut down; the old Church was declared illegal in Mexico. And the religion of Quetzalcoatl was declared to be the national religion of the Republic (382). Here, Lawrence seems to be influenced by Mexican revolution (1910-20) during which several Catholic institutions were attacked. During the regime of the President Venustiano Carranza in 1917, the rights of the Roman Catholic Church were curtailed.

During his stay in Mexico, Lawrence astutely observed what the Mexicans thought of the white men and women. He documents his observations in *Mornings in Mexico*. He writes that to the Mexicans a white man or woman is merely a sort of phenomenon, something to watch, laugh and wonder at. For the locals the white man is "a sort of extraordinary white monkey", who has learnt the "semi-magical secrets" of the world and made himself "boss of the show". Mexicans call these methods "monkey-tricks" and "monkey-virtues" (61). Their understanding of time, distance and money, Lawrence found out, was utterly different from those of the white people. Mexicans understood only three ways to measure time—morning, afternoon and night. They found the "white monkey's" fondness for exactitude in time, for instance, half-past nine, or five o'clock, horrible. Similarly, they measured distance not in terms of miles; for them a place was either near or far. Lawrence has put the ambivalent feelings of Mexicans towards the white men ironically:

> But the great white monkey has got hold of the keys of the world, and the black-eyed Mexican has to serve the great white monkey, in order to live. He has to learn the tricks of the white monkey show: time of the day, coin of money, machines that start at a second.... The strange monkey-virtue of charity, the white monkeys nosing round to help, to save! Could any trick be more unnatural? (61)

Lawrence has captured the seething anger of the locals who were upset at foreigners taking away their land, oil and metal. Don Ramon's hymns composed in the honour of Aztec God, therefore, captures the indignation of Mexicans, especially their desire to drive away foreigners, including their Christian God, to begin with.

Initially, like Gandhi, Don Ramon does not take resort to violence in his venture, not even when he is attacked and injured by the henchmen of the Church. He never himself penalizes his assailants but does not even object to it, when his loyal adherent General Cipriano sentences them to death. During the Mexican revolution and in the following years there was no escape from violence. Lawrence's servant Rosalino in Mexico had been conscripted to fight for the revolutionaries of the winning side.

When he refused to join them, he was beaten up so brutally by the soldiers that the "prevailing motive of Indian-Mexican life" must have become "Not to be caught!"[17]

The executions of Don Ramon's assailants depressed and shocked Kate Leslie but perhaps not as much as the slaughter of bulls. It gives her a mixed feeling of revulsion as well as attraction. She finds "something dark and lustrous and fascinating" in Cipriano and Ramon (351). It's perhaps this fascination with them as well as the new cult, which prevents her from leaving Mexico.

Conclusion

"I feel a stranger. I feel a stranger everywhere and nowhere," wrote D.H. Lawrence in 1921.[18] It is this lack of belongingness that Kate Leslie shares with her creator throughout the novel. She constantly oscillates between her denunciation of Mexican ways and her cravings for mystical experience. The narrator expresses her longings: "*Give me the mystery and let the world live again for me!* Kate cried to her own soul. *And deliver me from man's automatism*" (94). Here she merely articulates what Lawrence always craved for. But unlike the restless wanderer Lawrence, Leslie, becomes an active participant both in the myth of the new cult of Don Ramon, and also in her relationship with Don Cipriano. To conclude—the description of bull-fighting, vilification and racial profiling of Mexicans, myth of the serpent God stabilizing the earth, and the apprehensions of Americanization—are some of the key issues in Lawrence's writings on Mexico, which readers in India may find fascinating and empathize with. The renewed crisis on the US-Mexico border over the construction of wall to regulate immigration makes it imperative to revisit *The Plumed Serpent,* which deals with the tension between Americans and Mexicans in the 1920s. On the one hand, Lawrence's hero Don Ramon was worried about the increasing threats of Americanization of Mexico. On the other hand, the current Trump administration, which is at loggerheads with the US Congress over funding of wall along the Mexican border, appears to be worried about "Mexicanization of America".

Notes

1. For Lawrence's condemnation of Aztec Gods and Goddesses see *Mornings in Mexico,* p. 56.
2. Porfirio Diaz was a Mexican general and politician who served as President of Mexico from 1876-80 and again from 1884-1911. After an armed conflict during the Mexican revolution Diaz was removed from his post.
3. Lawrence's Letter to Catherine Carswell in *The Letters of D.H. Lawrence*. Ed. Aldous Huxley, p. 565.
4. See *D.H. Lawrence: The Critical Heritage*, Introduction, p. 18.
5. Cited in Michael Squires's *Foreword* to *Mornings in Mexico*, p. 1 from Lawrence's letter to Catherine Carswell, dated 21 December 1921 in *Letters of D.H. Lawrence*, p. 151.
6. Lawrence's letter to Catherine, dated 24 January 1922, Huxley, p. 534.
7. Letter to Lady Cynthia Asquith, dated 30 April 1922, Huxley, p. 545.
8. Letter to E.M. Forster, dated 20 Sept. 1922, Huxley, p. 552.
9. See Lawrence's essay "Red Trousers", Boulton, p. 137.
10. See Lawrence's essay "Return to Bestwood," Boulton, p. 15.
11. "Red Trousers," Boulton, p. 137.
12. See "E.M. Forster on Lawrence's art and ideas" in *D.H. Lawrence: Critical Heritage*, p. 343.
13. For Katherine Anne Porter's review of *The Plumed Serpent* in *New York Herald Tribune Books* see *Critical Heritage,* pp. 268-71.
14. Lawrence in his writings has used Indian for the native population of Mexico. I have used the word Indian in the essay for both the inhabitants of India as well as the people of Mexico. Though the context makes it clear which Indian am I talking about, nevertheless, whenever I thought that there might be some confusion, I have put Mexican in parenthesis after Indian to denote the local population of Mexico.
15. See Introduction to *The Plumed Serpent*, p. xx.
16. See Lawrence's letter to Catherine Carswell, dated 20 June 1925, Huxley, p. 636.
17. *Mornings in Mexico,* p. 76.
18. Letter to Catherine Carswell, dated May 17, 1921, Huxley, p. 517.

Works Cited

D.H. Lawrence: The Critical Heritage. Ed. R.P. Draper. London: Routledge, 2002.

Lawrence, D.H. *Mornings in Mexico*. 1927. New York: Tauris Parke Paperbacks, 2009.

———. *The Plumed Serpent*. 1926. Intro. Cedric Watts. London: Wordsworth Classics, 2009.

The Letters of D.H. Lawrence, Warren Roberts, Vol. iv. Cambridge: Cambridge University Press, 1987.

Millett, Kate. *Sexual Politics*. 1969. Chicago: University of Illinois Press, 2000.

The Cambridge Edition of the Works of D.H. Lawrence: Late Essays and Articles. Ed. James T. Boulton. Cambridge: Cambridge University Press, 2004.

The Letters of D.H. Lawrence. Ed. Aldous Huxley. London: William Heinemann Ltd., 1932.

7

Destitute Humanity and Impoverished Saint: An Indian Response to Lawrence's *Apocalypse*

Asima Ranjan Parhi

1

Lawrence's *Apocalypse* demands attention to the making of Western religious history, its cultural and political reconstruction amidst a deep philosophical and theological crisis. From Platonic imitative art, renaissance response to nature, geography and human potential to the far greater debates of human rationality of the 18th century and subsequent socio-cultural construction of the twentieth century, a cursory look at human evolution in the above inevitable contextual history seems to be a necessary technique in fathoming Lawrence's depth of analysis of human civilisation. It happens to be his last shot at the ignominy of institutional religion and mass hysteria in the face of a chosen conservative aristocracy of the select few with the capacity to hold on to individual integrity rather than behaving like slaves to an imposed order. Lawrence has pondered over the subject all through his essays with the same power and energy while his masterpieces in the fictional narrative provide a romantic solace out of the same inertia. Human 'Will' triumphs as individual 'Will', the collective 'Will' is an illusion; a faith that corrupts the individual self and its potential to connect with cosmos, laments the prophetic author.

In "The Reality of Peace" (*Phoenix*), Lawrence contends "where is there peace, if I take my being from the balance of pure opposition?" (690). And even if all men followed St. Francis or St. Bernard, the race of mankind could be extinct in a generation. "Whichever it is, I am only half, complemented by my opposite" (691). All we can infer is a critique of the gospel directing humanity for a collective will, collective peace or collective submission. This is anathema for Lawrence. This general approval of religious teachings and puritan Christian values repel Lawrence who would bat for the real, the ephemeral, the immediate existence of our flesh and blood. It is vital, elemental and physical in existence. The human, animal and inanimate worlds connect with each other and are a part of the cosmic. Lawrence furthers this in all his novels. Birkin and Ursula in *Women in Love* try for a star-like self-sustenance as well as love of the other, not sacrificing their individual ego resulting in self-contempt and desolation. Paul in *Sons and Lovers* gets disillusioned by Miriam because she surrenders completely and offers herself as a feast. This, Lawrence feels, is a culturally defines trait in the woman. So is Paul, coded in the Victorian socio-cultural norm yet struggling to get out of it. Lady Chatterley attempts a release from institutionalised marriage and a religion that would support its very basis. It is for this cosmic presence of the self in diverse communication with the life force not in term of the mind but body that Lawrence pleads for in his ideal romantic exploration of life on earth. Self is nothing but a unit like all other objects placed in their respective orbits of the cosmic force. Whether it is a man-woman love or the question of god, Lawrence preserves and instinctually reacts against any form of uniformity, submission or supreme revelation. There is no place of reconciliation. Darkness will never be light; neither will the one ever triumph over the other. "When there is an end of darkness, there is a an end of darkness, there is an end of light" (691). Lawrence again appeals in the same essay, "O death, give us to our single being. Release me from the debased social body, O death release me at last; let me find few men who are distinct and at ease in themselves like stars. Let me derive no more from the body of mankind. Let one desire direct from life or direct from death, according to the impulse that is in me" (687).

Much before institutionalized religion invented rigorous rituals and a frightening god, human beings got used to pose faith in the sun, moon, rain and all natural processes, lived with them and relied on them without any sense of fear or ideological preference. There was no sense of a Supreme God or Supreme Being other than nature. This is the contention of Lawrence in *Apocalypse* while he satirizes the high handedness of the Christian Gospel: "We cannot help hating the Christian fear whose method, from the very beginning has been to deny everything that didn't fit, or better still, suppress it" (41). Lawrence further makes a very point that exposes this superiority complex and homogenizing tendency of Christianity:

> Curiously enough, we do not look on the Greeks and the Romans, after about 600 B.C. as real pagans: not like Hindus or Persians, Babylonians or Egyptians, or even Cretans for example we accept the Greeks and the Romans as the initiators of our intellectual and political civilization, the Jews as the fathers of our moral religious civilization so these are 'our sort'. All the rest are mere nothing, almost idiots. (42)

In chapter Seven, he questions more fervently what our postcolonial theorist would profess much later:

> What of it? Because they lacked our modern mental and mechanical attainments, were they any less 'civilised' or 'cultured'...and have we anything as good as the Egyptians of two or three thousand years before Christ as a people? Culture and civilisation are tested by vital consciousness. Are we more vitally conscious than an Egyptian 3000 years B.C. was? (46-47)

Lawrence would lament the loss of impulse and imagination in us while being taken over by a dead boredom (48). Symbols, imagery and myths are of great importance to Lawrence. They embody certain great ideas related to the cosmos. And these symbols, imagery and myths act as clues to the religious past and take the mind back to the ancient ways of life and practice. Lawrence had a strong aversion towards the Christian ways of perceiving apocalypse which he explains by saying: "In the first place its splendiferous imagery is distasteful because of its complete unnaturalness" (6). To him such imagery can never exist in their natural state and hence can never be imagined. He further says "much of the imagery is utterly unpoetic and arbitrary, some of it really ugly, like all the wadings in blood, and the rider's shirt dipped in blood, and people washed in the blood of Lamb" (7).

Lawrence also talks about the oddity of tone which the book of revelation holds. There is more to annihilation and wiping cult than to actual salvation. One finds that the purpose is not to attain salvation but rather it is "about being saved, and sitting on the throne with the Lamb, and reigning in Glory, and having Everlasting life, and living in a grand city made of jasper, with gates of pearl" (8).

Lawrence gives us two versions of apocalyptic ideas. The first version holds its root in the pagan culture and signifies a glorious rebirth. As the seventh seal is opened, the winds from all the four directions are asked to be still by an angel because the new born is to appear. And with it comes a sort of glory followed by dazzling light of hope dressed in white. Lawrence writes: "And then those who 'went through the great tribulation', or initiation into death and rebirth, appear in glory, clothed in the white dazzling robes of their new bodies, carrying branches of the tree of light before the Almighty" (67-68). This unique experience is highly praised and appreciated by Lawrence. He seems to be taken aback by the palm-branch, white robes which give him the feel of some temple in Cybele. For a while he stretches upon his own experience and extraordinary power of imagination where he reflects upon the glorification of the new bodies along with the identification of merging the self with the god.

Chapter 11 of *Apocalypse* provides a deep insight to his actual beliefs and his attachment to the pagan world and its ways of celebrating religion. He complains that this beautiful scene with all truth is modified and scrutinised by the Christians to such an extent that the essence of the "Revelation" is dead. It is impious for any Christian to accept the kind of revelation which Lawrence talks about. According to it, "No Christian is allowed to rise up new and in a divine body, here on earth and in the midst of life. So we are given crowd of martyrs in heaven instead" (68-69). Lawrence here is utterly displeased by the way revelation is considered and welcomed by the Christians.

The apocalyptic vision of John of Patmos must carry the terrific lake of sulphurous fire which must be left burning till eternity so that the enemies can be kept roasted, grilled and tortured. The vision of eternity of all the Patmossers lies in the destruction of earth and sky. No doubt the death of cosmos and the terrible apocalyptic end is hailed. The heaven that is ever glorious must remain even if the cosmos is dead and there must remain the ever-burning fire of hell. The souls after reaching heaven are yet to attain their salvation and final contentment and that is only possible when the enemies are tortured in hell. Lawrence takes a deep sigh of disappointment and writes, "They could not be happy in heaven unless they knew their enemies were unhappy in hell" (76).

Apocalypse thus provides us with two different outlooks. As Lawrence writes, "one of the apocalypse put it in as a part of a theoretic scheme: the birth of the Messiah after the little death of earth and man. And the other apocalyptists left it there" (84). There is a new way to recover from the diseased cosmos in the first vision but the latter one comes with final death note for the already sick cosmos without any hope.

Any multicultural nation has a scope of looking at religion, salvation from different philosophical, ethical points of view. The relevance of *Apocalypse* in a world poised with religious intolerance and political affiliations of religious sects is immense. A world frightened by the IS, Jaish-e-Mohemmed, Al-Qaeda and the fanatic followers of such organizations who act by the name of god and a particular homogenising religious sect reminds of the apprehension raised by Lawrence in such fatality of human instinct, imagination and vitality of life.

Lawrence was a natural traveller and it is through travelling that he discovered the ancient civilisations. His last pilgrimage led him to the Etruscan ruins, north of Rome on which he wrote an account of his travel titled *Etruscan Places*. Lawrence rejected the contemporary views of scholars regarding time.

They put forth this view that Etruscans were inferior to the ancient Romans. It is true that there are hardly any scientific facts supporting it as it is highly personal. But it has successfully shaped the ideas of the modern readers related to this ancient civilisation. Lawrence visited many tombs just to cherish and read the relics of this beautiful civilisation. These beauties which exalted the body and faced death, not pursuing a journey towards the end but towards renewal still bear witness to their faith in an unending joy. And this is what the current society lacks. The present society is caught in an automatic process and almost is dead. There is hardly any hope for renewal of it soul. In the ruins of Etruscan buildings one would still feel the faint presence of the living cosmos. The current civilisation has lost it already. *Etruscan Places* celebrates the power of the imagination and carry us into other dimensions in search of the source of life. And the contemporary common mass is deprived of such imagination because of the established religious way of life. It is in these places where Lawrence could feel the essence of life. Thus in *Etruscan Places* he mentions about the loud noise of water like an eternal flow of life, a maddening sound in itself, like the sound of time, rustling and rushing and wavering but never ceasing. But life seems to cease for the new civilisation. And hence they are more drawn towards end and waiting for death to take over. Again in the same text we find Lawrence talking about a stillness that can only transcend the soul. This transcendent poise is like flames of forgotten darkness, he would suffice. And it is this feeling which he craves for throughout *Apocalypse*. Time and again he mourns for the forgotten and dead cosmos and points towards the hopelessness of its renewal.

In the introduction to *The Letters of D.H. Lawrence,* Huxley writes:

> Lawrence's special and characteristic gift was an extraordinary sensitiveness to what Wordsworth called 'unknown modes of being'. He was always intensely aware of the mystery of the world, and the mystery was always for him a *numen,* divine. Lawrence would never forget, as most of us almost continuously forget,

> the dark presence of the otherness that lies beyond the boundaries of man's conscious mind. (42)

Lawrence believes that preventing one's self from pure spirituality is a wrong approach to life in all its natural state. For example, love in all its form whether physical or not is a pure feeling but it is the crudity of mind that makes it appear sinful and forbidden. Making love is also a kind of liberation of soul, diving deep into the self. It is not only the physical act of merging but also uniting of two halves that forms the whole. But the sinful and unrefined minds of Puritans are unexposed to such forms of purity and are unable to perceive its deeper insight beneath the seemingly vulgar surface. He mocks the hypocrisy of the mass that has developed a 'grey disease of sex hatred' along with a 'yellow disease of dirt lust'. In his essay *Pornography and Obscenity* Lawrence writes:

> But in the degraded human mind being the deep instincts have gone dead and then the two flows (sex flow and excrement flow) become identical. This is the secret of really the vulgar and pornographic; the sex flow and the excrement flow is the same to them. It happens when the psyche deteriorates, and the profound controlling instinct collapse. Then sex is dirt and dirt is sex, and sexual excitement becomes a playing with dirt. (176)

And in *Apocalypse* we just get glimpses of this idea, for the cosmic as a whole is the central focus. The attitude towards religion is also the same. The essence of true religion has already received a deadly blow and is dead just like the cosmos. And it is the mob or the mass that is to be blamed for. As it goes without saying that 'the voice of mass is the voice of god'. And this mass is the second-minded people who are unable to distinguish between living and money, good and evil, earthly bread and heavenly bread. And the first-minded people, the aristocrats are individuals. And thus a religion like Christianity is not for the mob but for the aristocrats, the strong-minded people.

Lawrence draws from Dostoevsky immensely. In the chapter "The Grand Inquisitor" from *The Brothers Karamazov,* Ivan Karamazov voices what Lawrence would time and again emphasize in the *Apocalypse*. Here is Ivan:

> You promised them bread from heaven, but I again repeat can it stand comparison with earthy bread in the eyes of the weak, for the ever vicious and forever ingrate tribe of man? And even if, for the sake of bread from heaven, you are followed by thousands and tens of thousands, what will become of the millions and scores of thousands of millions of creatures unable to forgo the earthy bread for the sake of heavenly? (387)

He speaks to Alyosha, his younger brother, "you did not know, however, that as soon as man rejected miracles, he would immediately reject God as well, since it is not so much God that man seeks, as miracles" (390). Lawrence in his own essay titled *The Grand Inquisitor* talks about the inadequacy of Jesus while never discarding Jesus. He loved Jesus the lover but he hated Jesus the teacher. He struggles with this paradoxical search of god and feels that such teachings are not meant for the mass but for special individuals or the chosen ones. His views that men look for miracles is also the same as that of Ivan Karamazov who hardly finds god to be convincing enough for the world. And on the basis of these miracles the mass build its faith is as thin as the gossamer. And it does not take a longer time to be shattered. So a particular god or a particular faith today might triumph over another. The mass always demands mystery and rejoices in the miraculous. And this mass belongs to the second category of people called weakling who need a Christ like figure to bow down to. The mass finds it complex and is beyond comprehension. When they are far away from the reality of life it is futile to expect a sort of understanding of heavenly and earthly bread from them. Now there is a clear failure and incapability of differentiating "between bread, or property, money and vivid life." And then there are the elected ones, 'the few', who really understand the meaning and pass it to the mass who accepts all these as a gift to mankind. Christianity looks for limitations and the good in man. But mankind also includes bitter limitations and the evil. And this is where the inadequacy lies. Lawrence puts this:

> The essence of Christianity is love of mankind. If a love of mankind entails accepting the bitter limitation of

> the mass of men, their inability to distinguish between money and life, then accept the limitation, and have done with it (832). Albert Camus in the essay *Rejection of Salvation* talks about Ivan Karamazov's rational search and inability of the search of god. He says god is denied by Ivan, rather is looked for as an equal (836-41). This is a different approach to religion. There is no other reason for Ivan to question god except his compassion for the poor. Ivan puts forth this idea of mortality and questions the eternal thing which Christianity promises to offer. But if there is no eternity and there lies the mortality on the face of human life then there is no heaven and heavenly bread. And it is unjust to continue with a sort of faith during hard times. Faith in divine power is not going to end suffering for it is always the poor that suffers. And instead, it is the action that helps one to come up with a solution. Camus also talks about truth, the kind of truth that Ivan defines. According to Ivan truth is always unacceptable and always unjust and so there is an unending struggle between truth and justice.

Ivan does not say that there is no truth. He says that truth does exist, it can only be unacceptable. Why? Because it is unjust. The struggle between truth and justice is begun here for the first time; and it will never end. The question of virtue also makes its way. Truth, virtue and faith are there important aspects of life which Christianity preaches in order to get hold of the heaven bread. Lawrence speaks of this remarkable ease with which Christianity uses these three words. Well, if virtue is absent then 'everything is permitted' (Ivan in *The Brothers Karamazov*). But it is the rebellion of the human mind, especially individuals like Ivan that would notice this, points out Lawrence. And thus refers to the inadequacy of Christianity. *Apocalypse* reveals a deep understanding of what Lawrence calls a cosmos. And this cosmos is living one. The book is a quest which ultimately leads to self-realisation. In the introduction to *Apocalypse,* Aldington says: "*Apocalypse* which attempts to give ordinary people the clue to the kind of life he felt he had discovered" (9).

Although this book discusses Revelation and tries to interpret the ending as discussed in *The New Testament*, it poses philosophical questions on the nature of miracle, faith, mass and the relevance of such faith in the return of Christ. There is a hope for life and perhaps new beginning. Lawrence goes to the root of apocalypse and finds it to be of pagan origin. But he shows his disappointment in Christianity that has altered and uprooted itself from its origin by being rigid and dogmatic.

2

For Lawrence the actual flexibility of the term matters where he can have multiple ways of visiting and revisiting its origin, define its significance. Thus it becomes an intimate connection with the cosmic sources of life i.e. sun, moon, river, stars, planets. This is similar to the Hindu Concept of *Moksha,* a state of supreme consciousness and oneness with the absolute, that of carrying the entire cosmos in one's self.

It is true Lawrence supported both the sensual and spiritual aspects of life and he calls them truth. There is a harmony Lawrence would be impatiently looking for, between body and the animating natural life, human instinct and the cosmic rule. According to him both are connected and therefore in their distinct selves lie an assimilated whole that bids and individual to its cosmos. We get to know from Earl Brewster's book *D.H. Lawrence: Reminisces and Correspondence* that his affinity with Hinduism dates back to 1915. But it will not be untrue to claim that he had understood it much before his soul was dampened by the ritualistic Hinduism. Lawrence has always been wrongly interpreted and seen to be someone blindly glued to the physical and the vulgar. But there is a struggle he envisages in the very vital body overpowered by the sense of the ego, the self that holds on its unique identity which subsequently turns towards the metaphysical. It is directed towards uniting the supreme consciousness and the 'other' to attain *Moksha.* There is an urge for transcendence of soul, space, time and human conscious. *The Upanishads,* which are basic philosophical texts of Hinduism, defines *Moksha* as a state of total self-realisation and oneness with *Brahma,* the supreme divine. This *Brahma* is believed to reside in each and every individual. And one can only achieve *Brahma* by the process of self-realisation and only then there is the attainment of *Moksha* (Liberation). *Apocalypse* guides us through this holy quest of a self-realisation. The influence of Hindu philosophy is remarkable. Although we cannot claim its certainty but one can easily draw ideas from this text and find its extension in Hindu scriptures.

The Hindu mythology and community festivals around its gods, the pagan culture of pre-Christian civilisation impress upon Lawrence in the same way that the star-like lovers do as part of a war against the 'mentalists'. He brings the apocalyptic revelation to its non-Christian glory: In spite of the apocalyptist, the pagan initiate, perhaps in a temple of Cybele...Dazzled, reborn, wears white robes and carries the palm-branch, and the flutes sound out their rapture round him, and dancing women life their garlands over him (68). It is nothing but the image of *Vrindaban* in the Hindu mythology where Krishna, the shepherd-god plays his flute, dress in herbs, flowers encircled by *Gopis* (the milkmaids who accompanied Radha, Krishna's lover).

Behind all creation myths lies the grand idea that the cosmos always was that it could not have had any beginning. It could not have a god to start it, because it was itself all god and all divine, the origin of everything. The mass is an envious lot. It is a bunch of self-serving, irrational brutes. In contemporary culture and political sphere, the aggressive Left-wing ideologues in their ultra left, Naxalite affiliation have been synonymous with intolerance, violence and ill will. This wing hates anything that has a heritage value; entire culture of the aristocracy and wants to take an unreasonable revenge against the state, its armed forces that protect the country, its unity and nurtures a secret desire to wipe away all that is beautiful, all that has had a glory, the entire value of the past. It does not want progress in the material form but it rots with the mental illusion and lives only by protesting anything and everything. Lawrence quite easily anticipated this in the context of religious bigotry; how the lowest classes abhorred kings, their chariot, their wine, their villas, their cultural traces. They want to destroy it forever.

Lawrence brings the destruction of Babylon to be a result of this destructive instinct of the unnamed mass that is intolerant of anything to be cherished, great that stand out. He unravels this secret anarchic ideals of modern democracies; this desire to look at every individual as a fragment, not a free will or integration by its own autonomy. The collective is out of the fragment and so it lacks any organic bonding. There lies the malady of the conception of the collective self. He talks of Lenin as the beginner in modern society of this collective will. He would lament finally: Jesus said: to them that have shall be given, etc. but he had forgotten to reckon with the mass of the mediocre, whose motto is: we have nothing and therefore nobody shall have anything (120).

The collective whole is not an organic whole. It is unable to lift the human spirit. It only could drive us to suicide. The Christian cult today is a symptomatic reminder of the modern diseased political equation among people and states. While lamenting the obsessive desire of establishing the divine law in men Lawrence writes in the context of the Etruscan civilisation in his essay "Making love to music":

> There seems to have been a peculiar large carelessness about them, very human and non-moral. They seems to have had a strong feeling for taking life sincerely as a pleasant thing. Even death was a gay and lively affair. Moralists would say: Divine law wiped them not. The answer of that is, divine law wipes everything out in time, even itself. (164)

This reminds us of the Hindu concept of *Banaprastha* (leaving in the forest) after an active life called *Gribastha* (worldly life) without any fear of death. It is an ultimate desire of being alone, being not possessive of the mundane world and approving of an immaterial life. But it is not a divorce of the body or denial of the life of senses. It is an aftermath of life in Nature of creation, life in eternal cycle. Blake, Nietzsche and Lawrence seem to have led this argument of presentation of life against an assertion of a state of life devoid of the senses. The old civilisations made a treaty with life. The new questioned their active physical life and pursued the mechanical path of a corrupt divinity.

In *American Literature of the Nineteenth Century,* Fisher Samuelson and Reninger Vaid record (33-38) how Vedanta Philosophy has been a strong though current that reached New England by which writers like Emerson, Thoreau and Whitman were thoroughly influenced. 'Selfhood' as it has been portrayed in the Hindu scriptures of *Katha Upanishad* and *Bhagavad Gita* when elaborated further gives a philosophical and spiritual doctrine of self. The *Upanishad* states: The self within you, the resplendent, immortal person is the internal self of all things and is the universal Brahman. The transcendentalists in America too emphasize similar concepts. Emerson in his essay, "Plato, or the Philosopher" writes, the 'ecstasy' of losing 'all being in one Being' finds its highest expression chiefly in the Indian scriptures in the *Vedas, the Bhagavad Gita* and the *Vishnu Purana* (34). His poem 'Brahma' echoes the same Vedantic rendition of selfhood,

> I am the doubter and the doubt,
> And I the hymn the Brahmin sings.
> The strong god pine for my abode,
> And pin in vain the sacred seven;
> But thou, meek lover of the good!
> Find me, and turn thy back on heaven. (35)

Thoreau and Whitman also record strong impression of the Hindu ethos in their writings. Evidently Lawrence who goes on exploring the pagan past from across the world would afford to lose sight of this. *The Upanishads* further expand the idea of Brahman as the ultimate reality, the very core of being and source of our existence around. Lawrence is very much touched by this idea of ultimate reality and the supreme unconscious. He is not looking for mere 'truth' or 'faith' but something beyond it. He looks for certain infinity that the Brahma holds. *The New Testament* talks about the 'true' and 'faithful' to be a trap for the common mass. He would say it is hard to hold over this truth and faith on the part of the mob because there is something beyond its superficial meaning and hence this is only meant for the strong minded people, the aristocrats. There is the truth of the living cosmos which is a vast entity just like Brahma. It is true that the universe has meaning only if we put the observer at the centre of it. And that centre holds the Brahma. It is possible to be capable of understanding the true essence of this universe when one is close to the living cosmos.

What is fascinating about Lawrence is his devotion to life which is beyond anyone's mere mental consciousness. The concept of *Shakti* (the universal creative power) in the Hindu principle of life is well understood by Lawrence even though he was never deeply involved in studying it. One can easily find similar ideas taking their shape in most of his works. Without this *Shakti* the world cannot function at all. It is the 'other' which Lawrence keeps talking about in *Apocalypse.* So comes the concept of the three eyed god, the ultra monk, Lord *Shiva. Shiva* and *Shakti* are two halves that make a whole. Lawrence mentions about the reverence paid to the phallic symbols by the old civilisations. And in Hindu philosophy we have the *Shivalinga* (the phallus of Lord Shiva) which is the male counterpart of *Shakti.* It is the source of cosmic energy and dynamic force. *Shakti* is known to be the consort of Lord *Shiva.* And together, they form this cosmos and stand for the Supreme Consciousness. And hence one is incomplete without the 'other' in *Yajur Veda* we have references to *Matru deva bhava* along with *Pitru devo bhava,* i.e., honour your mother as goddess and father as god. This also indicates the equal presence of the 'other' in divine invocations. There is always the 'other' and this sense of 'otherness' adds to the meaning of existence and helps us understand the cosmos better by offering the real bread of heaven.

Brewster, in his book *D.H. Lawrence: Reminiscences and Correspondence,* writes that he is moved by Lawrence's expansion of the Seven-Sealed Mystery. He argues that Lawrence's interpretation of this Seven-Sealed Mystery reminds him of the Hindu idea of seven *Chakras.* These seven *Chakras* are like the seven types of spiritual awareness in the body. His philosophy is deeply influenced by this mystical body. The universe is a vast entity and the human being is the small part of it, caught in its pattern. This 'Seven-Sealed Mystery' is just like the seven centres of spiritual consciousness and need to be unlocked. Liberation of self and the merging with Brahma to attain *Moksha* (liberation) is only possible when one solely dedicates himself to unlock these seven *Chakras*. This attraction towards Hindu philosophy is because of its primitive existence. Lawrence believed that the old races carry cult-lore. And this cult-lore is the wisdom. In *Apocalypse,* Lawrence writes about a nation that was, in a very old sense, a church, or a vast cult-unit. "From cult to culture is only a step, but it took a lot of making. Cult-lore was the wisdom of the old races. We now have culture" (47).

The cult-lore made one exposed to the great sensual awareness and sense knowledge which was developed through instincts and not reasons. But then the culture that replaced it made men strip of their emotional and imaginative reactions leaving them dead and empty. This might be the reason why Lawrence often seems critical about Buddhism and was repelled by the rigidly of Christianity. He searches for the primitive roots of *Apocalypse* and is moved by the original and pagan symbols rather than the Christian ones. The process itself is the way to liberation. It will be a false statement if one says that Lawrence is against Christianity or for that matter any religion. It is the arbitrary and fixed understanding of Christ and Christianity that he opposes. Because of the arbitrary and fixed meaning of *The Bible,* people tend to understand it in its superficial or popular meaning and that is why *The Bible* stops being interesting. And it is this fixed interpretation of *The Bible* that makes one's mind stubborn. And it is this *fixed* interpretation that has been unable to convey that what exactly is revealed. To the common mass it's just a revelation they need to bow to accepting the end.

The Hindu scriptures like *The Upanishads, The Vedas* and *The Bhagavad Gita* unfold their beauty by citing different interpretations. There are layers of meanings that these holy texts would often focus. This is the approach that Christianity lacks in its reading of *The Bible.* Hence, *The Bible* remains the same mundane text that is supposed to be only memorised and repeated. Lawrence has his logical reservation towards the precise way philosophers or scientists attempted to prove truth as an ontological as well as an empirical entity. His belief in the 'pure' and 'passionate' is based on the physical response of an organism in nature. This 'pure' and 'passionate' are spontaneous and can only be achieved when one is in his whole being, which is a contribution of mind, emotion and soul. And any precise way to approach them reduces the subjective truth to that of expecting a laboratory experimentation of reality. The attempts which Lawrence has made through *Apocalypse* is to break through the usual pattern of thought prevailing in Christianity. This has a relevance to contemporary times when religion has been reduced to an identity formation for opportunities is political and social spheres, *Jihadi* (holy war) cause and ego-fulfilment, playing the often cited minority tag across nations or similar ideological practices suitable to the current material society. There is always a presence of 'deeper consciousness' or supreme conscious which Lawrence presents with the help of certain symbols like cosmic, blood, and phallic. He seems to have a flexible way of understanding god and his conception for a deeper cause. It is similar to the way we perceive or understand god in the Hindu culture. The diversity of understanding is what Lawrence focuses on in *Apocalypse*. And his constant effort is to connect his reader to guide through a journey of self-realisation by defining and introducing them to the living cosmos.

The cosmos is the whole and we are all equal parts of it, starting from a small insect to all other, more complex forms of life. The *Brahman* is the all-pervading consciousness. It is the beginning and end of the whole being. It is formless yet encompasses all diverse forms around in order to sustain the complexities of the universe. This also defines Lawrence's idea of god. In *Apocalypse*, he writes that god is revealed spontaneously in every element of nature. Hence, the *Brahman* dwells in unity. The idea is to unfold the concept of god and preserve the natural sense. And the physical aspect denotes to the revelation of this mystic process and urge to take the form finally uniting with cosmos. To extend the argument further on the connections of Lawrentian understanding of the universe and that of Hindu philosophical, religious ethos I would like to state that in multiple devotional hymns of certain cultures god is simultaneously and object of adoration, companionship and satire. And this is exactly what Christianity doesn't allow. There is no sense of proximity with the lord. And it is this fixed and rigidity of Christianity that Lawrence discards. He is uncomfortable with the portrayal of the one-dimensional Christ in Christianity and searches for a spiritual release in *Apocalypse*.

3

There is an attempt to trace life back to its origin through religious symbols, myths and rituals of ancient societies that involve Etruscans, Egyptians, Chaldeans, and the Hindu culture. This happens to be the best way to rediscover the deep, unearthed realities of the world and cosmic powers which are lost due to the monotony of scriptures in general and Christianity in particular as opposed to life lived in flesh and blood. One can clearly notice the influence of animistic philosophy in his works. There are instances of Lawrence referring to early Greek writers as Herakleitons and Anaximander. This enchantment with the flow and balance of ancient civilization and culture and their religious flexibility, profess a significant departure from institutionalised and dogmatic religions. But in the end it is the 'living cosmos' that has bewitched his soul and mind. This cosmos needs to come to be recreated and it can only be possible when there will be living organic connections. The text of *Apocalypse* comes to an end with such a message by Lawrence:

> What we want is to destroy our false, inorganic connections, especially those related to money, and re-establish the living organic connections, with the cosmos, the sun and earth, with mankind and nation and family. Start with the sun and the rest will slowly happen. (125)

It is the recognition here and now, that of the mundane and immediate world which talks about the presence of the highly specific, concrete and individual self in all and the presence of all in the self. The mass is incapable to grasp this and hence one can only look for uplift through an inner vision and strength flowing within the subconscious mind. However somewhere or the other even Lawrence fails to maintain the harmony he prophetically visualises. He was afraid to give up his individuality and unite with Brahma. Therefore he looks for his own way of redemption. There is always a longing for connection with the universe in him but there are intermittent mental blocks which scares him to commit to anything lest he would lose own singleness. Thus, he remains content in polarity. However, he has this unusual of going along with the undying rhythm in the flux of life smitten with the divine music of the cosmos.

Works Cited

Brewster, Earl and Achsah. *D.H. Lawrence: Reminiscences and Correspondence.* London: Martin Secker, 1934.

Camus, Albert. "The Rejection of Salvation". *The Brothers Karmazov,* Ed. Ralph E. Matlaw. New York: Norton Critical Edition, 1976.

Chand, Devi. Trans. *Taittiriya Upanishad* i.11.2, V.V.R.I. Shikshavalli Press, 1959.

Christy, Arthur. *The Orient in American Transcendentalism: A Study of Emerson, Thoreau and Alcott.* Columbia: Columbia UP, 1932.

Carter, Fredrick. *D.H. Lawrence and the Body Mystical.* London: Denis Archer, 1932.

Dostoevsky, Fyodor. *The Brothers Karamazov* (1879), Ed. Ralph E. Matlaw. New York: Norton Critical Edition, 1976.

Huxley, Aldous. quoted in Andrews, W.T. Ed. *Critics on D.H. Lawrence.* First published, London: George Allen and Unwin Publisher Ltd., 1970. Reprint, New Delhi: Universal Book Stall, 1995.

Lawrence, D.H. *Apocalypse.* Harmondsworth: Penguin Books, 1931.

Etruscan Places. New York: Viking Press, 1957.

"The Grand Inquisitor". Ed. Ralph E. Matlaw. New York: Norton Critical Edition, 1976.

The Letters of D.H. Lawrence. Ed. Aldous Huxley. London: Viking, 1932.

Lawrence, D.H. "Making Love to Music". *Phoenix: The Posthumous Papers of D.H. Lawrence.* Ed. Edward McDonald. London: Viking, 1936.

———. "Pornography and Obscenity". *Phoenix: The Posthumous Papers of D.H. Lawrence.* Ed. Edward McDonald, London: Viking, 1936.

———. "The Reality of Peace". *Phoenix: The Posthumous Papers of D.H. Lawrence.* Ed. Edward McDonald. London: Viking, 1936.

Paramanand, Swami. Trans. *The Upanishads.* Boston: The Vedanta Centre, 1919.

Padhi, Bibhu. *D.H. Lawrence: Modes of Fictional Style.* Troy NY, Whitson, 1989.

Parhi, Asima Ranjan. "The Religion of Self and Impersonality: Revisiting Shelley, Hardy and Lawrence". *Reassessing British Literature.* Ed. S.K. Paul and A.N. Prasad. New Delhi: Sarup and Sons, 2008.

Reed, Elizabeth. *Hinduism in Europe and America.* Calcutta: Brahmo Samaj Press, 1942.

Samuelson, Fisher and Vaid, Reninger. *American Literature of the Nineteenth Century.* New Delhi: Eurasia Publishing House, 1955.

Wendell, Thomas. *Hinduism Invades America.* Beacon Press, 1930.

8

London in the Time of War (1914-1918): Re-reading D.H. Lawrence's Letters

Joyjit Ghosh

> The Town has opened to the sun.
> Like a flat red lily with a million petals
> She unfolds, she comes undone.
>
> D.H. Lawrence, "Bombardment"

D.H. Lawrence did not like cities in general whether it was London, New York or Paris. He believed that in the cities the weather was "always benzene, or else petrol fumes/lubricating oil, exhaust gas", to quote a couple of lines from his poem titled "In the Cities".[1] Lawrence always preferred the countryside to a metropolis. His reference to London in his letters often verges on the negative. London is "all smoke", he wrote to Arthur McLeod on 26 October 1913 (II. 90). And around this time he wrote to Walter de la Mare, "One breathes so much freer out of London" (II. 84). A close reading of his letters reveals how his dislike of the city of London reached its peak during the First World War. The "magnificent" city of his youthful vision turned into "a hoary, ponderous inferno" as the war broke out. The present paper attempts to explore Lawrence's responses to London during the First World War as reflected in his letters, and in the course of discussion it also seeks to address the issue of Lawrence's attitude to war in general.

Let us start our discussion with Lawrence's response to London when he was appointed assistant master in the Davidson Road

School, Croydon. He wrote to Blanche Jennings on 9 October 1908 that London seemed to him "pompous, magnificent capital of commercialdom, a place of stately individualistic ideas, with nothing Gothic or aspiring or spiritual". He felt "remarkably at home in London, remarkably cheerful and delighted". He was also favourably exposed to the Londoners: "the people in London do not feel so strange; they are folk who have come down the four winds of Heaven to this centre of convergence of the Universe". Interestingly, he even compared the Londoners with the "people in Manchester and Stockport and the awful undignified provincial towns" and described the latter as "races of insects running over some food body". In Lawrence's idea, "one naturally gravitates to London; one naturally flees from the cotton centres" (I. 80). A week later Lawrence again wrote about London in glowing terms:

> Here I stand with all London rumbling round me, thinking of you. I wish you could see the shops and the folks here—do, my dear, come down for a day with Fran[ces], you would enjoy it. (I. 83)

Lawrence thus had a tremendous fascination for London during his youth. Both the city and its people seemed to him "cheerful". Interestingly, Lawrence's late essay titled "Why I don't like living in London", published in *Evening News* on 3 September 1928, also reveals his early admiration of the city:

> Twenty years ago, London was to me thrilling, thrilling, thrilling, the vast and roaring heart of all adventure. It was not only the heart of the world, it was the heart of the world's living adventure. How wonderful the Strand, the Bank, Charing Cross at night, Hyde Park in the morning![2]

The thrice use of the word "thrilling" brings home the point that Lawrence was passionately attached to the "living adventure" at the heart of London in the days of his youth. However, as we read in *Kangaroo,* "In the winter of 1915-16 the spirit of the old London collapsed, the city, in some way, perished, perished from being a heart of the world, and became a vortex of broken passions, lusts, hopes, fears, and horrors" (*Kangaroo*, 216).

The First World War brought a chapter of "nightmare" in the life of the author. Jane Costin rightly observes that Lawrence was a non-combatant but he was bitterly opposed to the war from the start (Costin, 93). The war made Lawrence a depressed man as he wrote to Lady Cynthia Asquith, "The war finished me. It was the spear through the side of all sorrows and hopes" (II. 268). The present essay will initially try to explore how the war darkened his vision of the city of London and the Londoners during the war, and as the discussion will move forward, it will shed light on Lawrence's views of war and nation.

Before delving deep into the discussion on the author's letters one may here quote a few lines from Lawrence's poem titled "Town in 1917":

> There are no gleams on the River,
> No goggling clock;
> No sound from St Stephen's;
> No lamp-fringed frock.
> Instead
> Darkness, and skin-wrapped
> Fleet, hurrying limbs,
> Soft-footed dead[3]. (9-16)

London thus lost its splendid lights and became a ghostly city in 1917. The images of darkness are all pervasive in the poem and suggest the gloom which the war cast on him. It is interesting to note, Lawrence's letter addressed to Cecil Gray on 17 October 1917 captures the same mood of gloom and despair although in a language that is much more stark than that of the poem:

> London is really very bad: gone mad, in fact. It thinks and breathes and lives air-raids, nothing else. People are not people any more: they are factors, really ghastly, like Lemures, evil spirits of the dead. What shall we do, how shall we get out of this Inferno? (III. 170)

Earlier also Lawrence wrote about his cordial dislike of the Londoners in a letter to Lady Cynthia Asquith (dated 5 September 1915): "The sight of the people of London strikes me into a dumb fury. The persistent nothingness of the war makes me feel like a paralytic convulsed with rage" (II. 386). So, London which seemed awfully "thrilling" to him in the past turned out to be an "Inferno" during the wartime vortex, and the sight of the Londoners made him not only depressed but filled him with feelings of "dumb fury".

War made Lawrence's approach to place and people fairly cynical. In an early letter addressed to Ottoline Morrell on 14 May 1915, Lawrence wrote:

> My eyes can see nothing human that is good, nowadays: at any rate, nothing public. London seems to me like some hoary massive underworld, a hoary, ponderous inferno. The traffic flows through the rigid grey streets like the rivers of Hell through their banks of dry, rocky ash. (II. 339)

The passage quoted above starkly represents the writer's mood of despair. London is once again imagined here as an "inferno" and the hectic traffic flowing through the "grey streets" is compared to the "rivers of Hell". These images have a point of similarity with those that are available in T.S. Eliot's portrayal of London in "The Waste Land" (1922) which in its own fashion reflects the post-war disillusionment.

Lawrence's representation of London may remind an informed reader of another modernist writer, Ezra Pound. Lawrence was then in Hampstead. We see him write to Lady Ottoline Morrell on 11 November 1915: "London *does* strike a blow at the heart, I must say: tonight, in a black rain out of doors, and a tube full of spectral, decayed people" (II. 434). These sentences may bring to one's mind Pound's celebrated poem "In a Station of the Metro":

> The apparition of these faces in the crowd:
> Petals on a wet, black bough[4]

Pound does not portray any particular city. It can be London, New York, Paris or any other city across the world. But his portrayal of a Metro Station is deeply suggestive. The use of the word "apparition" is significant in this context, and the said word is in harmony with the Lawrencian expression "spectral, decayed people". One may remember at this point how Shelley in "Ode to the West Wind" imagines the rotten leaves as "Pestilence-stricken multitudes"[5]. Lawrence seems to suggest that the war has sucked the vitality of the city-people. They no longer look like living human beings but are apparitions at best. The use of the colour "black" in both Lawrence ("black rain") and Pound ("black bough") is also worthy of mention. It suggests that death prevails in all corners of human existence.

It is also important to note how in the Lawrencian vision London became associated with sickness/disease in the inter-war years. We see him write to Lady Cynthia Asquith on 26 April 1917, "It was the evil influence of aggregate London made me ill: suddenly I start to be sick. It is all very vile" (III. 117). The phrase "the evil influence of aggregate London" is indeed loaded. Lawrence does not elaborate his idea here but we may assume that the ambience of the dehumanizing war in the city made his soul sick. One may in this context refer to another letter, addressed to Stanley Hocking on 30 October 1918:

> We went to London about a month ago, intending to stay some little time. But Mrs Lawrence immediately became ill—the doctor said pleurisy—and she was so depressed that we fled away here again to the country as soon as she could travel.... The flu is really like a plague, everywhere—London absolutely stricken. (III. 294)

The sentences quoted above help in evoking the image of London as a distempered cause. The city is "absolutely stricken" and it makes people (who come from outside to stay in) ill. The words in the letter are charged with an existential anguish—anguish of a man who never could come to terms with London under the shadow of the war.

During the war London figures time and again in Lawrence's letters as a city ridden with trouble and anxiety. The letter which I am going to cite now is addressed to Eoa Rainusso, dated 16 September 1915:

> We are here in London for one winter. The other evening we saw a German Zeppelin in the sky. My wife was very frightened. The bombs fell, very many houses are destroyed.... The war goes on and will go on for a long

> time. Oh God, the world is too sad and cruel. That winter of peace which we spent in Fiascherino now seems a paradise to me, now that the whole world has turned into hell.[6]

The passage sharply brings home the trauma of the Lawrences as they experienced the devastation caused by German warships. Lawrence's words, "the whole world has turned into hell" voices the agony of a man who never forgave the war describing it as a "colossal idiocy" (II. 212).

Lawrence's letter to Lady Ottoline Morrell on 9 September 1915, however, seems to be more poetically charged:

> Last night when we were coming home the guns broke out, and there was a noise of bombs. Then we saw the Zeppelin above us, just ahead, amid a gleaming of clouds: high up, like a bright golden finger, quite small, among a fragile incandescence of clouds. And underneath it were splashes of fire as the shells fired from earth burst. Then there were flashes near the ground—and the shaking noise. It was like Milton—then there was war in heaven. But it was not angels. It was that golden Zeppelin, like a long oval world, high up. (II. 389-90)

Lawrence here alludes to *Paradise Lost* (Book VI) but the purpose of alluding to Milton is ironic. For he himself clarifies that it is no "cosmic order" that he speaks of here rather "a new order, a new heavens above us." In this "new order" a Zeppelin (a German type of large warship) is "golden like a moon, having taken control of the sky" (390). This reference to "Zeppelin" that has taken "control of the sky" is a precise one for Zeppelin warships bombed London and eastern countries on 8 September 1915, killing 20 people (II. 390, n. 1).

One may remember Lawrence's poem "Zeppelin Nights" and I quote it at length

> Now, will you play all night!
> Come in, my mother says.
> Look in the sky, at the bright
> Moon all ablaze!

> Look at the shaking, white
> Searchlight rays!
>
> Tonight they're coming!
> It's a full moon!
> When you hear them humming
> Very soon,
> You'll stop that blooming
> Tune—[7]

Kate McLoughlin observes, "'They' and 'them' are not identified in the body of the poem: the undisclosed threat draws on the terrors of the dark, the menace of what might come out in the moonlight and the ominous connotations of 'humming'" (McLoughlin, 53-54). The observation compels conviction. The mother's warning "Tonight they're coming!" fails to draw the attention of the children who being innocent of the horrors of warfare continue to sing the "blooming tune" but it strikes terror in the hearts of the adult readers who (whether they have gone through the traumatic experiences caused by war or not) always warn humanity against war and violence.

While speaking on Lawrence's response to the First World War, John Middleton Murry writes, "He [Lawrence] suffered under a prophetic vision of the war as a portent of the imminent doom of modern civilization and modern man" (Murry, 30). This is indeed an insightful observation. Lawrence was concerned about humanity and human civilization and not about nation as is sharply reflected in his letters from time to time. He wrote in a letter dated 18 April 1916:

> I don't care a straw what the Germans do. Everything that is done, *nationally*, in any sense, is now vile and stinking, whether it is England or Germany.... I hate the whole concern of the nation. Bloody false fools, I don't care what they do, so long as I can avoid them, the mass of my countrymen: or any other countrymen. (II. 597)

The war was indeed "a wicked mistake" to Lawrence. And the warriors (whether Germans or Englishmen) were all "Bloody false fools" in his vision. But the war was "dreadful" as well. He thus wrote to Harriet Monroe on 17 November 1914:

> The war is dreadful. It is the business of the artist to follow it home to the heart of the individual fighters—not to talk in armies and nations and numbers—but to track it home—home—their war—and it's at the bottom of almost every Englishman's heart—the war—the desire of war—the *will* to war—and at the bottom of every German's. (II. 233)

D.H. Lawrence here candidly criticizes the "*will* to war" of opposing forces. This criticism sounds compelling because it is honest and not clouded by narrow nationalist sentiments. George A. Panichas in "D.H. Lawrence's War Letters" (1963) rightly observes, "In these war letters, it can hardly be denied, the extraordinary diversity of Lawrence's temperament and attitudes is closely interlinked with a relentless integrity and sensibility" (Panichas, 400). To Lawrence, both the Germans and the Englishmen are evil-minded when they cherish "the desire of war". But what is perhaps most important to note in the passage quoted above is Lawrence's observation on "the business of the artist". An artist should talk about the dreadfulness of war; he must focus on the agony of an individual fighter and not about "nations" and "numbers".

In this context a reader of Lawrence may be reminded of his poem titled "Eloi, Eloi, Lama Sabachthani?" that begins with a reference to the agony of the speaking subject who is obviously a soldier:

> How I hate myself, this body which is me;
> How it dogs me, what a galling shadow!
> How I would like to cut off my hands,
> And take out my intestines to torture them!
> But I can't, for it is written against me I must not,
> I must preserve my life from hurt.
> But then, that shadow's shadow of me,
> The enemy! (1-8)

The soldier here is a split personality. He is at war with himself. He hates his own body which he describes as a "galling shadow". And when he kills his enemy, he actually kills his own "shadow's shadow". Finally, a grim realization dawns upon him:

> This death, his death, my death—
> It is the same, this death[8]. (31-32)

Lawrence's war poetry is not valorised like Owen's or Sassoon's. Lee M. Jenkins comments that his war poems "are still stranded in a definitional no-man's land" (Jenkins, 36). But a poem like "Eloi, Eloi, Lama Sabachthani?" pierces a reader's heart and brings home in the fashion of a poem by Owen that war is the other name of death. This attitude to war is time and again reflected in the letters.

A close study of Lawrence's letters reveals that he hated the war from the bottom of his being. In a letter dated 5 May 1916 Lawrence wrote:

> When I think of the degenerate and insect-like stupidity of the men now, my heart stops beating. That England should go on destroying herself to fight this chimerical Germany, whilst all the time the Allies, like great insatiable leeches, hang on her body and glut themselves; that she should destroy her own body, tearing her own limbs, wilfully defiling and desecrating herself like an obscene fakir, to make a meaningless war on Germany, for the sake of Allies, who gloat and feed like enormous rats on her dismemberment, this one cannot see, and live. (II. 603)

Lawrence here lets out a stream of invective against the Allies of England in the war. One may note the use of language in the passage which carries the burden of satire. The Allies are thus compared to "insatiable leeches" hanging on the "body" of England or to "enormous rats" feeding on her "dismemberment". But England that engages in "a meaningless war" with "chimerical Germany" does not also escape from his censure. She is compared to "an obscene fakir" whose body has been wilfully corrupted. This is how Lawrence makes a scathing attack on the very idea of war.

We often speak of a prophetic remark—"Out of evil cometh good". But Lawrence was convinced that no "good" would come out of the war. We see him write to Amy Lowell on 23 August 1916:

> I am glad you think the war is virtually over. Official London seems to be saying, with much confidence, two years more of it. But nobody knows, God help us if this is going on for two years more. These last two years have made one at least two centuries older. In two years more, we shall have ceased to be human beings at all.... What will be the end, when the war is at last over, the mind refuses to consider: but it will be nothing good. (II. 644)

Lawrence's implication that with the end of the war, "we shall have ceased to be human beings at all" sounds terrible. According to Lawrence, the "lowest truth" which leads a nation to engage in warfare is the worship of Mammon, that is, "money is honor and glory". He passionately believed that a nation should be built up "according to a living idea, a great architecture of living people, which shall express the greatest truth of which we are capable" (II. 379). Lawrence does not clarify what he suggests by the "greatest truth" but it may very well suggest (among other things) an all-encompassing love/ fellow-feeling which is "in direct opposition to the principle of war" (II. 424).

In Lawrence's vision (as we read in his letter to Lady Cynthia Asquith, dated 2 November 1915) the war is a "disintegrating autumnal process" and love is "the great creative process, like Spring, the making an integral unity out of many disintegrating factors" (II. 424). This is the voice of a preacher who with zeal preached the love of life to his fellow human beings. George A. Panichas in his article titled "D.H. Lawrence: The Hero Poet as Letter Writer" (1988) judiciously states that "in his furious protestations against the war, Lawrence discloses an independent lyrical note and his language becomes infused with tragic grandiloquence, as well as excessively self-righteous pleas and feelings" (Panichas, 256). One may in this connection quote a few lines from Lawrence's letter to Lady Cynthia Asquith in 1918 that contain "an independent lyrical note", to echo the words of Panichas:

> The spring is here, the cuckoo is heard, primroses and daffodils are out in the woods, it is very lovely. I feel

> that the buds as they unfold, and the primroses come out, are really stronger than all the armies and all the war. I feel as if the young grass growing would upset all the cannon on the face of the earth, and that man with his evil stupidity is after all nothing, the leaves just brush him aside. (III. 117-18)

This is how Lawrence glorifies the "principle of life" above everything that suggests death and disintegration. Lawrence believed, "all art is *au fond* symbolic, conscious or unconscious" (VII. 476). Lawrence's letter to Cynthia Asquith goes beyond the limits of a private correspondence and emerges as a piece of literary art. The "primroses" and the "young grass" are among other things symbols of life and they are stronger than "all the canon on the face of the earth".

Lawrence was convinced, "One should stick by one's own soul, and by nothing else" (III. 118). The First World War to him was "utterly wrong, stupid, monstrous and contemptible". It embittered his soul, it brought a sharp change in his attitude to London but it could not alter his "beliefs or visions" (II. 218). Lawrence believed that only love could subdue the spirit of war and conquer death. His war-letters indeed bear a testimony to that. The last words to the essay may come from Lawrence's poem titled "The Turning Back" that finds its place in his letter to Lady Cynthia Asquith on 2 November 1915 (II. 421-23):

> We have gone too far, oh very much too far;
> Only attend to the noiseless multitudes
> Of ghosts that throng about our muffled hearts
> Only behold the ghosts, the ghosts of the slain,
> Behold them homeless and houseless, without complaint
> . . .
> What matters any more, but only love?
> There's only love that matters any more.
> There's only love, the rest is all outspent. (33-37; 42-44)

Notes

[All references to the letters of Lawrence except the letter to Eoa Renusso are from *The Letters of D.H. Lawrence*, Vol. I: September 1901-May 1913, ed. James T. Boulton (Cambridge: Cambridge University Press,

1979); Vol. II: June 1913-October 1916, eds. George A. Zytaruk and James T. Boulton (Cambridge: Cambridge University Press, 1981); *The Letters of D.H. Lawrence*, Vol. III: October 1916-June 1921, eds. James T. Boulton and Andrew Robertson (Cambridge: Cambridge University Press, 1984) and *The Letters of D.H. Lawrence*, Vol. VII: November 1928-February 1930, eds. Keith Sagar and James T. Boulton (Cambridge: Cambridge University Press, 1993)].

1. See the poem in *D.H. Lawrence: The Complete Poems*, collected and edited with an Introduction and Notes by Vivian De Sola Pinto and Warren Roberts (Harmondsworth: Penguin Books, 1993), p. 703.
2. The essay "Why I Don't Like Living in London" is available in *D.H. Lawrence: Late Essays and Articles,* ed. James T. Boulton (Cambridge: Cambridge University Press, 2004), pp. 120-22.
3. See the poem in *D.H. Lawrence: The Complete Poems*, collected and edited with an Introduction and Notes by Vivian De Sola Pinto and Warren Roberts (Harmondsworth: Penguin Books, 1993), pp. 170-71.
4. See the poem in Ezra Pound: Poems Selected by Thom Gunn (London: Faber and Faber, 2005), p. 23.
5. The relevant lines from "Ode to the West Wind" are:

    Thou from whose unseen presence the leaves dead
    Are driven, like ghosts from an enchanter fleeing,
    Yellow, and black, and pale, and hectic red,
    Pestilence-stricken multitudes

6. This letter is cited from "Further Letters of D.H. Lawrence", John Worthen and Andrew Harrison, *Journal of D.H. Lawrence Studies* (A Publication of the D.H. Lawrence Society of Great Britain), Vol. 3, No. 3, 2014, ed. Susan Reid, p. 9.
7. The poem is available in *D.H. Lawrence: The Complete Poems*, p. 755.
8. See the poem in *D.H. Lawrence: The Complete Poems*, pp. 741-43.

Works Cited

Costin, Jane. "Senses of Touch: Henry Moore, D.H. Lawrence and the First World War". *Journal of D.H. Lawrence Studies,* ed. Susan Reid, Volume 3, Number 3, 2014: 87-108. Print.

Jenkins, Lee M. "'A Propos of the War': D.H. Lawrence's 'All of Us'. *Journal of D.H. Lawrence Studies,* (A Publication of the D.H. Lawrence Society of Great Britain), ed. Susan Reid, Volume 4, Number 2, 2016: 25-46. Print.

Lawrence, D.H. *Kangaroo*. Ed. Bruce Steele. Cambridge: Cambridge University Press, 1994. Print.

McLoughlin, Kate. "*All of Us*: D.H. Lawrence's First World War Poems for the People". *Journal of D.H. Lawrence Studies*, ed. Susan Reid, Volume 4, Number 1, 2015: 45-66. Print.

Murry, Middleton. *Love, Freedom and Society*. London: J. Cape, 1957. Print.

Panichas, George A. "D.H. Lawrence's War Letters". *Texas Studies in Literature and Language*. Vol. 5, No. 3 (Autumn 1963): 398-409. Print.

——. "D.H. Lawrence: The Hero-Poet as Letter Writer". *The Spirit of D.H. Lawrence: Centenary Studies*. Ed. Gamini Salgado and G.K. Das. London: Macmillan, 1988. Print.

9

Wheels Within Wheels: D.H. Lawrence's *Study of Thomas Hardy*

Rajan Joseph Barrett

My paper tries to look at the *Study of Thomas Hardy* and negate claims that it is not about Hardy but D.H. Lawrence's own philosophy. It looks at the positions that Lawrence uses to construct his argument, right from the artificial vs the natural, the economic and political: self-preservation, the male-female principles and the aristocratic principles. It also looks at the notion of the State which Lawrence has and tries to show that besides his anti-establishmental stance in this study and in real life Lawrence is unaware of the malevolent being the state can become to the writer and the individual. It tries to argue that Lawrence needs to define and explain a lot of systems in his own subjective, if not idiosyncratic, manner to find the language to discuss Hardy.

Is the *Study of Thomas Hardy* about Hardy's work or Lawrence's own philosophy?

D.H. Lawrence's *Study of Thomas Hardy* begun in 1914 and not published till 1930 after Lawrence died it makes us ask the questions: 'Does the title advertise text as a cheap gimmick?', 'Does the title mislead by using the name of Thomas Hardy when it perhaps has little to say about Hardy or so it seems?' or 'Is the text an enterprise which must make the reader work out the connections of what is said in it to understand Hardy's oeuvre?' In other words, the title seems to be misleading and not about Hardy in the larger scheme of things that Lawrence ventures into. It appears that Lawrence had another topic in mind got from the French Troubadour poets *Le Gai Savaire*[1] which would mean the gay skill or the gay science and was used as a title of a work by the philosopher Nietzsche.[2] That Nietzsche is quoted in the work is no surprise at all. One also might seem to wonder if the style of the argument is modelled on Nietzsche's style as the *Gay Science* has 'a prelude in rhymes and an appendix in songs' and the name comes from the French Troubadour poets.

The text per se is intense as Lawrence's writing is always so. It does make it possible for a reader who has no notion of the history of publication, and the motivation for the writing of the text, to indulge in a hope that the theorizing, which Lawrence undertakes, is perhaps leading into a deep understanding of the works of Hardy. The text certainly locates Hardy in the European Tradition, something Lawrence does with Walt Whitman by locating the soul of America in Europe. It also makes the attempt to say what is not quite right with the novels of Hardy with a position that is Lawrence's subjective position based on his theorizing of what literature, culture and art does and ought to do.

It leaves one with no doubt by the text's engagement with musicians, philosophers, playwrights and artists of Europe, that Hardy is a product of European thought and culture, even though vernacularization of culture in Wessex is noticeable There is no hint given that Hardy could have perhaps thought outside the framework of European History and European discourse and elides the regionalism of Hardy's fiction. Though Hardy was aware of postcoloniality, perhaps not as critically as a subject who had experienced or thought about the cultural constraints of postcolonialism, as he lived at the zenith of English Imperialism the notions of the standardized from of the English Language and Culture and its Wessex variant as a resistance to the modernization is perhaps something which Lawrence is not concerned with as he sets out to give Hardy a place in the scheme of European consciousness and culture with the confidence that more than two hundred years of imperial advantage have inscribed. In fact, the dialectical variants one finds in Hardy to locate his novels in Wessex is something that other dialects of English have in the postcolonial commonwealth of Britain.[3]

The Complexity of Engaging with Hardy as Lawrence Does

One of the views about *Study of Thomas Hardy* is that it is more about Lawrence's philosophy than about Hardy.[4] It is important that one as a reader who approaches the text as criticism by one novelist and poet about another novelist and poet sees the closeness and distance between each other. This insight that might help us to think about Hardy and about Lawrence as practitioners of the same art seems to have an analysis of their culture and ethnicity, however, the regional and also the notion of a developing history of the English Novel and its place within the canon of English Literature might be a consideration in reading the *Study of Hardy*. Lawrence in his own unique manner makes the reader engage with Hardy in no easy manner, without extrapolating the material of the text—its art history and criticism, musical knowledge and its place within the being of Europe and the philosophical understanding on European principles, along with the author's own principles that he constructs about the male and female principles, something that Lawrence is known for, if anyone pretends to have even a slight acquaintance of Lawrence. Another principle that he uses is the aristocratic principle, which forms a part of his study. Be that as it may, besides these principles Lawrence recounts frameworks that make one think not only about Hardy's novels but about systems, categories, definitions that are redefined as part of a philosophical process of building up a careful argument, circuitous and oblique though it may seem to be.

Direct References to Hardy among the Oblique and Circuitous Argument

It might be gathered by now that I don't stand with those who think that Lawrence's *Study of Thomas Hardy* is a narcissistic adventure into the systems one has constructed to theorize one's own philosophy. I do contend with the fact, though, that one might assert the right to read the text precisely in that manner as the concepts and concerns of the author seem to be screaming out loudly for recognition, with the idiosyncratic ways in which he lays them down for analysis. One might even go on to say that except for Chapters III, V and IX there is nothing about Hardy, it's all Lawrence's esoteric philosophy canvassing for itself as principles to read any novel with the principles of conflict and compromise worked out and explained according to Lawrence's subjective frameworks. There are also influences of Nietzsche on Lawrence and well documented too as the manuscripts and typescripts suggest that the name he wanted to give is was 'Le Gai Savaire'.[5] That many were influenced by Nietzsche as an energetic release from the chaos and confusion of the seeming darkness of the Victorian age is perhaps common knowledge. Lawrence shows his tendencies towards the Germanic philosophy[6] and the notions of being from plant life to mechanical life and notions of productivity across modes of being. He thus constructs the purpose of the human subject from anthropological fictions[7] that he creates to illustrate his point in symbolic and metaphorical language often personifying the poppies, the lily and other flowers.

The Elements of Colour, Form and the Metaphorical Associations for Analysis

There is a long tradition of the white and the red signifying death and which is perhaps most seen in the colour symbolism in *Tess of the D'Urbervilles*. Lawrence uses the colour symbolism along with interpretations form anthropology and economics. The anthropological is however linked up with the notion red as excessive and out of proportion, but for a purpose. This Lawrence links up with the blood and procreation however the red of the rose and the red of the poppy he links up with utilitarianism where in the excessive of the pastry batter is made as rose on the pastry pie.[8]

Half-natural, Half-artificial

It becomes even more complicatedly linked to the Victorian notion in art, architecture and landscaping as the half natural and half artificial of the rose on the pie has no natural colour and is artificially made to be present on the pie. The natural and the artificial are again linked up to the colour of the poppy and the colour of the flame of the phoenix when it sets itself alight. The connections of the flame to passion, is not quite colour alone but the purposefulness of burning oneself out to *be*. Thus, Lawrence exploits symbols to the maximum and signifying much more than a one to one metaphorical relationship between the object or image and the meaning attached, which accounts for the rich texture of his symbols and images, which is a quality of Thomas Hardy in his prose and literary pieces. Though Lawrence begins with the poppy he does not abandon it, but uses it at a motif through his argument. He does this to draw at the multifaceted implications it has whether it be: height and hierarchy, or the Christian dictum to love one's neighbour, or the notion of red, and the ant and the grasshopper story paralleling the lily and the poppy.

The phoenix image is also an image whose symbolic meaning is linked to the history and culture of the European people. Lawrence is discussing perpetuation and preservation of the self from the initial part of the argument till the end. Though this self-preservation is sometimes used tongue in cheek as we see in references to the German people and the war.[9]

Creating Frameworks for Analysis of Hardy's Work

The gamut of sexuality, political economy, desire and drive along with the nothingness and self-destruction, which seems to be what the First World War was doing, has complex arguments, which co-occur in the interplay of the conflicting desires of passion and the instinct of self-preservation. With these interlocking systems that Lawrence builds up he used traditional frameworks of Christianity and the *Bible*, the Greek and European Epics and Literature, Greek and European Philosophy, notions of being, notions of art and architecture, and music to give *Study of Thomas Hardy* a shape. These interlocking systems are linked up to all that he was engaging with to theorize the art of the novelist and poet, Hardy.

It might be curious that *Study of Thomas Hardy* begins with a chapter called 'Of Poppies and Phoenixes and the Beginning of the Argument' The poppy is considered as a wild and a useless weed, while the lily is like the hard working ant, in the story of the ant and the grasshopper. The wildness of the poppy is perhaps of some importance as after the Romantics wildness and nature uncultivated, gains importance. However, the Utilitarian logic which persists into the Victorian age has a gradation of 'usefulness' and economic value from the eighteenth century. Lawrence pits the poppy against the bound cabbage. Binding of cabbages was a way of making them marketable commodities.[10] The poppy is looked down upon as a flower, and referred to as not having a use value, despite its bright red colour. Lawrence gives us the picture of a poppy field with the red splashed all around it and asks what the purpose of being is. This is again linked up to the notion of holidaying and living life for no other purpose but to live it. Living for the pure purpose of being might seem aristocratic for a post-Marxist world. However, Lawrence has his own definition of aristocracy.

The phoenix is associated with the flame and passion is similar to red and its associations, but it also burns itself out to recreate itself and give a new phoenix out of its ash. The cyclical is also a reference to the wheel of preservation and destruction to preserve. The references to the *Bible* take us to the 'Parable of the Talents' and is linked to the cabbage that vegetates on its market bound adventure. Bound and not free the cabbage is unlike the poppy or the phoenix. This is because the poppy and the phoenix do not have the market at the end, but life and newness, which Lawrence finds in the poppy, the phoenix and Dido. It seems as if Lawrence is stating, in romantic and classical metaphors the essence of an artist. An artist is not bothered about the market or respectability, but exists in his/her own right: a notion which has been traditionally linked with freedom of the artistic self. Self-preservation, which is talked about throughout the study, is perhaps asking the question about the poppy and the phoenix, who use different means of self-preservation. This certainly is not the self-preservations of the market bound cabbage, and the writer or artist who writes, paints or sculpts. So the questions seem to be 'What is the purpose of the writer?', 'What is the purpose of writing?' and 'Why write?' I think that after his metaphorical journey into the being of the poppy, the phoenix and the cabbage that Lawrence discusses the purpose of being:

> The final aim of every living thing, creature or being is the full achievement of itself. This accomplished, it will produce what it will produce, it will bear the fruit of nature. Not the fruit, however but the flower is the culmination and the climax, the degree to be striven for. Not the work I shall produce, but the real Me I shall achieve, that is the consideration; of the complete Me will come the complete fruit of me, the work, the children. (12-13)

The flowering is more important in Lawrence's scheme of things. This is the highest point of being for an artist though the metaphor is Romantic and from nature. However, the notion of Victorianism, which seems to be a synthesis of the Romantic and the near Neo-classical age of Britain, emphasised by the half-natural and half-artificial, works on Lawrence too with the notions of the labour movements and the woman's suffrage movement. The latter seem artificial or seem rather to confront the artificial while preserving the natural in as much as the labour movements are talking of the living man pitted against the machine. The woman's suffrage movement considers the location of the body and the location of the mind as the half-artificial and half-natural. Lawrence is at pains to explain this in his male-female principle. More importantly it is the natural confronting the artificial.

'Self-preservation' as a Trope with Multiple Significations

His notion of self-preservation is linked to the discussions on the purpose of work is not only about the artist but the need for work in a post-capitalist world, and it looks like a formulaic norm in the Modern world: 'work is essential for the self-preservation of the human being'. The economic aspects of needing a means of survival is one aspect of self-preservation and the other is the notion that an artist has to think about art and self-preservation in *being*. This probably goes beyond the monetary and the notion of self-preservation in the ordinary sense of the term but hints at self-preservation of a culture, art forms and writing. Thus, Lawrence takes the argument beyond the individual and into a sociological understanding of self-preservation, which touches the political as the self confronts the world. I might be tempted to use the notion of the 'Selfish Gene' by Richard Dawkins, but will restrain myself from doing so and perhaps look at the characters that Hardy creates, who by conservative estimates are going to destroy themselves because of them trying to be different from the culture and environment one is born into. This is a standard reading of Hardy as a writer, and Lawrence too has alluded to it. So when we have so much in Lawrence that is crying out for self-preservation, where does the artist go to? Are artists like the poppies that Lawrence alludes to, or do they change and perhaps flower even after they are no more, or stop producing art, which in Hardy's case is to stop writing novels? The simple kind of equation that the readers of Hardy perhaps seem to like the insight of the individual not pushing beyond the conservative estimate of society, and getting destroyed because they do so. This is a politics of keeping people conservative and not attempting the modern as 'choice of a different way of being'. Lawrence says:

> It is urged against Thomas Hardy's characters that they do unreasonable things—quite, quite unreasonable things. They are always going off unexpectedly and doing something that nobody would do. That is quite true, and the charge is amusing. These people of Wessex are always bursting suddenly out of bud and taking a wild flight into flower, always shooting something out of a tight convention, a tight hide-bound cabbage state into something quite madly personal. It would be amusing to count the number of special marriage licences taken out in Hardy's books. Nowhere, except perhaps in Jude, is there the slightest development of personal action in the characters: it is all explosive. Jude, however, does see more or less what he is doing and act from choice. He is more consecutive. The rest explode out of the convention. They are people each with a real, vital, potential self, even the apparently wishy-washy heroines of the earlier books, and this self

> suddenly bursts the shell of manner and convention and commonplace opinion, and acts independently, absurdly, without mental knowledge or acquiescence.[11]

Lawrence's reading is sophisticated, looks at Hardy's tragedy on a comparative scale with the great epics and classics, where a tragic hero actually revolts against the metaphysics of the Universe and thereby is meant for death. Lawrence looks at the tragic in Hardy being standing against the immediate social system and thereby suffering for it. Lawrence decries modern tragedy for this saying:

> ...the weakness of modern tragedy, where transgression against the social code is made to bring destruction, as though the social code worked our irrevocable fate. Like Clym, the map appears to us more real than the land.
>
> Short sighted almost to blindness, we [pore] over the chart, map out journeys and confirm them: and we cannot see life itself giving the lie the whole time.[12]

The accusation against the English is that they are a conservative lot of people in spite of seeing that they have produced a Newton and a Darwin to shake the world and the conception of the world. I tend to believe that in the romantic principles of changing the world, and the neo-classical principles of adhering to existing forms, is what Hardy adopts to bring out the uniqueness in his characters. It seems as if, the tension between the individual and society produces some lesser promethean figures like Jude, Tess, Sue, and others. These protagonists pay for their difference of choice, and being in the world on different terms given the technologies that were not available to their ancestors. Lawrence does not precisely mention the existential but alludes to the coincidental mismatches that a lot of the characters have in Hardy's novels.

Siding with the Romantic

However, it seems as if the romantic, or promethean urges people have, is what Lawrence sides with:

> Where is the source of all money-sickness, and the origin of all the sex-perversion?

> That is the question to answer. And no cause shall come to life unless it contain an answer to this question. Laws, and all State machinery, these only regulate the sick, separate the sick and the whole, clumsily, oh, so clumsily that it is worse than futile. Who is there who searches out the origin of the sickness, with a hope to quench the malady at its source?
>
> It lies in the heart of man, and not in the conditions—that is obvious, yet always forgotten. It is not a malaria which blows in through the window and attack us when we are healthy. We are each one of us a swamp, we are like the hide-bound cabbage going rotten at the heart. And for the same reason that, instead of producing our flower, instead of continuing our activity, satisfying our true desire, climbing and clambering till, like the poppy, we lean on the sill of all the unknown, and run our flag out there in colour and shine of being, having surpassed that which has been before, we hang back, we dare not even peep forth, but safely shut up in bud, safely and darkly and snugly enclosed, like the regulation cabbage, we remain secure till our hearts go rotten, saying all the while how safe we are.[13]

I think that this above quotation shows where Lawrence stands with regard to not taking a conservative position. The understanding of why there is a war he links up to the idea of self-preservation, and it being perverted to such an extent where people have no space to be creative or romantic enough to follow their own inner being. It must be said that this is in Chapter II which he titles as "Still introductory: about Women's Suffrage, and Laws, and the War, and the Poor, with some Fancyful Moralising".

He is critical of Law as it cannot create anything new but that it only alters what is already there.[14] The notion of the political with the notion of Law and creativity in conflict and often with no compromise, whether in the novels of Hardy or in society, is a hard and bitter fact that Lawrence notes. In the above quotation it is as if Laws are meant to regulate the sick and cannot deal with the notion of freedom of people like the freedom of the blossoming or flowering poppy.

The comparison between the poppy and the hide-bound cabbage though taken from the natural, stand for the natural versus the artificial and the non-commercial versus the market driven. He is already against the homo economicus who is killing off the human and is more economic, or only economic, as a facet of its living. It is actually discussing the human condition, which in a post-capitalist world makes the human being rot psychologically. Self-preservation that is economically driven, is death of the creative spirit of the individual, and perhaps also of society also.

When we consider the hide-bound cabbage it spells out unfreedom chosen for political and economic ends. Unfortunately, when we consider the economic and the legal as technologies of the self, it seems as if Lawrence is asking: "How much do these technologies free us as human beings, and make us productive to create something new?" The echo in Hardy is certainly against these artificial instruments, which are all pervasive and perverse to the human being and creative spirit. Both Hardy and Lawrence seem to advocate this position. Thus the theorizing of Lawrence appears to meet Hardy's notion of the human consciousness in a post-capitalist world, which we often refer to as modern, with all the inconsistencies of the terms. The Language of Law, the Language of Capital or Utilitarianism are considered Modern coming out form the Enlightenment. This anti-modernity of Hardy perhaps is already well-known and accepted.

Against the staid establishment, to choose life

It is often assumed that everyone in the modern world must work. Lawrence does not take that as an essential to the life of the human being, and probes the question. Is having to work an essential for every person? Does one have to work to live? Or does one have to work to eat? These are actually questions that people in the modern age don't answer quite honestly. This is problematic as one perhaps does not know when, or why to stop working. The irony is that even if one has provided for oneself one thinks that one must work, as Lawrence says 'to feed the poor'. These are kind of lame excuses and working for self-preservation of a culture, and for the self-preservation of an art, is something that, according to Lawrence, a miniscule of people actually do.

Does work provide satisfaction, or is one done to death by working without interest in the job, till one is a prisoner of one's own designs. Many would like to ask when they should stop working but who do they ask this question to? This ties up with the notion of holidays and the poppies who flower, seemingly without a purpose. The conflict between a romantic understanding of the world based on a pro-nature and pro-life choice and one of an industrial age seems the crux of the argument. In the latter case it seems that it is already allotted, by consensus or belief, that one has to work till one either dies, or is done to death with the job, and never has the time for what is called creative living.

Lawrence discusses what he considers the outcome of the work-centric approach to life: one is produced as an expert when one keeps doing a job with speed and efficiency. This is matched to the perfect machine, which is what the human being in the industrial age becomes. We might recall the prose of Charles Lamb and his essay "Superannuated Man" where the persona actually is incapable of living the life of a superannuated person, but finds it hard to live without the job that has structured and made itself a habit of his life, and which he can't get rid of. It is indeed important that Lawrence takes up the notion of the political economy of a job and how the job operates the human being instead of the human being knowing when to detach himself, or herself, from a job and do something different, new or creative.

The notion of the human being approximating to a perfect machine is a pat on the back for many who are congratulated on their precision and efficiency. This is something the industrial age gifts to the repertoire of congratulatory phrases to be used to praise someone. However, the language and the practice that work on the individual, to divest him/her of his/her humanness, is the worst casualty in the process of being made into a perfect machine. The implications seem to be seen in the long prose piece by John Ruskin 'Unto this Last' where the inquiry into 'What is a just wage?' throws up questions about the industrial age and exploitation. It does not seem that there is a break with the Victorian Age, which is the age of the Industrial Revolution in which peoples' lives are brutally restructured, according to the rhythms and timing of machines like the train, etc. The human being becomes less a human being, and more of a machine and laps up the praise for it as if it is a marker of achievement.

Different Orientations Plant, Human, Machine

Lawrence is bringing together the beings of various life forms and machine forms. The life forms, which are seen to be in a holiday mood as the poppy, to the hide-bound cabbage with its being dead except for being prepared for the market. Of course, these are metaphors for people to learn from life in a typically Romantic vein. However, the demands on the human subject by the oppression of the Industrial Age is contrasted with, and compared to the flowers and nature. How close are the hide-bound cabbage fit for the market, and the human being called the perfect machine. The comparison strikes anyone as a lampoon on the Industrial Age, and what it has made of willing subjects who bow down to the regimes of power, without a question or even a battle. These conformists, become mechanical cogs in the wheel of the giant system called the Industrial Age, but at the same time, sacrificing all that is human in them. The kind of slavery and competition with a machine might seem challenging, but it is dehumanizing in itself and over a period of time without any resistance it tends to become the norm.

Lawrence finds that the purpose of being is truncated, because of the consent to become a perfect machine. The real purpose that most human beings desire of life is to have time to be, which is sadly not available when the shackles of work are finally done away with, according to Lawrence. Placing this in Chapter IV in the *Study of Thomas Hardy* the notion of what should be the purpose of being, for all human beings, is posited. However, when it is juxtaposed with the imposed purpose of being, bequeathed to the modern subject in a post-industrial and post-capitalist world, the purpose is defeated or skewed with tragic consequences as discussed above.

However, Lawrence as philosopher opting for new life, and a longing for liberty form work, to live a creative life and be says:

> But, satisfied for the time being of that which has been and remains now finite, he wearies for his own, limitless being, for the unresolved, quivering, infinitely complex and indefinite movement of new living, he wants to be free.

Political Economy, Privilege and Need

Lawrence is asking the question that Thoreau asked before him in *Walden*, and is asked again and again which is 'How much does a person need?' Lawrence's scheme of things thus take on the creative spirit and the question of the homo economicus, who no longer goes by need but by greed. This greed is created by a false value system, when self-perseveration is taken to an extreme, and one really cannot draw the limits to how much one actually needs of money. He compares money and food assuming that people know where the limits of eating lie, and also when to stop making money. Perhaps Lawrence has not experienced the experiments of those who create oversized men and women. In their desire to create high calorie food for the labour classes they create bodily imbalance and health problems. The creation of living spaces for the working classes also is a design of governance not in the best interest of the people concerned.

Lawrence perhaps pretends to have no understanding how oppressive the State can be when he says:

> Which is greater, The State or myself? Myself, unquestionably, since the State is only an arrangement made for my convenience. If it is not convenient for me, I must depart from it. There is no need to break laws. The only need is to be a law unto oneself.[15]

Yet what he says should be the norm. But we know that the notion of the totalitarian state perhaps is not theorized or well known in his time. We know that the state was oppressive to Lawrence, his writings and paintings, but that does not figure in this exposition. At the same time the notion of the migrant as we face today had perhaps never occurred to Lawrence when he says "If it is not convenient for me, I must depart from it." The notion of citizenship, immigration, and migration after the notion of the nation state becomes a hardened concept in the 20th century, which puts people into a lot of inconvenience and discomfort and so they have to migrate as refugees due to persecution. Only the fortunate can migrate at will, because they want to be. Lawrence is privileged enough not to have to be a refugee though he does face oppression for his paintings. Also, his artistic freedom is curtailed by the state and the law.

Cultural Opposition and State Repression

It becomes imperative to ask "What has this to do with the study of Hardy?" Was the hardship that Hardy had to face with his last two novels *Tess* and *Jude* and the opposition to it bad enough to move away from the state physically though the state did not act against Hardy but the people reacted to his books. It is probable that Lawrence is talking about a mental movement away from an oppressive state, which might have been possible as long as the Law did not get to one. The idealized State and the real state are set in contrast to each other by the statements of Lawrence. The question of cultural and ethnic intolerance by the State, and curbs on Artistic Freedom are certainly not the same, though both could be equally oppressive. In some cases the curbs on artistic freedom by the state might be so oppressive that one might have no other option but to leave the state. Here too the notion of privilege comes in, which perhaps none of Hardy's characters are endowed with.

Lawrence is also pointing at the privilege of some to obtain and secure the work they like and who are economically equally well-endowed to shrug off a job when it comes to artistic choice and freedom. In principle, however, Lawrence is talking of ideal conditions of work, pay, economic conditions and choice. If any of Hardy's characters had the privilege of moving away inwardly, or outwardly, they perhaps would not be the characters that would occur in his novels. Then again by Lawrence's own notion of the modern tragedy in Hardy we find that they are not being harassed by the State but by the notion of culture and societal norms which are not the same as the Law and the State.

Cementing the Judeo-Christian and the Greco-Roman in a World of Science

I wish Lawrence had not used so many allusions to Christianity, though they are interesting in themselves, as he tries to be non-binary in the resolution between the law of the Father—God the Father, the law of Love—God the Son, Christ, and the resolution of the difference in the person of the Holy Spirit. However, as his argument goes it seems as if he is consolidating the idea of European Culture, and has little to do with the rest of the world. When he starts writing the *Study of Thomas Hardy* in 1914 the war and the effects of the war and totalitarianism have not become issues, yet. But his inter locking of his principles of the flesh and the feminine principle attached to it, and the notion of the male principle are used along with the principles of physics, such as the centripetal and centrifugal forces.

He also combines the story of human consciousness along with the consciousness of matter and the principles of gravitation. He discusses the notion of the continental drift theory of the SiAl floating on the SiMa[16] and links these up to mechanical productions like the wheel, which is a major evolutionary step in the history of locomotion and the human subject's consciousness as it uses the artificial that it creates to be. We must recall that Lawrence considers the price of liberty, as the price of being, as the highest purpose of living. According to Lawrence kings and everyone else strive for it.

The State becomes for Lawrence an artifice, which is meant to foster the individual. The notion of the half-natural and half-artificial cannot be wished away from his scheme of things. If there a balance sought by Lawrence between these traits that signify a Victorian mode of thinking, is not easy to say. He glorifies the poppy and disparages the hide-bound cabbage, and stresses the notion of self-preservation which slowly builds up in oblique manners through the *Study of Thomas Hardy*. But the physics and the centripetal and centrifugal forces are coupled with the hub and the rim: two metaphors for stasis and movement. The interlocking devices between the male and female principles, the trinity and the conflict between father and son, law and love and the resolution because of the spirit are slowly built up over the pages in the *Study of Thomas Hardy.*

Talking about the Male Female Principle with the Renaissance Artists

I think the *Study of Thomas Hardy* is incomplete without all the art history analysed from Lawrence's unique perspective, and his application of the male and the female principle, the rim and the hub, which are used to study the paintings. What purpose do these two chapters serve? I would think that they serve two purposes one is to locate Hardy in the pantheon of European artists, with all their flaws according to the notion of male and female principles. By these principles, Lawrence shows how even if the form is a female form she might fail the test for being female and the same is true about the male forms.[17] When reading the schema of Hardy's novels the cartography, the journeys of characters and images are something one would not be able to miss out on, as geography is one of the tools of the language of modern consciousness. We might protest about the standardization of this tool, without which we have problems in communicating and understanding spatiality. While Lawrence looks at the female flesh as withholding all knowledge of itself, which is his own esoteric schema of things the analysis of the paintings and sculptures seem plausible and well worked out. More than ever, Lawrence is able to convince the reader that his analysis is sound and valid. Most of all the principles adhere to the analysis in a coherent manner when he comes back to Hardy in Chapter IX of the study after making mention of him in Chapter V where he discusses *Desperate Remedies* and says:

> In *Desperate Remedies* there are scarcely any people at all, particularly when the plot is working. The tiresome part about Hardy is that, so often, he will neither write a morality play nor a novel. The people of the first book, as far as the plot is concerned, are not people: they are a heroine, faultless and white; the hero, with a small

> spot on his whiteness; the villainess, red and black, but more red than black; the villain, black and red; the Murderer aided by the Adulteress, obtains power over the Virgin, who, rescued last moment by the Virgin Knight, evades the evil clutch. Then the Murderer, overtaken by vengeance, is put to death, whilst Divine Justice descends upon the Adulteress. Then the Virgin unites with the Virgin Knight, and receives Divine Blessing.[18]

What catches Lawrence's eye is the kind of anti-aristocratic stand that Hardy takes, and an aristocrat is going to be turned into a case of tragedy according to him in Chapter V. This is a unique reading by Lawrence as it uses class as a trope, which is identifiable in Hardy's novels:

> So that we have, of men, the noble Lord in *A Pair of Blue Eyes*, Sergeant Troy, Wildeve, de Stacy, Fitzpiers, and Jude all passionate, aristocratic males, doomed by their very being to tragedy, or to misfortune in the end.
>
> Of the same class among women are: Elfride, Lady Constantine, Marty South, and Tess, all aristocratic, passionate, yet necessarily unfortunate females.
>
> We have also, of men Manston, Farmer Boldwood, Henchard, Alex d'Urberville, and perhaps Jude, all passionate, aristocratic males, who fell before the weight of the average, the lawful crowd, but who, in more primitive times, would have formed romantic rather than tragic figures.
>
> Of women of the same class are Miss Aldclyffe, Eustacia, Lucetta, Mrs Charmond.
>
> The third class, of bourgeois or average hero, whose purpose is to live and have his being in the community, contains the successful hero of *Desperate Remedies*, the unsuccessful but not very much injured two heroes of *A Pair of Blue Eyes*, the successful Gabriel Oak, the unsuccessful left-preacher Clym, the unsuccessful but not very much injured astronomer of *Two on a*

> *Tower,* the successful Scotchman of Casterbridge, the unsuccessful and expired Giles Winterborne of *The Woodlanders*, the arch-type, Angel Clare, and perhaps a little of Jude.
>
> The companion women to these men are, the heroine of *Desperate Remedies* Bathsheba, Thomasin, Paula, Henchard's daughter, Grace in the Woodlanders, and Sue.[19]

This seems quite a reading of Hardy and he later states that Hardy is like Tolstoy who "always stands with the community in condemnation of the aristocrat."[20] This is an important observation, and though Lawrence thinks that Hardy as an artist has the individual against the community, he somehow chooses these aristocratic individuals. One perhaps would not come to such a conclusion unless they have engaged with all the novels seriously. It is important to note that in his personal life Lawrence came from a working class background, but we cannot draw on that connection quite easily to say that his background led him to observe class carefully. But the French Revolution and Tolstoy are perhaps important markers where in the targets are aristocrats. So it seems the accusation against Hardy is that he has not got over the influence of the French Revolution and Tolstoy.

We might also like to look at the fact that Lawrence uses words like 'heroes' and 'heroines' to discuss what today will be called protagonists and at the most protagonists and antagonists instead of heroes, heroines, villains and villainesses. There seems to be a conceptual difference in using these terms as perhaps none of Hardy's characters are heroes and heroines, or villains and villainesses and to us they seem more complex characters who are human and therefore flawed though they stand out as protagonists in the novels. They also have better aspects of their personality but if one wants to look at aristocrats and their tragedy then there is the romantic urge to look as loss and gain from a class perspective which is too easy to class Hardy's complex plots and thereby characters in.

Defining the Aristocrat from a Socio-psychological Perspective in Relation to the Other

I think that the notion of the flesh and the depiction of Hardy's characters through the female and male principle might give them a fairer treatment on some concrete principle as Lawrence does with the paintings and sculptures of the great artists that he discusses. However, the class angle would be still a strong element of analysis and in the still early days of criticism of the British novel it certainly is a welcome insight into character and character types as Lawrence tries to study them. At the same time what is insightful on the part of Lawrence is the definition of the aristocrat. The conventional notion of the aristocrat is one who does not have to work for a living, and acquires social position because of accumulated capital both cultural and economic. However, Lawrence is looking at how the notion of the aristocrat is defined in the modern world, where everyone is expected to have a job. It is quite evident that Hardy's Tess does not have the capital assets that a traditional aristocrat has probably in both senses of the term. However, Lawrence thinks differently:

> This Tess knew, unconsciously. An aristocrat she was, developed through generations to the belief in her own self-establishment. She could help, but she could not be helped. She could give, but she could not receive. She could attend to the wants of the other person, but no other person, save another aristocrat,—and there is scarcely such a thing as another aristocrat,—could attend to her wants, her deeper wants.
>
> So it is the aristocrat alone, who has any real and vital sense of the "neighbour", of the other person; who has the habit of submerging himself, putting himself entirely away before the other person: because he expects to receive nothing from the other person. So that now, he has lost much of his initiative force, and exists almost isolated, detached, and without the surging ego of the ordinary man, to exclude him.[21]

Thus, Lawrence though he talks of the characters of Hardy's being aristocrats he also in dealing with them as fictional characters creates a character type not resorting to the acquired economic and cultural capital that might be conventional notion of an aristocrat. But Lawrence tries to show how agency is mutated in a modern world where the aristocracy has little or no place. From the above quotation it seems that the aristocrat has not been able to live in an equal world, where giving and receiving is an important transaction that signify equality and oneness. The giving and receiving, whether in abstract or in concrete terms is something that an aristocrat is incapable of doing which is the crux of Lawrence's definition. When we think of the traditional notions of the aristocracy, we might have looked at how primogeniture and acquisitiveness would play a part in the power relations. Also the unequal exploitation of labour, with the notions of an old family, or an old Lord which is either semi-feudal or feudal would probably be compensating the workers in kind. Sexual exploitation was a part of the tradition of the aristocracy as part of the order of societal power. However, Lawrence marks Alec d'Urberville out as an aristocrat in his accusation of Hardy discussed above. Now he goes back to the aristocratic principle he develops in spite of Hardy not doing Alec the honours. Lawrence says:

> And just as the aristocratic principle isolated Tess, it had isolated Alec d'Urberville. For though Hardy consciously made the young betrayer a plebeian and an impostor, unconsciously, with the supreme justice of an artist, he made him same as de Stacy, a true aristocrat, or as Fitzpiers, or Troy. He did not give him the tiredness, the touch of exhaustion necessary, in Hardy's mind, to an aristocrat. But he gave him the intrinsic qualities.
>
> With the men as with the women of old decent: they have nothing to do with mankind in general, they are exceedingly personal. For many generations they have been accustomed to regard their own desires as their own supreme laws. They have not been bound by conventional morality: this they have transcended, being a code unto themselves. The other has always

> been Present in their imagination, in the spectacular sense. He has always existed to them but as something other than themselves.
>
> Hence the inevitable isolation, detachment of the aristocrat. His one aim, During centuries, has been to keep himself detached. At last he finds himself, by his very nature, cut off.[22]

The issue at hand is that Lawrence finds the way out for Alec in seeking the woman in Tess. He looks at Jude as similar to Tess with the aristocratic principle in mind. He also finds that there is no reconciliation but death for these characters.[23] Somehow or the other, Lawrence puts his male and female principles to work along with his aristocratic principle, and the tripartite Christian understanding of the world with the Father and the Son being reconciled by the Holy Spirit, and with the Greek notions of Themis and Nemesis.

The male in the flesh and the male in the spirit have to match with the female in the flesh and the female in the spirit otherwise for Lawrence there is discord. Thus, the *Study of Thomas Hardy* is certainly Lawrence's own philosophy carefully and uniquely defined and rigorously argued. However, it is putting the novels of Hardy to test in this framework he has built with the aid of aesthetics, art, music, his own principles of the man and the woman, and aristocracy. Of course, he keeps the Judeo-Christian and the Greco-Roman cultures in mind and relates and places Hardy within these frameworks. Though it is not easy to discuss all the complex sets of systems which interlock in the *Study of Thomas Hardy,* one might like to consider that there has to be so much explanation of different systems to come to an understanding of the characters of Hardy. Though there is not much to do with the plot of the novels, the complexity of engaging with systems of metaphysics, religion, aesthetics, law, nation states, etc. are a different way of doing a study in fiction. The interlocking wheels of a system, which is also tied up with histories of different times, gives us a plethora of wheels within wheels, which create a framework from which Lawrence can discuss Hardy's novels with clarity.

Notes

1. Bruce Steele the editor of *The Cambridge Edition of the Works of D.H. Lawrence: Study of Thomas Hardy and Other Essays* (Cambridge: Cambridge University Press), 1984, has *Le Gai Savaire* as a title in brackets and in his introduction gives the genesis of the text as Lawrence was asked to do a work on Hardy.
2. Bruce Steele says in his introduction "Throughout 1915 Lawrence made several frustrated attempts to rewrite 'Le Gai Savaire'." *The Cambridge Edition of the Works of D.H. Lawrence: Study of Thomas Hardy and Other Essays* (Cambridge: Cambridge University Press), 1984, xxx.
3. One for instance finds that Tess speaks the Wessex dialect and also knows standard English. "Between the mother, with her fast-perishing lumber of superstitions, folk-lore, dialect, and orally transmitted ballads, and the daughter, with her trained National teachings and Standard knowledge under an infinitely Revised Code, there was a gap of two hundred years as ordinarily understood. When they were together the Jacobean and the Victorian ages were juxtaposed." *Tess of D'Urbervilles* by Thomas Hardy, 1891. (N.Y.: Global Grey) 2018, 21.
4. Lawrence says "The book I wrote—mostly philosophicalish, slightly about Hardy—I want to re-write and publish in pamphlets. We must create an idea of new, freer life, where men and women can really meet on natural terms, instead of being barred within so many barriers. And if the money spirit is killed, and eating and sleeping is free, then most of the barriers will collapse. Something must be done and we must begin soon." *The Letters of D.H. Lawrence* Vol. II. Ed. George J. Zyataruk and James T. Boulton, Cambridge: Cambridge University Press, 1981, pp. 292-93.
5. Bruce Steele, *The Cambridge Edition of the Works of D.H. Lawrence: Study of Thomas Hardy and Other Essays* (Cambridge: Cambridge University Press), 1984, xxxv.
6. "Let there be an end then of all this welter of pity, which is only self-pity reflected on to some obvious surface. And let there be an end of this German hatred. We ought to be grateful to Germany that she still has the power to burst the bound hide of the cabbage. Where do I meet a man or a woman who does not draw deep and thorough satisfaction from this war? Because of pure shame that we should have seemed such poltroons, living safe and atrophied, not daring to take one step to life. And this is the only good that can result from the 'world disaster': that we realise once more that self-preservation isn't the final goal of life; that we realise that we can still squander life and property and inflict suffering wholesale.

That will free us, perhaps, from the bushel we cower under, from the paucity of our lives, from the cowardice that will not let us *be*, which will only let us live in security, unflowering, unreal, fat, under the cosy jam-pot of the State, under the shelter of the social frame." *The Cambridge Edition of The Works of D.H. Lawrence: Study of Thomas Hardy and Other Essays* (Cambridge: Cambridge University Press), 1984, pp. 16-17.

7. "Working in contradiction to the will of self-preservation, from the very first man wasted himself begetting children, colouring himself and dancing and howling and sticking feathers in his hair, in scratching pictures on the walls of his cave, and making graven images of his unutterable feelings. So, he went on, wildly with gorgeousness taking no thought of the morrow, but at evening, considering the ruddy lily." *The Cambridge Edition of the Works of D.H. Lawrence: Study of Thomas Hardy and Other Essays* (Cambridge: Cambridge University Press), 1984, p. 7.
8. *Study of Thomas Hardy and Other Essays* (Cambridge: Cambridge University Press), 1984, p. 9.
9. See foot note 5 above.
10. Lawrence uses this term constantly for the humdrum and dull existence of eating, breeding, and sleeping.
11. *The Cambridge Edition of The Works of D.H. Lawrence: Study of Thomas Hardy and Other Essays* (Cambridge: Cambridge University Press), 1984, 20.
12. *Ibid.*, p. 30.
13. *Ibid.*, p. 15.
14. *Ibid.*, p. 14.
15. *Ibid.*, p. 35.
16. SiAl and SiMa, SiAl = Silica + Aluminium, SiMa = Silica + Magnesium.
17. *The Cambridge Edition of The Works of D.H. Lawrence: Study of Thomas Hardy and Other Essays* (Cambridge: Cambridge University Press), 1984, 38.
18. Chapters VII and VIII are an exposition of the male and female principles of Lawrence and they become clear when he discusses paintings and sculpture and how they conform to the male and female principles or detract from them.
19. *The Cambridge Edition of The Works of D.H. Lawrence: Study of Thomas Hardy and Other Essays* (Cambridge: Cambridge University Press), 1984, p. 45.
20. *Ibid.*, pp. 48-49.
21. *Ibid.*, p. 49.

22. *Ibid.*, p. 98.
23. *Ibid.*, p. 99.

Works Cited

Dawkins, Richard, *The Selfish Gene*. Oxford: Oxford University Press, 1976.

Hardy, Thomas, *Tess of the d'Urbervilles*, 1891. New York: Global Grey, 2018.

Lawrence, D.H., *Studies in Classic American Literature*, ed. Ezra Greenspan, Lindeth Vasey, and John Worthen. *The Cambridge Edition of the Works of D.H. Lawrence*. Cambridge: Cambridge University Press, 2003.

———, *Study of Thomas Hardy and Other Essays* ed. Bruce Steele in the *Cambridge Edition of the Works of D.H. Lawrence.* Eds. James T. Boulton and Warren Roberts. Cambridge: Cambridge University Press, 1984.

Nietzsche, Friedrich, *The Gay Science: With a Prelude in Rhymes and an Appendix of Songs*, Tr. and ed. Walter Kaufmann. New York: Vintage, 1984. (This translation is based on the second edition of Die fröhliche Wissenschaft, published in 1887.)

Thoreau, H.D., *Walden and Civil Disobedience.* New York: Penguin, 1986.

10

Censorship and the Self in the Art of D.H. Lawrence

Deeptha Achar

1

> What then is involved in making explicit? Explicit is to implicit as explication is to implication: these oppositions derive from the distinction between the manifest and the latent, the discovered and the concealed.
>
> *The Theory of Literary Production*, Pierre Macherey

Most engagements with the work of D.H. Lawrence tend to focus on his fiction and his poetry, and there is little focus on his painted works. The fact that they were confiscated from the gallery where they were on show and literally banished to the United States by law often appears as an addendum to his more well-known skirmishes with censorship qua *Lady Chatterley's Lover* and *The Rainbow* as well as *Pansies*. In this context, would it be productive to examine the question of censorship in relation to his painted works independent of his fiction?

This paper will focus on Lawrence's take on censorship that followed the confiscation of his paintings. The attempt would be to examine the manner in which he stages his critique of censorship and addresses the charges of obscenity in his art work. I will work away from an approach that would attribute obscenity, or not, to the works themselves. In that sense, obscenity would not be an attribute that inheres within the work itself but rather, it will be seen as being produced by social and political contexts that articulate obscenity in relation to the work. This being the case, my concern is more to pursue the Laurentian argument around censorship, with his painting as an entry point. The particular focus of this paper is an essay "Pornography and Obscenity"[1] written by Lawrence almost as a response to the confiscation of his works. Here he is not interested in castigating the "censor-morons"[2] so much as articulating the social lie of the land that engendered such a hostile response to his work.

The paper will start with an account of the events surrounding the confiscation of his work. In the second section, the focus will be on unpacking the question of censorship. Here, I offer a reading of Lawrence's "Pornography and Obscenity" in order to open out his analysis of censorship and the "obscenity" of his paintings.

2

An exhibition of twenty-five of Lawrence's paintings was put on display at the Dorothy Warren Gallery in London.[3] The exhibition also featured a limited run of the paintings printed in book form with Lawrence's essay "Introduction to these Paintings".[4] The show opened on 14 June 1929 to a mixed response: the reviews were both highly favorable and deeply negative. Jonathon Green observes that the "authorities noted those [negative] criticisms were based more on moral than aesthetic ground" (322). *The Observer* called the paintings "frankly disgusting" and *The Daily Telegraph*, "gross and obscene".[5] Addressing a complaint made by a member of the public, an inspector and sergeant of police visited the exhibition on 5 July, went back to report and then returned to confiscate thirteen of the paintings on display among which were Boccaccio's Story, Fight with an Amazon, Leda and the Swan and Under the Mango Tree and deposited them in a cell. Lawrence believed that it was the visible pubic hair in some of the works that landed the seized works in court. The hearing at court surely seems like a travesty today. Lawrence, who was in Italy for treatment of the tuberculosis that eventually killed him, was not able to be present at the hearing. Green, in his account of the hearing, says:

> The octogenarian magistrate Frederick Mead who heard the case at Marlborough Police Court on August 8 apostrophized the works as 'gross, coarse, hideous, unlovely, and obscene'. He refused to hear such expert witnesses as Augustus John and Arnold Bennett, declaring that it was 'utterly immaterial whether they are works of art or not. The most splendidly painted picture in the universe might be obscene...' and should be 'put an end to, like any wild animal which is dangerous.' (322)

Lawrence, following his lawyer's advice, paid a fine of five guineas and retrieved the works on the condition that he would not exhibit these works in Britain again. The paintings eventually made their way to the United States, and can now be found in New Mexico and Texas. The catalogues of reproductions were destroyed. This judgment clearly had a long shadow: in 1951, Green reports that the U.S. Customs "refused to permit the import of the privately printed *Paintings of D.H. Lawrence*, ordered by one of his biographers, on the grounds that it was obscene" (322).

Jonathan Jones, in his perspicacious article "A Life in Pictures" has commented on Lawrence's surprising reaction to the judgment. Instead of fighting "a cultural battle" around the seizure of his paintings and making a claim for the freedom of the artist, Jones remarks, Lawrence responded with "distress, rather than glee" in spite of the broad support he received from Virginia Woolf, Jacob Epstein, Roger Fry and others. It is this, Jones observes, that marks Lawrence away from the "cultural theatre of outrage" which characterizes the contemporary moment. For Jones, the works themselves are naïve and not quite skilled. He describes the work as "paintings with an argument". Jones says:

> Lawrence painted erotic visions with a reverence for the naked heroic body and extensive quotations of the physically explicit art of Renaissance Italy. Renaissance themes in his Boccaccio's Story and Leda and the Swan unfortunately don't mean a Renaissance confidence in depicting bodies. Arms and legs taper bizzarely, heads

> are tiny, torsos warp in odd ways; everyone looks slightly deformed—the women more than the men.

He points out that Lawrence's portrayals of men were more sophisticated than his representation of women, almost a parallel to the erotic charge of the scene in which two men wrestle in *Women in Love*. The work Dandelions, in which a peasant is painted urinating, he finds, is a case in point. The overemphasis of the heroic singular phallic figure, according to Jones, is out of sync with the world we inhabit today. Lawrence's battles that centered around sex are not our battles: "The war is over; sex won. Lawrence was in the advance guard, but like many an old soldier he has been pensioned off.... Sex [today] is far too big to require his services." In spite of his somewhat derogatory reading of Lawrence's paintings, he offers an important insight into their significance when he casts them as a part of an argument that equally involves Lawrence's seminal essay introducing his paintings.

Picking up a cue from Jones in his assertion that the essay and the paintings are a part of a composite argument, it would be apposite to take a look at Lawrence's contentions in the introduction. It is significant that nowhere does ITP refer to or seek to explicate Lawrence's own art work. Instead, the essay is an engagement with art historical moves that sought to characterize modernity in art at that time, particularly in the work of Roger Fry. Taken in conjunction with the exhibition, Lawrence's essay could be read as an intervention into the manner in which a possible future could be imagined for British modernism. Jeff Wallace, in a careful reading of ITP, suggests that the text can be divided into three sections.[6] The first section is an exposition on "the fear of the body which entered the English, and later American, consciousness, at the Renaissance and which is galvanized by the 'great shock' of syphilis and its impact in C16";[7] Lawrence points, for example, to the anxiety ridden jokes around the pox and clap that haunt sixteenth and seventeenth century English society to buttress this view (ITP, 553-54). In the second section, says Wallace, Lawrence focuses on the implications of this fear on the trajectory taken by English art while setting up "a parallel, extended analysis of French visual culture"[8] where Lawrence suggests somewhat problematically that the French did not quite labor under the fear that had taken over British consciousness. In the last section, Lawrence offers an assessment of Paul Cézanne, who, he declares, "is the first artist in centuries to rupture the established pattern of fear and evasion of the body."[9] It is in this section that Lawrence takes issue with Roger Fry. Though his and Fry's estimation of the significance of Cézanne did not significantly diverge, there is a sense in this section that Lawrence is developing a critique of Fry's book *Cézanne: A Study of Development*.[10] He declares "And so we can return to modern French painting, without having to quake before the bogy, or the Holy Ghost of the Significant Form" (ITP, 567); instead of framing Cézanne's work in and through the category form as proposed by Fry (ITP, 572). Lawrence suggests that the constitutive conflict that underwrote Cézanne's work "was not between the artist and his medium but between the artist's *mind* and the artist's *intuition* and *instinct*" (ITP, 573; italics in the original). Indeed, he argues that Cézanne could be put "among the heroes" because "He would *not* abandon his own vital imagination" (ITP, 571; italics in the original).

Given the careful articulation of Lawrence's laudatory assessment of Cézanne, and since Lawrence wrote the essay as an introduction to his own paintings, it would perhaps be productive to look at the conjunctions obtaining between his reading of Cézanne and his works on show. While one would agree with Jones's assertion that the significance of Lawrence's works lay more in their position in cultural history, it might also be quite instructive to take a look at some of the work itself. However, it will be critical to do so in a manner in which the primary mode of evaluation is structured not through a formal analysis of the work but through its function as a part of a composite argument proposed by Lawrence. Since Lawrence does not reference his own work while yet terming the essay "An Introduction to these Paintings", one could assume that he was trying to set up some alignments between his paintings and the work of Cézanne. This is not to say, however, that he was proposing a simple equation between the two, but was rather trying to suggest that there were points of convergence in questions of method and a vivifying intention.

What, then, are Lawrence's central contentions about Cézanne? Certainly, he saw Cézanne as the heroic embodiment of a kind of bravery constituted by a resolve to be true to his intuitive self. Such a resolve was all the more significant because it overcame the pull to be fearful about the procreative body. Lawrence sees this as a counter movement to British (but later universal) fearfulness with regard to the procreative body that manifests as an overemphasis on "mental consciousness" (ITP, 556). Lawrence seems to suggest that Cézanne draws on a French tradition of engagement with the body that is not quite so mired in anxiety. Instead, Cézanne works with an intuitive instinctual engagement with the substantial body, says Lawrence, and this enables him to rework conventional form and clichéd representations that are underwritten by "mental consciousness": Lawrence writes, "...Cézanne, far too inwardly proud and haughty to accept the readymade clichés that came from his mental consciousness, stoked with memories, and which appeared mocking at him on his canvas, spent most of his time smashing his own forms to bits" (ITP, 578). By taking such a position Lawrence seems to move away from the prevailing formalism of the time, which read Cézanne's work, as Fry did, in mostly formal terms. In fact, his reading of Cézanne uses a historico-social framework which, Lawrence argues, played a critical role in shaping his art. Lawrence underlines Cézanne's Provencal bourgeois background: "He was a bourgeois and one must never forget it. He had a moderate bourgeois income. But a bourgeois from Provence is much more real and human than a bourgeois in Normandy. He is much nearer the actual people, and the actual people are much less subdued by awe of his respectable bourgeois money" (ITP, 571). Both the independence that his class offered him and his regional affiliations which do not quite allow him the status of a "bourgeois from Normandy" enable him to forge close living ties with "actual" people who are presumably closer to their intuitive selves.

Most assessments of Lawrence's art work focus on considering whether the paintings are obscene. Such assessments offer analyses of the paintings which lead to the conclusion that either the works are obscene or they are not.[11] Another variation of this approach is a freedom of the artist position which would take a detour around the obscenity question in order to assert that the artist should be free to create regardless of the "obscenity" of the work.[12] Jones, in contrast, analyses Lawrence's paintings on the basis of their formal qualities and their level of skill. Lawrence, he says "never claimed to be a skilled artist, and he was right to be modest".[13] If, instead of using these approaches, one could examine the works in line with the criteria that Lawrence set up in ITP, it may be possible to understand the significance of these works in a different way. To do this would be to bypass both the morality-based obscenity argument and the technique and skill-based aesthetic argument. This would mean that the ITP and the paintings would be read together in order to tease out the contours of the aesthetic and moral dimensions of Lawrence's argument.

Even a casual glance at Lawrence's paintings will show an assemblage of nude bodies in a variety of poses and positions, indoors and out. Wolves and other creatures participate in the action. Quite a few of them are structured almost like an orgy. Conventional sexual mores count for but little if at all. Some invoke the Bible and in others, pastoral landscapes reference Renaissance painting. Andrew Graham-Dixon says: "Most of the paintings showed nude men and women embracing or otherwise communing with themselves and one another in Arcadian landscapes of an abstract character.... Some were comical and burlesque in mood, others melancholic, others ecstatic."[14] They suggest visions of complex sexual dreams that have been rendered apparently unedited. The images have a sense of the looming masculine, with a preponderance of men and phallic objects decidedly on view. The strangely composed bodies belie the structure of the human torso. In fact, the painterly naiveté and the technical gaucherie of the paintings have been widely commented upon.[15]

These are the qualities, rather than the out there sexuality of the paintings, which we view today with a faint embarrassment. Yet it is not difficult to see that the paintings, with their overrepresentation of the body in sex, are interwoven with Lawrence's celebration of the "procreative body" which he argued was underrepresented in British art. It can be seen qua Cézanne as a brave, even heroic attempt to stay true to the intuitive impulses which for him was the lynch pin of a fearless art. Lawrence's bodies in sex stand in contradistinction to the history of art that has been produced through "mental consciousness". Since Lawrence ties intuition and instinct to the body in sex, his lack of technical skill becomes immaterial in the context of his larger project. From such a perspective, the works themselves become a critique of formalism. His naïve renderings of the human form can be read as a rejection of the overly formalist demands being made then on contemporary art and in tune with his extended criticism of Fry's notion of "Significant Form" in ITP. Further, his paintings can also be seen as pushing ahead with his attempt to make the question of class more thematic to the understanding of the art-making process. His portrayal of peasant life in contexts outside both a life of labor and a sense of nostalgia as also his specific manner of thematizing "actual" life in class terms quietly underscores this position.

A look at his work, Holy Family, can be illustrative. The work pictures three figures, parents and son in a peasant's home. The parents are posed against a table: the father, large moustached, in the collarless shirt of the peasant; the mother, broad shouldered, bare breasted. The man grasps her breast and she places her hand on his, intimately. However, she looks past him while he looks ahead. The child sits behind his parents at the table from where he watches his parents with bemused interest. Their gazes do not engage the spectator in anyway. From a round window, one can see a phallic structure in the landscape beyond; Calvary? A lighthouse? All three sport halos, somewhat at odds with the humble dwellings and peasant clothes they wear. The halos surely call to mind the Renaissance groupings of the Holy Family. But how can this oddly modern, peasant family be so simply equated with the Holy Family? The blasphemy of this gesture shocks quite as much as the manner in which the figure of the son is drawn into the ambit of a profane love. The sexualization of childhood laid over the secularization of the Holy Family horrifies us. Perhaps it contributes to the "obscenity" of the work far more than the nudity of the woman. However, the sexualization of the son also pulls in another direction; the family has been newly sexualized by Freud at that point, we remember. Thus, the oedipal triangle too comes to represent the Holy Family. Within the erotic energies of this naïve painting it is still possible to unpack an argument about the social figured by an arrangement of bodies.

3

Obscenity in art, and censorship have been stitched together in a profound way at least since the nineteenth century. This is the period in which censorship essentially got relocated into the secular domain. Hitherto censorship was a provenance of the Church and the State, which kept their watchful eyes on heresy and treason respectively and even when obscenity came to be a charge that could be prosecuted in a court of law, the focus of obscene libel was mostly tied to a breach of peace. It is only around the nineteenth century that cultural and moral as opposed to political censorship became ascendant. Green notes "The wider moral censorship that was to come as a product of the 18th and 19th centuries abandoned any connection with a breach of peace but instead saw its purpose to simply maintain control of "dirty books" (and, later, films, television and other media)—ushering in the modern concept of "obscene publications".[16]

Fear lies at the center of censorship. Censorship is premised on the idea that the object to be censored threatens the order of things: Green suggests that censorship stems from the "belief that if the speech, book, play, film, state secret or whatever is permitted free exposure, then authorities will find themselves threatened to an extent they cannot tolerate" (Introduction, xviii). Another way of thinking about censorship is to see it as a process, that is, not through the objects that are censored but through the modes by which censorship is instituted. In this context, we can characterize the censorship imposed upon by the authorities as regulative. In contrast, constitutive censorship refers to the ideological bases through which censorship engenders control. Parul Singh argues that constitutive censorship suggests "censorial regimes such as (self-) censorship where the boundaries are blurred" between an enforced censorship and one that accepts hegemonic power in either a deliberate or instinctive way.[17] In constitutive censorship, one can say, control over prohibited work is put in place by systems that play a key role in constituting the self, either consciously or unconsciously. Where in regulative censorship, the domain in which censorship is seen to operate is on the object itself, in constitutive censorship it operates across the complicated terrain between the self and society.

The taking down of Lawrence's exhibition became the occasion for him to write on the question of censorship. It was an occasion for him to think through why the exhibition was taken down, why the policemen who came to shut the exhibition down were confused about what was to be removed, and what could be the criteria through which one can think about obscenity. Significantly, the essay "Pornography and Obscenity" scarcely focuses on figures of the moral and legal authorities who were instrumental in the exercise of censorship over the charge of obscenity. Instead, the essay focuses on the manner in which obscenity is forged and how it operates through public opinion. It focuses on the idea of censorship that is not a mere operation of law but a process that involves attitudes and beliefs that are historically constructed.

His argument hinges on the historicity of the category obscenity. He offers a programmatic sketch of the history of obscenity, tracking it from its etymological meaning "that which might not be represented on stage" ("PO", 170). He dwells on the fact that obscenity changes with time and context "*Hamlet* shocked all the Cromwellian Puritans, and shocks nobody today"; what is obscene for one is not obscene for another "What is obscene to Tom is not obscene to Lucy or Joe" ("PO", 170). He pushes further to make a more significant point: he suggests that obscenity is constructed though the operation of the majority: "If a play shocks ten people in an audience, and doesn't shock the remaining five hundred then it is obscene to ten and innocuous to five hundred; hence the play is not obscene, by majority" ("PO", 170). Should the majority find the play obscene, then it would become so. Since obscenity is changeable and resides with the majority, it is the majority which is the judge of obscenity and this power is translated into law based on the principle of *Vox populi, vox Dei.* Since the majority, by way of its indiscriminate use of its majoritarian power, determines the obscene, it is nothing but a mob. In other words, Lawrence implies, it is the majority or the mob who decides what is obscene. By invoking the notion of the mob, Lawrence seems to be suggesting hegemonic processes of ideological control. One can also extrapolate here that this is the way regulative forces, including the state, come to take charge of what is considered obscene. What Lawrence implies is that there is no negotiation possible around the question of meanings as meanings are fixed and established by the power of the mob. This is a violent process, he suggests, particularly since meanings are volatile, precarious entities, negotiated through and across social and historical contexts ("PO", 171). The meanings of the obscene object are the meanings attributed to the object by the mob, "if you are talking to the mob, the meaning of your words is the mob-meaning, decided by majority" ("PO", 170). Yet, the mob is not a simple agglomeration of a majority, every member of the mob constantly has to negotiate between "an individual reaction and a mob reaction" ("PO", 171). This negotiation within the self which manifests as a questioning of alternative meanings, between alternative reactions, is at the heart of process of the attribution of obscenity to a word or scene or image.

The centering of the self in negotiations around the obscene takes Lawrence to censorship. How does the obscene get censored? Sigmund Freud had proposed that censorship (*die Zensur*) operated at two levels. At one level he posits an explicit censorship that was located on the outside and at another level, an implicit censorship that was built into the psyche. In "A Note on the Unconscious" (1912), he lays out a schema where the censor is positioned between the unconscious and the conscious, whose function is to prevent the leaking of the secret impulses of the unconscious into the conscious: "...picture a large entrance room (the unconscious) joined by a passageway to a drawing room (the conscious), with a 'watchman' or a 'censor' guarding the doorway between them, allowing only certain individuals (impulses) to pass and even, occasionally, jettisoning some from the drawing room back into the entrance room"[18] Lawrence's conceptualization of the unconscious ran counter to Freud and he had laid out his points of difference with the Freudian schema in *Psychoanalysis and the Unconscious*. In ITP, too, he makes a case for "the whole consciousness of man working together in unison and oneness" (574). He seems to go along with the Freudian notion of the unconscious,[19] in that he characterizes it as a repository of the instinct, impulse or intuition. However, instead of imagining the unconscious as an arena marked by repression and by the policing of *die Zensur*, he imagines it as a resource that is available to the conscious self: "instinct, intuition, mind, intellect all fused into one complete consciousness, and grasping what we may call a complete truth, or a complete vision, or a complete revelation in sound" (ITP, 574). This sense of "whole consciousness" is applicable to the process of creation as well as "genuine appreciation" (ITP, 574). In other words, where for Freud the self is characterized by a secrecy produced by the censor, for Lawrence it is characterized by an open traffic that bears no mark of such policing.

In "PO", pornography becomes the signifier of the unconscious. It is marked by its underground character; the undercover manner in the way it circulates, as pornographic postcards and texts, is but an index of this: "The whole question of pornography seems to me a question of secrecy. Without secrecy there would be no pornography" ("PO", 177). He refuses to link pornography and obscenity on the basis of "sex appeal" or "sex stimulus" ("PO", 174). He distinguishes the two in that pornography is marked by the furtive and the covert and obscenity, by open, public, majoritarian disavowal. Pornography comes into being by transforming sex into "a dirty, little secret" ("PO", 177) and its central function is to constitute the world at large as pure and sexless: "the vast public lie of purity and the dirty little secret" ("PO", 184). It is this which is genuine pornography, says Lawrence, and it is this that he would censor, "rigorously" ("PO", 175). He argues that this particular structure emerges with the full force of social sanction in the nineteenth century. Hence, from the nineteenth century, references to sex become surreptitious or masked or punished. Pornography enters, he says, when we can perceive "a desire to spite the sexual feeling, to humiliate it and degrade it" ("PO", 177). Read from such a perspective, he says, we must acknowledge that even a text such as *Jane Eyre* tends towards the pornographic: "Mr. Rochester's sex passion is not 'respectable' till Mr. Rochester is burned, blinded, disfigured, and reduced to helpless dependence. Then, thoroughly humbled and humiliated, it may be admitted" ("PO", 176-77).

The pornographic attitude of the nineteenth century is to be found embodied the "grey elderly ones belong[ing] to the last century" ("PO", 183), who are full of "the grey disease of sex-hatred and the yellow disease of dirt-lust" ("PO", 176). They are left over from the nineteenth century in "And [yet] they rule us. They rule us with the grey, mealy-mouthed, canting lie of that great century of lies..." ("PO", 183). The grey elite continue to have ideological control of the mob, the majority whose views construct public opinion, and we can see this, says Lawrence, in their attitude towards sex. Closely mirroring the pornographic stance of the elite, the mob finds the "dirty little secret" "infinitely precious" ("PO", 177). The mob comprises "the great pornographic class—the really common men-in-the-street and women-in-the-street. They have as great a hate and contempt of sex as the greyest Puritan..." (176). It is interesting to note that Lawrence does not suggest that the mob is led by the elite, "the grey men", but rather, suggests that the mob and the elite together operate with a shared ideology that works to shrink the lived possibilities of more open, more equal, more exuberant relationships in sex. Since such an attitude engenders hostility towards to the opposite sex, human beings are cocooned in a singular, self-enclosed, masturbatory, non-reciprocal relationship with one's own self (179).

Boccaccio is for Lawrence an exemplary figure who can counter the purity-dirty dichotomy with regard to sex. Boccaccio is medicine for Lawrence: his "gay Renaissance stories... would help to shake off a lot of grey self-importance, which is our modern, civilized disease" (175). Boccaccio's orientation towards sex is "quite open and wholesome" (177) and Lawrence prescribes it as a cure and an antidote: "Today Boccaccio should be given to everybody young and old, to read if they like," says Lawrence, "Only a natural fresh openness about sex will do any good, now we are being swamped by secret or semi-secret pornography" (177). Perhaps it is this view of Boccaccio that led him to attempt the painting of Boccaccio's Story. He painted the work in December 1926 while he was writing *Lady Chatterley's Lover*. In a letter to a friend, he describes doing a canvas of "Boccaccio's story of the nuns and the gardener: nice improper story that tells itself."[20]

The painting depicts a peasant, strongly built, moustached, sleeping under a tree in a garden. His clothes are in disarray and his penis in view, almost at the centre of the painting. He is the only vivid object in what is a sea of pastels. He is stretched out across the canvas, head towards the lower half and legs splaying diagonally outwards. His thighs, partly because of the angle in which he is positioned, appear massive and catch the gaze. His gardening tool—quite clearly a phallic object—lies beside him and in the background, one sees furrowed land, both thinly disguised sexual metaphors. His foot seems to point at the row of nuns, described by Lawrence as "nuns in frocks like lavender crocuses"[21] who are passing by but are arrested by the sight of his member. They look on, not with horror, but perhaps with amazement and with frank curiosity. There is no show of embarrassment. Is it because he is sleeping and cannot engage their looks? Is it because they employ him that they can look him over? Though they are positioned in the margin (like a bed of flowers?), they stand over his supine figure, reversing the standard structure of many works where men look at the figure of reclining women. In one way, this work can be read as an illustration of a story (first story, third day) from Boccaccio's *Decameron*. The story is of Masetto, a peasant who pretends to be mute in order to gain employment as a gardener in a convent, both to secure his livelihood and sexual access to the eight young nuns and the abbess there. Although it appears that the work is an illustration of the story, in fact, it condenses two separate incidents to construct a composite image. In the first incident, he pretends to sleep so that he can facilitate the young nun's plans to seduce him; in the second incident, he is actually asleep after having sex with the young nuns when he is seen by the abbess. What does Lawrence achieve by overlaying these separate incidents on one another? The focus, perhaps, falls on the manner in which nature comes into its own overcoming man-made rules, and "open and wholesome" sexuality wins out. This is in line with Lawrence's arguments in PO, his contention that the artistic representation of sex, which is the very fount of human life, needs to be portrayed without a grey pornographic stamp. It would be this that rescues, according to him, the work from the charge of obscenity. For Lawrence, Boccaccio's brilliance lay in his ability to represent sexuality without a pornographic taint, and one can postulate that his attempt in this work was to replicate this. But the work also invokes class in a significant way. It portrays a laboring man as erotic and opens out the possibility of more complex representations of class. Resonating with the *Decameron* tale, it also represents sex as labor. At the same time, the body, exhausted, also seems to signify the life of labor. The literal meaning of the furrowed garden, the interleaved notions of livelihood and labor skew a simply sexual account of Boccaccio's Story.

What this paper has sought to do is to think through the category of censorship in relation to D.H. Lawrence, in his art and in this thought. To that extent, his paintings and writings on art have been viewed as a composite body of work that articulates consistent arguments. They can be seen as a serious intervention into the Western art history of the time, a commentary on trans- and intercontinental trajectories of art making and an argument against formalism. These ideas often feed into each other, and also across the verbal and the visual. Also significant is the way he presses into play his critique of the Freudian schema while acknowledging at the same time the value of the concept of the unconscious and conscious self to an understanding of art and society. Censorship here has emerged as a site where complex articulations of the social have been staged, not least with regard to ideas such as obscenity and human consciousness. One can argue thus that in the Laurentian imaginary, his art work carries the intention that is laid out in his critical writing. Yet, if one decenters the idea of an artist's intentionality, one might possibly arrive at other meanings that circulate in these paintings.

Notes

1. *Phoenix: The Posthumous Papers of D.H. Lawrence.* Edward D. McDonald Ed. and Introd. (London: William Heinemann, 1936). Henceforth PO in the text.
2. D.H. Lawrence uses this phrase in a letter to Morris Ernst: He wrote "Our civilization cannot afford to let the censor-moron loose." Quoted in Chuck Stone, "The Censor Morons of the World: Ubiquitous Usurpers of the Four Literary Freedoms", *The D.H. Lawrence Review*, Vol. 24, No. 3 (Fall 1992), 206.
3. The account of the exhibition is largely drawn from the entry on D.H. Lawrence in the *Encyclopedia of Censorship* Jonathon Green. Nicholas J. Karolides, Rev. (New York: Facts on File, 1990), Rev. 2005.
4. *Phoenix: Posthumous Papers of D.H. Lawrence.* Edward D. McDonald Ed. and Introd. (London: William Heinemann, 1936). Henceforth ITP in the text.
5. Jonathan Jones, "A Life in Pictures", *The Guardian*, 8 November 2003. Url: https://www.theguardian.com/artanddesign/2003/nov/08/art.classics. Retrieved 16 May 2020.
6. Jeff Wallace, "Educability and Art: D.H. Lawrence, Paul Cezanne, Herbert Read." Etudes Lawrenciennes, Vol. 47 (2016). Url: https://journals.openedition.org/lawrence/252?lang=en. Retrieved on 17 May 2020.
7. *Ibid.*
8. *Ibid.*
9. *Ibid.*
10. Roger Eliot Fry (1866-1934) is described as an "Ënglish philosopher of art, artist, art critic, and curator, one of the foremost Formalists in aesthetics, a salient critic and advocate of modern painting and art, especially of Post-Impressionism, and a prominent exponent of Paul Cezanne" by the *Oxford Encyclopedia of Aesthetics* (Oxford: Oxford University Press, 2014), 2nd Edn.

11. This would be the position of Frederick Mead, the judge who declared that Lawrence's paintings were obscene. In contrast Gwen John who reviewed the show found the works as "pictures of great vitality and beauty". Wikipedia: https://en.m.wikipedia.org/wiki/D._H._Lawrence.
12. All arguments regarding the freedom of the artist from conventional mores would fall in this bracket.
13. Jones, "A Life in Pictures", *The Guardian*, 8 November 2003. See also Maev Kennedy, "Lawrence 'Obscenities' Finally Get a Showing." *The Guardian*, 22 November 2003. Url: https://www.theguardian.com/uk/2003/nov/22/books.arts Retrieved 18 May 2020.
14. Andrew Graham-Dixon, "Rude Awakening", *The Telegraph*, 5 November 2003. Url: https://www.telgraph.co.uk/culture/art/3605916/Rude-awakening.html Retrieved 18 May 2019.
15. For example, Maev Kennedy says, "What is most shocking to some viewers of the exhibition [today] is not the plentiful buttocks, penises and breasts, but Lawrence's shaky grasp of anatomy", "Lawrence 'Obscenities' Finally Get a Showing"; Andrew Graham-Dixon calls the paintings "vigorously naive", "Rude Awakening", and Jonathan Jones calls the paintings "awful and a bit weird" populated with "[aesthetically] bad bodies", "A Life in Pictures".
16. "Introduction" *Encyclopedia of Censorship*, Jonathon Green. Nicholas J. Karolides, Rev. (New York: Facts on File, 1990) xix. Rev. 2005.
17. Parul Singh, *The Invisible Realm: The Poetics and Politics of Self-Censorship in Contemporary Visual Art*. Unpublished M. Phil. Dissertation (Delhi: Jawaharlal Nehru University, 2017), 3.
18. Sigmund Freud, *Complete Works*, Ed. Ivan Smith (2010), 3392. Web. Retrieved 18 May 2020.
19. D.H. Lawrence, *Psychoanalysis and the Unconscious*.
20. Keith Sagar and Lindeth Vasey, *D.H. Lawrence: A Calendar of His Works* (Manchester: Manchester University Press, 1979), 156.
21. *Ibid*.

Works Cited

"D.H. Lawrence," Wikipedia: https://en.m.wikipedia.org/wiki/D._H._Lawrence Retrieved 4 May 2020.

"Fry, Roger Eliot", *Oxford Encyclopedia of Aesthetics* (Oxford: Oxford University Press, 2014), 2nd Edn.

Freud, Sigmund. *Complete Works*, Ed. Ivan Smith. 2010. Web. Retrieved 18 May 2020.

Graham-Dixon, Andrew. "Rude Awakening", *The Telegraph*, 5 November 2003. Url: https://www.telegraph.co.uk/culture/art/3605916/Rude-awakening.html. Retrieved 18 May 2019.

Green, Jonathon. "Introduction", *Encyclopedia of Censorship*. Jonathon Green. Nicholas J. Karolides, Rev. New York: Facts on File, 1990, xvii-xxii. Rev. 2005.

_____. "Lawrence, D.H." *Encyclopedia of Censorship*. Jonathon Green. Nicholas J. Karolides, Rev. New York: Facts on File, 1990, 32. Rev. 2005.

Jones, Jonathan. "A Life in Pictures", *The Guardian*, 8 November 2003. Url: https://www.theguardian.com/artanddesign/2003/nov/08/art.classics. Retrieved 16 May 2020.

Kennedy, Maev. "Lawrence 'Obscenities' Finally Get a Showing." *The Guardian*, 22 November 2003. Url: https://www.theguardian.com/uk/2003/nov/22/books.arts. Retrieved 18 May 2020.

Lawrence, D.H. *Psychoanalysis and the Unconscious*. Spastic Cat Press, 2012.

_____. "Introduction to these Paintings," *Phoenix: The Posthumous Papers of D.H. Lawrence*. Edward D. McDonald Ed. and Introd. London: William Heinemann, 1936.

_____. "Pornography and Obscenity," *Phoenix: The Posthumous Papers of D.H. Lawrence*. Edward D. McDonald Ed. and Introd. London: William Heinemann, 1936.

Sagar, Keith and Lindeth Vasey. *D.H. Lawrence: A Calendar of His Work*. Manchester: Manchester University Press, 1979.

Singh, Parul. *The Invisible Realm: The Poetics and Politics of Self-Censorship in Contemporary Visual Art*. Unpublished M. Phil. Dissertation. Delhi: Jawaharlal Nehru University, 2017.

Stone, Chuck. "The Censor Morons of the World: Ubiquitous Usurpers of the Four Literary Freedoms", *The D.H. Lawrence Review*, Vol. 24, No. 3 (Fall 1992), 203-14.

Wallace, Jeff. "Educability and Art: D.H. Lawrence, Paul Cézanne, Herbert Read." *Etudes Lawrenciennes*, Vol. 47 (2016). Url: https://journals.openedition.org/lawrence/252?lang=en. Retrieved on 17 May 2020.

11

Lawrence's *Studies in Classic American Literature*: Revisiting the Narratives of Freedom and Democracy in America

Santosh Dash

From Newspaper to Lawrence

It might look uncanny that this paper on Lawrence starts by referencing a piece of news reported in *The Times of India* in February 2020 with the title: "We Need To Build a New Capitalism".[1] The original piece, written by Marc Benioff, the Chairman and co-CEO of Salesforce, was published in *The New York Times* that talked about 'profound inequality' in America and how it was time for a new, more equal and sustainable capitalism. Benioff, excitedly, remembers his great grandfather's time:

> Capitalism, I acknowledge, has been good to me. Over the past twenty years, the company that I co-founded, Salesforce, has generated billions in profits and made me a very wealthy person. I have been fortunate to live a life beyond the wildest imaginations of my great-grandfather, who immigrated to San Francisco from Kiev in the late 1800s.[2]

What needs to be underlined here in this public assertion by one of America's wealthiest corporate executive is that much of its force comes actually from his having lived "a life beyond the wildest imagination of (his) great-grandfathers", which reads like an American dream come true. What also needs to be underlined is that Beinoff's public assertion comes at a time when there is a "profound inequality" in America and the support for capitalism has dropped, especially among young people.

On the same day, *The Times of India* carried on the same page an interview with another American, Kim Polman, an environmentalist, social thinker, the Chairperson of Reboot the Future Foundation and a writer of *Imaginal Cells: Visions of Transformation*, where she has raised issues like climate change and inequality in present-day America. In her interview, Polman reiterates, like Beinoff, the point about huge inequalities which has become a challenge to democracy itself. In all earnestness she says that "It is not only about people on earth, it's about all of life. A more equitable world, for everybody". She particularly talks about the need for a more "conscious capitalism".[3] She alludes to the founding fathers of America and talks about how "when Benjamin Franklin and John Adams were writing the US constitution, they actually consulted Native Americans who had formed an Iroquois confederacy. They had this wonderful system of government which was adopted to the US constitution". Here, Benioff and Polman, it appears, are not just talking about America and the Americans. In fact, they are talking about creating a more just society and the need for capitalism to "Treat others and the planet as you wish to be treated." Their voices constitute an important moment in what can be called American self-reckoning.

Doesn't it sound a little strange that these two American executives are talking about capitalism, inequality, democracy and about grandfathers, Founding Fathers, the Constitution, native Americans and the Iroquois confederacy almost in the same breath? But, the question remains: How then are these reflections offered in 2020, relevant to the study of D.H. Lawrence and his study of American Literature? Does Lawrence's *Studies in Classic American Literature*[4] possess resources to reflect on some of the dilemmas that America needs to address at this point of time? How does a book on American literature written in the 1920s purport to speak to the American present?

Is Lawrence's book literary criticism or a treatise on American society and culture? Is Lawrence's *SCAL,* a critical, a political, a historical, a sociological, a psychological or a mythic work?[5] The answer to these questions, as we would see, would rest on a careful unravelling of the narrative strategies that Lawrence employs in order to address issues that majorly occupied the American mind in the 1920s.

Lawrence and His Critical Manifesto

Here, an attempt would be made to read the *Foreword* and the book's first chapter *The Spirit of Place* together. The benefit of such a reading would be that it might help us sketch an outline of Lawrence's artistic beliefs, his motives and the mode of his criticism. *SCAL* was published in 1923, and the individual essays in the book were published over a period of time, starting sometime in 1917. Looking at the tone and tenor of the first chapter, one could possibly conjecture that Lawrence might have written these two sections together when he might have felt the need to articulate his critical brief in the book. Taken together, these two sections of the book could be seen as constituting a critical manifesto giving expression to some of Lawrence's ideas about art practice in America, on the one hand and some of his very perceptive takes on the early history of America, on the other. It is also clear that the individual essays on Benjamin Franklin, Hector John de Crevecoeur, two eighteenth century writers and the six nineteenth century writers Fenimore Cooper, Edgar Allan Poe, Nathaniel Hawthorne, Richard Dana, Herman Melville and Walt Whitman, are products of very intense reflections on these authors whose occupations in the domain of literature, politics and religion occupied Lawrence's imagination in the 1920s.[6]

It is important to remember that Lawrence published these essays in the 1920s when the national mood in America was running high in confidence. The buoyancy in the atmosphere was palpable and Lawrence seems to have captured this mood clearly in his *Foreword*:

> Listen to the States asserting: 'The hour has struck! Americans will be American. The U.S.A. is now grown

> up artistically. It is time we ceased to hang on to the skirts of Europe, or to behave like schoolboys let loose from European school-masters—'[7]

At this time Lawrence was very aware of the tendency among the Americans to dismiss old American literature as mere "mass of words", as "all so unreal". The new America, Lawrence thought, could be described in a space of just five contiguous words: "Telephone, tinned meat, Charlie Chaplin, water-taps, and World-Salvation, presumably", indicating perhaps its materialism, industrialization and the world historical ambitions.[8] What is equally significant is that Lawrence noticed at this point of time a clear anxiety around European influence and so, a loud assertion against it.

As the *Foreword* to the book indicates, Lawrence was not singularly critical of America, he was acting more like a European interlocutor trying to understand American achievements in the field of arts, literature, politics and social engineering. It is for this reason he points out that it is "no good merely asserting": "Where is this new bird called the true American? Show us the homunculus of the new era. Go on show us him", asks Lawrence of the new American of the 1920s. In the face of such a confident American assertion, Lawrence advises introspection, *not* opposition to Europe: "he must be somewhere inside you, Oh American. No good chasing him over all the old continents." Instead, the best place to look for their inner selves is "under the American bushes. The old American Literature to start with."

We could thus see in the *Foreword* itself the reason why Lawrence chooses to study the American authors. He chooses to look for the living American self in the old American literature. He also prefers to read this literature against the grain of Europe, in order to see what images of the American they have put together in their writings in the first place. He separates their art from that of contemporary American writers like Sherwood Anderson. He points out how the old masters are more "modern" than their contemporaries. Their art, Lawrence feels, is comparable only to the Russian masters like Tolstoy, Dostoevsky, Chekhov and Artzibashev but, he regards them as different in their method and approaches to art making:

> ...the Russians are explicit and hate eloquence and symbols, seeing in these only subterfuge, whereas the Americans refuse everything explicit and always put up a sort of double meaning. They revel in subterfuge.

Lawrence does not pursue this idea of the modern any further in relation to Russian literature but, what he achieves in this part of the *Foreword* is locating the "subterfuge" as an important function of American art speech before he ventures to study how the art of subterfuge works in the old American authors.

Lawrence takes forward this idea of subterfuge in "The Spirit of the Place", the first chapter of *SCAL* that contains the nucleus of all his arguments in the book. Here, he attempts two things: first, he elaborates on his views about art, particularly American art and second, he takes us, much like a historian, on a brief detour into the early history of America. He begins by making an affirmation: "the old American art speech contains an alien quality, which belongs to the American continent and to nowhere else" (11). Here, his objective, it seems, is to get his readers to discover American art speech as essentially American. If at present it looks "alien", Lawrence suggests, it is mostly because of a certain tradition of reading which is Eurocentric and which insists on "reading old European inferences over the top of Poe or Hawthorne" (11). It misses out on the historical character of this art speech "which belongs to the American continent." The critical task for Lawrence, therefore, is how to rescue this historical character of American art speech from its Eurocentrism.

Lawrence knows that his critical enterprise entails work on two fronts: first, he has to describe the precise nature of American art speech and second, he has to challenge some of the historical misgivings and falsehoods perpetuated by Eurocentric writing. It is for this reason that Lawrence begins by listing out his views on art: "Art speech is the only truth. An artist is usually a damned liar, but, his art, if it be art, will tell you the truth of his day" (12). "[A]rt is a sort of subterfuge," he says, "But thank God, we can see through the subterfuge" (12). All these sweeping pronouncements over a space of a page tend to lead us to one of his major formulations about the function of a critic:

> The artist usually sets out—or used to—to point a moral and adorn a tale. The tale, however, points the other way, as a rule. Two blankly opposing morals, the artist's and the tale's. Never trust the artist. Trust the tale. The proper function of a critic is to save the tale from the artist who created it. (12)

Lawrence then goes on to align his brief in *SCAL* with his formulations on art and criticism: "Now we know our business in these studies: saving the American tale from the American artist," giving us to believe that his views on American art are not separate from his views on criticism and his role as a critic (13).

In his next critical manoeuvre, Lawrence confronts some of the historical misgivings about early American history by way of raising questions about the American artist: "How did he ever get to America, to start with. Why isn't he a European still, like his father before him?" (13). These questions strategically allow Lawrence an entry into the early history of New England and its European past. Next, Lawrence offers a quick account of historical events, starting from the Renaissance to post-Renaissance Europe, the large scale emigrations over the Atlantic and the history of the Pilgrim Fathers. According to Lawrence, Renaissance in Europe almost destroyed kingship, on one hand and fatherhood, on the other. It was also a time when, according to Lawrence, "Europe drifted into a dangerous half truth: of liberty and equality" (17). Lawrence contends that the Pilgrim Fathers, who emigrated to America, did not come for freedom of worship. Rather, they came because they were disenchanted with developments in Europe, particularly in the ways the state exercises in liberty and equality unfolded in Europe. The motivation for emigration, therefore, was not only religious, as traditional historians would have us believe, but it was also political. Besides, Lawrence believed that, much like Europe, America too fell into "this dangerous half-truth of liberty and equality". In fact, America went one better than Europe in its pursuit of liberty and equality. It experimented with "masterlessness" as a form of freedom: "Do away with masters, exalt the will of the people" (18).

Masterlessness became a paradigm for development in America. In its effort at defining democracy in its own terms, America might have escaped the European ways of emergence into democracy. But, Lawrence believed that America needed to confront the shape democracy has taken, the ways in which the ideas of liberty and equality have historically unfolded in America: "You have got to pull the democratic and idealistic clothes off 'American utterance'", says Lawrence (18). Lawrence leaves this task, an essentially historical task, at the doorstep of the classical masters of American literature with the belief that it is in their art speech that one can locate the subtle and intricate ways in which these clothes have been woven in America and the way democracy is still a work in progress.

In the Name of God and in the Name of Nature: Franklin's Pattern American and de Crevecoeur's Children of Nature

Lawrence starts his studies with the Founding Fathers of America in order to tease open what he calls "the democratic and idealistic clothes" that they have woven through their art. His studies of Benjamin Franklin and Hector St. John de Crevecoeur are sharp and passionately argued engagements, which sometimes read like very personal, impressionistic reflections drawn from his own experiences, sometimes like a cultural analysis of people and places across continents, and yet other times like a very carefully and consistently pursued line of argument involving movements of people and of ideas across the globe in general. For example, the clothes he invokes, democracy and idealism, are part of the textile which has spawned across the globe since at least the time of the Renaissance in Europe and has been part of the general wear and tear of most of the people across the world.

Lawrence's assessment of Benjamin's life and work begins on a stern and serious note as he counters him on the issue of the perfectibility of man. He is aware that Franklin, whom he calls the "Old Daddy", was the one who set America and the Americans on a theocratic and materialistic path (30).

Lawrence refers to Franklin's *Poor Richard's Almanac*, a yearly almanac that was a household name in America and Europe, from the eighteenth century when they were first published and remained popular even up to Lawrence's time. He says how he, as a child in England, grew up reading these almanacs. They were actually conduct books with little anecdotes, morals and humorisms, he recalls, and remembers how he learnt some of his most lasting moral lessons on life from these "scrubby yearly almanacs" bought for him by his father[9] (24). He also shares that it took him "many years and countless smarts to get out of that barbed wire moral enclosure that Poor Richard rigged up" (24). Lawrence reads himself as the product of this moral technology which Franklin had put together.

Lawrence further points out how Franklin's moral technology was forged in the language of religion, in the name of God and Providence and had a set of handles and levers, the operation of which ensured the production of what he called a "perfect" citizen (30). Franklin thought that man can be designed to function like a moral machine working more or less in the same way a keyboard worked. Given the moral inputs in the keyboard, of temperance-silence-order-resolution-frugality-industry-sincerity-justice-moderation-clealiness-tranquility-chastity-humility, Franklin thought, would produce a "pattern" American or a "dummy" American (30). Franklin "practiced this enticing list with assiduity" (23) but by putting this up as a national example, he expected to produce, according to Lawrence, a "virtuous little automaton" (26) or at best, a "dry, moral, utilitarian little democrat" out of every American (31). Lawrence debunks the grandeur of this Franklinian technology by insisting that man is not a mechanical contrivance. In fact, Lawrence goes on to say that Franklin's "pattern American" has not only been damaging to America but it has "done more to ruin the Old Europe than any Russian nihilist" (31).

He points to the ways in which America, in its attempt to free itself from masters, has been "mastered by the machines of its own making" (31). He refers to the twin process of aggressive "Americanizing" and "mechanizing" of man which has ensured that "clever America lies on her muck-heaps of gold, strangled in her own barbed wire of shalt-not ideals and shalt-not moralisms" (31). For Lawrence, America in the 1920s is not an image of an inspiring "living, organic, *believing* community, active in fulfilling some unfulfilled, perhaps unrealized purpose" (16). Instead, Lawrence paints an image of America that is "shut up in her own 'productive' machines like millions of squirrels running in millions of cages" (31). The European interlocutor in Lawrence feels that America is on a false course and that the progressive American consciousness is only a false dawn. Hence Europe should stay clear of the road—theocratic and materialistic—which America has taken from the days of Benjamin Franklin to Woodrow Wilson (30).

In order to cite an instance of the negative practice of democracy and the way it has progressed in America, Lawrence shows how Franklin in his frequent parleys at the court of France was actually collecting money and plotting "the first steps of the overthrow of all Europe, France included" (30). In his enthusiasm to overthrow the monarchies in Europe, Franklin thought he was putting together the pattern of a perfect citizen and, along with it, the pattern of a democracy for America. But, Lawrence in line with his critical promise, pulls off the democratic and idealistic cloth that Franklin uses to adorn his tale about American democracy by showing how his advocacy for democracy was shallow and how his democratic imagination had little space for the Indians.

By drawing from histories of settlement with the Indians in which Franklin played an archetypal role, Lawrence shows how these crucial junctures in American history are infused with moral seriousness and are not just about questions of cultivation alone. The ease with which Franklin, the colonial administrator, short circuits his moral qualms in one such settlement issue with the Indians and talks of extirpation of a tribe with such ease, becomes a moment of real disenchantment for Lawrence. That Franklin, in order to promote cultivation, would justify his action by saying "if it be the design of providence...to extirpate these savages in order to make room for the cultivators of the earth, it seems not improbable that rum may be the appointed means" (25), is morally nauseating to Lawrence because such modes of governance of tribes through the ideology of rum is a devious form of governance. What is more nauseating is that the "most moral Benjamin" approves of such forms of action with full knowledge that it is rum which "has already annihilated all the tribes who formerly inhabited all the sea coast..." (25).

Lawrence's reading of Crevecoeur follows a similar line of unveiling the democratic and idealistic clothes with which Crevecoeur had adorned his tale of America. According to Lawrence what Franklin wanted to achieve in the name of God, Crevecoeur wanted the same in the name of nature. "He wanted to put Nature in his pocket, as Benjamin put the Human Being. Between them, they wanted the whole scheme of things in their pocket, and the things themselves" (34-35). They both together cultivated two important aspects of the American character. Franklin was the "practical" prototype of the American and Crevecoeur was the "emotional" prototype (33). One cultivated the mind and the other the heart. One was to produce the practical American and the other the emotional American. Crevecoeur, much like his friend Franklin was also occupied with issues of land and cultivation but his methods were more covert and more refined ideologically.

According to Lawrence, Crevecoeur was the first to have spotted in America the value of nature much before Thoreau and Emerson. Crevecoeur's romanticism was not simply that of an American Farmer, it clearly had an appeal beyond America.[10] He was a darling of the English and French Romantics. Lawrence, however, reads Crevecoeur's romanticism and idealization of nature in the context of the American War of Independence, particularly in the context of Crevecoeur's negotiations with the Noble Red Man. A reading such as this is also in line with Lawrence's purpose of pulling off the democratic and idealistic clothes off the American utterance. He deliberately chooses to read Crevecoeur's idealism about nature alongside some of the most uncomfortable issues involving race and violence in early America. As Lawrence puts it, there is no doubt that "Crevecoeur the idealist puts over us a lot of stuff about nature and the novel savage and the innocence of toil" but "Crevecoeur the artist gives us glimpses of actual nature, not writ large" (35).

Lawrence takes up Crevecoeur's classic book *Letters from an American Farmer* in order to show how Crevecoeur is the perfect example of an artist who "usually intellectualizes on top, and his dark under-consciousness goes on contradicting him beneath" (35). Crevecoeur, the idealist paints "a world of the Nobel Savage and Pristine Nature and Paradisal Simplicity and all that gorgeousness that flows out of the unsullied fount of the ink bottle" (32). The details of his writing seem to be geared towards showing how "nature is sweet and pure, that all men are brothers and equal, and that they love one another like so many cooing doves" (40). In his letters we come across ample instances of romantic longing for a life with the Red Men, a desire for a life in the wigwam, for "a tented home near the Indian village" (39). The Indians, for Crevecoeur, were "the noble children of Nature who peopled his predetermined fancy" (39).

Crevecoeur, according to Lawrence, was determined to propagate the idea of the noble savage and the noble Indian mostly for the satisfaction of his own fancy, even when his own writing shows it to be otherwise. Lawrence also points out how Crevecoeur refrained from mentioning in his letters how the Indians had burnt his farm several times simply for the reason that it might invalidate his most precious belief that "the natural man is an object of undefiled brotherliness" (39). But, by doing so he merely succeeds in sustaining a lie in the face of hard facts of history of which he himself is an important part. It is this lie built around a certain idealism, a certain romanticism that takes Crevecoeur on a journey of mere wish-fulfilment in his letters where finally "we are left to imagine him retiring in grief to dwell with his Red Brothers under the wigwams" (39). We are told in the letters that "he will leave the civilized coasts, where man is sophisticated, and therefore inclined to vile" (39).

But, according to Lawrence "it all a swindle" (39), a deception, at best an adornment because, in actual life, "he trotted back to France in high-heeled shoes, and imagined America in Paris", much like his friend Franklin. He not only figured in the literary saloons but took refuge in commerce and the material world. A good businessman that he was, he also arranged a line of shipping between France and America. The life of the American farmer finally ended in "materialism, really. But, the letters tell us nothing about this", Lawrence reminds us (38-39).

Much like Lawrence's reading of Franklin's "moralism" which leaves us with the image of Americans as "millions of squirrels running in million of cages", his reading of the idealism of Crevecoeur leaves us with the image of Americans as "white savages, with motor-cars, telephones, incomes and ideals!" (43). Lawrence seems to suggest that the idea of the noble savage is a fertile contrivance of the white mind and it has succeeded in producing, in real historical terms, white savages who are always in a state of self-denial because that would mean destruction of idealism and romanticism around which the white men have built their civilized empires against all "the brutishness of unchristian darkness" (39).

Idealisms of Class, Race and Love: On Reading the American Tales of Cooper, Poe and Hawthorne

Having discovered the existence of a dual feeling in the American vis-à-vis the Red Indian in the writings of Franklin and Crevecoeur, Lawrence then points out how such dual feelings about the Indian persist even today: "the desire to extirpate the Indian and the contradictory desire to glorify him—both are rampant still today" (45). While writing in the 1920s, he observes: "The Aztec is gone, and the Incas. The Red Indian, the Esquimo, the Pantagonians are reduced to negligible numbers" (44). Lawrence refers to 'the great white swamp' in America. Regarding the relation between white people and Indians, Lawrence observes that the relations between these two races have no longer remained simply about "grabbing his land" but it has turned into a "silent, invisible, but deadly hostility between the spirit of two races" (45).

In the context of such hostility, Lawrence points to a tendency among "a minority of whites who try to intellectualize the Red Man and laud him to the skies" (45). But, this minority, he says, is "a high-brow minority with a big grouch against its own whiteness" (45). This is a minority which sees no possibility of "any real reconciliation, in the flesh, between the white and the red" and therefore, it tries to achieve a "reconciliation in the soul" as an exercise in "expiation and oneing" (47), as a kind of atonement. According to Lawrence, Cooper is probably one writer who has done more than any other writer to present to the white man, this aspect of atonement, expiation and oneing of races, and it is perhaps for this reason that Cooper's novels were very popular in America. His novels performed a very important function of what Lawrence called a "popular wish-fulfilment" (47). It is precisely this aspect of wish-fulfilment which Lawrence feels critical about because it this which "makes it so hard for the real thing to come through, later" (47).

Lawrence classifies Cooper's novels into two categories: the white novels and the Leatherstocking novels, each performing a different function. The White Novels which include *Homeward Bound, Eve Effingham, The Spy, The Pilot* are novels that study the social and class aspect of the white American life, whereas the Leatherstocking novels study the complex, nuanced relationship between the white men and Natives Americans and are thematically more in akin to Crevecoeur in their study of race relations.

Lawrence's focus in the white novels is on the Effinghams and their relations with Mr. Septimus Dodge. The Effinghams are of an aristocratic lineage and they are homeward bound from Europe to America. Their daughter Eve Effingham has finished her education in Europe and we are told "England, France and Italy and Germany have nothing more to teach her" (48). She is a woman of "perfectly good taste, clever and assured in her speech, like a man, but withal charmingly deferential and modest before the stronger sex" (48). The character of Eve Effingham, for Lawrence, is a perfect metaphor for an American who has been brought up systematically in the manners of European aristocracy and who has acquired a natural sense of superiority. It is not just the daughter, all the Effinghams have a sense of superiority in relation to Mr. Septimus Dodge who is a typical representative of "the American self-made man" (48).

According to Lawrence, Septimus is the other type of American, "the parvenu, the demagogue, who has 'done'

Europe and put it in his breeches pocket, in a month" (48). He has not only seen Europe but sucked it dry. Lawrence is very critical of this demagogue of an American who claims he has "done" Europe. His attitude towards Europe is nothing more than that of a visitor. For example, he has seen the Venus de Milo and for him she is as if "a fish he has hooked, and he is off to America with her, leaving the scum of a statue in the Louvre" (48). According to Lawrence, Septimus's attitude is an "American way of vandalism" (48). Lawrence is scathing in his opprobrium:

> And there you are. When a few German bombs fell upon Rheims Cathedral up went a howl of execration. But there are more ways than one of vandalism. I should think the American admiration of five-minutes tourists has done more to kill the sacredness of old European beauty and aspiration than multitudes of bombs would have done. (49)

Talking about the German bombs and American vandalism in the same breath in the 1920s would have certainly demanded courage on Lawrence's part but by doing so he is vindicating the American narrative of freedom and at the same time making an appeal to the American mind to go inward, to look at its innermost self, through an engagement with its own classic past. Through a reading of Cooper's white novels, Lawrence has in fact tried to offer a possible meaningful dialogue between Effinghams and Septimus Dodge. The interaction between them, it is suggested, remains superficial because they are limited by the standards and ideals of American democracy which treats them as equal. Lawrence seems to suggest that class relations in America are bogged down by "the democratic pin" (54) and cause of much social disengagement in America. "As a historic phenomenon, it is amazing, ludicrous, and irritating" (53), Lawrence says:

> When America set out to destroy Kings, Lords and Masters, and the whole paraphernalia of European superiority, it pushed a pin right through its own body, and on that pin it still flaps, buzzes and twists in misery. The pin of democratic equality. Freedom. (53)

Cooper's Leatherstocking novels perform a similar function by straddling race relations in America. These novels are part of the same popular wish-fulfilment genre which Crevercoeur had put together. Natty Bumppo, the protagonist of most of Cooper's Leatherstocking novels, is the object of Cooper's wish-fulfilment. According to Lawrence, "Fenimore, in his imagination, wanted to be Natty Bumppo" (59). The Leatherstocking novels, therefore, carry this conflict of desires in Cooper to a point of irresolution but, as the readings of his novels by Lawrence suggest there can be no abiding love stories across races in Cooper's novels because "evidently Cooper—or the artist in him—has decided that there can be no blood-mixing of two races, white and red. He kills them off" (68). The love stories don't carry any creative purchase with Cooper, the American gentleman. Still, everything in his novels unmistakably point towards reconciliation in soul, if not flesh, everything is geared towards a resolution of race conflicts in art, a sort of American wish fulfilment.

Poe's novels, Lawrence recognizes, have nothing to do with Native Americans or Nature. He was occupied with the American psyche. He was more like a scientist focused on a "chemical analysis of the American soul and consciousness" (74). Moralists found his stories "morbid" (74), they were clueless about why such stories were written in the first place. But, for Lawrence, these stories performed a very important function by capturing a very important psychic process involving the American artist and his art speech. Lawrence found in the morbidity of Poe's stories an expression of what is essentially a cultural and psychic process which also reflected an important American art activity: the "disintegrating and sloughing of the old consciousness, meaning the old European consciousness" (74). Lawrence believed that "the old white psyche has to be gradually broken down before anything else come to pass" (74) and Poe's stories registered this process of disintegration of the white psyche. In Poe, one therefore finds "ghastly stories of the human soul in its disruptive throes" (75). What is striking about these stories is that they are all love stories and there are two blankly opposing morals in these stories: one that of the author and the other, of the stories themselves. Lawrence's self-professed job in reading Poe then is to save these stories from its author.

According to Lawrence, Poe was a fearless man when it came to his own belief and experience. He believed that love is the greatest thing in life and he yearned for the ecstasies of extreme spiritual love. This passion for spiritual love found its expression in terms of characters who carried this frenzied passion even to the point of death. A reading of Poe gives us an insight into this disease which, according to Lawrence, is the cause for much of "the neuroticism of the day" (77). Lawrence's contention here is not just that Poe has woven his stories around such a disease, that he has taken us into "vaults and cellars and horrible underground passages of the human soul" (91-92) but that he has made this disease look attractive. It is in this success of Poe's stories, in their popularity that Lawrence sees "the inevitable falseness, duplicity of art, American art in particular" (92).

By organizing a careful and intense reading around Poe's stories like "Ligeia", "Eleanora", "Berenice", "The Fall of the House of Usher" and "The Cask of Amontillado", among others, Lawrence shows how in each one of these tales, morbidity, or a certain type of fever and frenzy envelops the chief protagonists who are eventually driven either to death or disease by their extremities of love or hate. Lawrence believes that the manifestation of such neuroticism in character is the consequence of an excess of what he calls "the human will, the 'will to love' and the 'will to consciousness', asserted against death itself" (85).

American neuroticism, according to Lawrence, is the product of a wilful violation of two central laws of all organic life: one, that each organism is intrinsically isolate and single in itself, and the other that each individual organism is vivified by intimate contact with fellow organisms. According to Lawrence, love is a field where two organisms enter into contact. But, he argues, though vivifying each other's lives these organisms should not forget the first law of life, that they have to go back to their original state of isolation. Both the laws should find a balance between isolation and contact. When this balance is not maintained and when an inordinate will to oneness sweeps across human consciousness, it leads to states of neurosis, as one sees in Poe's characters. Lawrence seems to suggest that the reason America has fallen into this neurosis is because in its attempt to break away from what is an essentially European conception of love, constructed around the binary of the sacred and the profane, between the spiritual and the sensual, it has fallen into extremities of love in complete violation of the laws of organic life.

Hawthorne too wrote romances, his novels are also stories of love but they are not written in the style of old romances such as *Morte d'Arthur*. As Lawrence observes Hawthorne's *The Scarlet Letter* is not "a pleasant pretty romance" (93). Instead, "it is very much an earthly story with a hellish meaning" (93). Lawrence says that one has to be careful while reading this blue eyed darling of America because he is a master of disguise: "you *must* look through the surface of American Art, and see the inner diabolism of the symbolic meaning" (93). On the surface, Hawthorne's novels were as nice as pie, goody-goody and lovey-dovey but that is only on the surface. Lawrence, therefore, undertakes the task of exposing the inner diabolism of his art speech by way of reading the symbolic meaning of Hawthorne's art consciousness.

On the surface, *The Scarlet Letter* would read like a love story with a moral, perhaps a spiritual lesson, with clear Christian messaging: "*Be good! Be good!* warbles Nathaniel. *Be good, and never sin! Be sure your sin will find you out*" (94). Obviously the novel depicts the fall of a saintly parson to the charms of a seductress. One sees Dimmesdale losing his manliness to Hester Pryne, his manliness that comprises in heeding the "be good, and never sin" injunction. Dimmsedale sins and wants to keep it a secret. But his secret is found out and he is held guilty for sinning against the divine father and for violating the Christian injunction he was supposed to uphold. It looks like the novel returns us to the Christian belief of "Be good, be good". That is the reason why Lawrence says: "There was no change in belief, either in Hester or in Dimmesdale or in Hawthorne or in America" (102). They all have their belief in "the Spirit, in Purity, in Selfless Love, and in Pure Consciousness, they would go on following this belief, for the sake of the sensation of it" (102).[11]

On the surface, Hawthorne's *The Scarlet Letter* seems to reaffirm the Christian belief in the superiority of the Spirit over the Body.[12] Lawrence feels that we will miss the point if we choose to read it simply as a reaffirmation. He, therefore, tries to complicate the tale's moral by pointing out to the struggle in the narrative over larger cultural and moral issues involving Europe and America. Extending the story beyond the relationship between Dimmesdale and Hester and by focusing on the character of Chillingworth, the ex-husband of Hester, Lawrence gives a new spin to the narrative. According to Lawrence, Chillingworth is portrayed as a figure representing medieval England, with his belief in the pre-Christian world, the dark sciences, the Hermetic philosophies, alchemy and magic, whereas Dimmesdale stood for Puritan England, fiercely reformist and Christian. Both Dimmsedale and Chillingworth fail in their relation with Hester, with their own male authority because, Lawrence argues, they are either stuck in their medieval European past or they are unwilling to engage with their own manliness, their male authority.

Hawthorne's *Blithedale Romance,* takes the character of Pearl, the child born out of Hester and Dimmesdale's secret passion and presents her as the prototype of a new age woman, a woman who believes that she cannot do wrong. Her mother, Hester was troubled by the knowledge of her own wrongdoing. Pearl has no such hang ups. She has no belief in the Divine Father, she has grown up into the devil of a modern woman. She has disowned her "papa both big and little" (113). Thus, Hawthorne's tales clearly point to the way White America has dealt with the question of love and sex and how it is poised very precariously in its relation with the question of gender. Lawrence seems to suggest that America needs to find a way out of the gender troubles, the extremities of love and freedom to which it has driven itself and to which the classics of American literature testify.

Homeland and Beyond: The Sea Stories of Dana, Melville and Whitman's Poetry

Lawrence notices a persistent strain in American art to move away from under the European tutelage and chart out new routes to freedom and democracy. Lawrence also observes how in its effort to not "hang onto the skirts of Europe" (Foreword), America has slipped into idealisms of various kinds, whether it is in matters of race, class or even love. Just as there is an idealization of the Spirit and of Land, there is an idealization of the Sea in American consciousness. Just as there are stories of Land, there are also stories of the Sea. These stories, according to Lawrence, are instances of "imaginative conquests", of Land as well as Seas (124). Lawrence invokes European stories of Swineburne and Conrad, the Greek stories of the Argonauts and Ulysses as a counterpoint to the American stories. Like the Europeans, the Americans like Melville didn't personify or sentimentalize the sea. Lawrence says that the American sea stories displayed a frenzied relationship, a maniac's attitude towards the sea. They were driven by one overarching motive:

> Away, away from humanity. To the sea. The naked salt, elemental sea. To go to sea, to escape humanity. (146)

Through a systematic engagement with Dana's *Two Years Before the Mast* and Melville's *Typee*, *Omoo* and his epic novel *Moby Dick*, Lawrence shows how their sea stories are actually about things which are nagging Americans continually and from which they are trying to escape, mostly, questions of race and class in American society. As with Poe, Lawrence's attempt is to save these American sea stories from the American artist and also from American and English critics who read these novels for their metaphysical and philosophical content or for their style.[13] For this purpose, he devises a method of reading which pries open those portions of the stories where the class and race aspects are more clearly noticeable. Lawrence divides the action in these stories into two sets: one set of actions taking place within the ship and the other set involving those of the ship with the outside, with islanders and creatures of the sea. Lawrence begins by taking us straightaway to a scene aboard Dana's ship: the captain of the ship is seen flogging a sailor named Sam, with Dana as a witness. There are other witnesses, such as seaman John and his companions. Dana is visibly disturbed and feels remorseful, feels nauseated, whereas seaman John and his mates, fired by their idealism, intervene and try to play the role of the saviour: "why are you whipping this man, sir?", they ask (131). Lawrence is critical of these saviour figures because of their sentimental attitude to labour, for their sententiousness and for their innocent queries: "But, flogging? Why flogging? Why not use reason or take away jam for tea?" (129). Such interventionist behaviour, Lawrence believes, violates what he terms as "the strange interflow of master-and-man, the strange reciprocity of command and obedience" (129).

By reading this scene of flogging which is obviously a violent scene as a "natural event" (132) as "nothing abnormal" (133) and seeing flogging as "passional" (132) justice Lawrence runs the risk of putting himself on the wrong side of the class struggle. But Lawrence is quick to juxtapose Dana's scene alongside a similar scene from Melville's *White Jacket*, where Melville narrates how he once escaped from being flogged unjustly by his captain due to the timely intervention of a mediator. By juxtaposing these two flogging scenes and driving a distinction between modes of intervention and mediation in both the cases, Lawrence seems to suggest that "Justice is a great and manly thing" (131) but the Salvationist and saviourist orientation towards justice is artificial and is mostly born out of theoretical idealism because it seems to be aligned to labour in a way that does not differentiate between a just and an unjust flogging. What Lawrence's reading makes clear is that Dana's and Melville's novels are about issues like class, mediation and justice and not simply mystical or philosophical.

Lawrence then turns to those portions of Dana's and Melville's narrative where the transactions between the crew on board and the islanders are the most apparent. Lawrence cites the way Dana reminisces, in *Two Years before the Mast*, about his relationship with Hope, a South Sea Islander, who is suffering from syphilis, the white man's disease. Lawrence, however, points out to the ephemeral nature of Dana's sentimental attachment to Hope and his suffering. Dana's love for Hope, Lawrence observes, is only like "pity, tinged with philanthropy. The inevitable saviourism. The Ideal being" (135), a perfect denouement for all hardcore American idealists and democrats (135).

Similarly, in tracking such transactional moments in Melville's *Typee*, *Omoo* and *Moby Dick*, Lawrence picks out "savage" races such as the Maoris, the Tongans, the Marquesans, the Fijians, the Polynesians, the Nukuhevas and others which feature in Melville's sea stories. He offers a glimpse into America's engagement with people of the Pacific islands. For Melville, the islanders are "gentle, laughing lambs compared to the ravening wolves of his white brothers, left behind in America and on an American whaleship" (147). Lawrence shows how Melville's crew consists of not just white men but also of men like Queequeg, a South Sea Islander, Tashtego, a Native American and Daggo, an African American. The *Pequod* is a microcosm of Melville's America, for Lawrence, representing "many races, many peoples, many nations, under the Stars and Stripes" (163). But, what is tragic about this mad pursuit of the whale is that Ahab is not alone in his monomania, he has roped in a range of people, of dark races and pale, red, yellow, black, east, west, Quaker and fire-worshippers, turning them all into partners in "this ghastly maniacal hunt which is our doom and our suicide" (173). The great denouement to this epic story, according to Lawrence, comes actually when, in this war against the white whale, that great American pride machine, the *Pequod* sinks and with it sinks the entire American crew: "negro and Indian and Polynesian, Asiatic and Quaker and good, business-like Yankees and Ishmael" (173-74) metaphorically leaving the white American soul virtually adrift yet again in the sea, like flotsam.

It is in the context of the white American soul that Lawrence's reading of Whitman becomes meaningful. He sees Whitman as the one great architect in whose poetry one found the most powerful articulation of man's relationship with soul. Lawrence thought, Whitman mapped the soul in its disintegration, in its death throes and so he as "a poet of the soul's last shout and shriek" (183). For him, Whitman's disease was that he was given to a certain generalization and universalization of both the self and the soul; his poetry displayed something "superhuman": "I am everything and everything is me and so we're all One in One Identity" (177). It is this orientation which leads Lawrence to call it Whitman's "Myself monomania" (186). His *Song of Myself* remains, for Lawrence, essentially a poem about "merging" (180). It is this philosophy of merging: "Walt becomes in his own person the whole world, the whole universe, the whole eternity of time" (178) which in fact animates Whitman's other poems such as *Democracy*, *En Masse*, and *One Identity*. His poetic aspirations are epic in dimension, he wants to "reach the state of ALLNESS" (179). But, Lawrence observes how his poems ultimately remain "songs of myself" (179). Lawrence recognized the importance of such a vision but still pointed out how such a vision is that of an automobile. Lawrence shows how Whitman's vision is like an automobile driver driving "with a very fierce headlight, along the track of a fixed idea, through the darkness of this world. And he saw everything that way. Just as a motorist does in the night" (179).

In spite of his reservations about Whitman's vision, Lawrence admits to his achievement as an American seer and the ways in which Whitman had moved away from two dominant Christian traditions of knowledge about the self and the other and their oneness in love and charity, inspired by Christ and St Paul. In place of Christ's Love and St Paul's charity, Whitman proposed "sympathy" (186) as a point of emergence for the self and the other. He proposed this idea in the context of an equally grand idea of the soul. Lawrence appreciates Whitman's idea of souls travelling down independently of each other in an "open road" (185) without any goal, having no known direction even, with only the soul remaining true to herself in her going, their point of contact being only in sympathy (185). But, Lawrence was critical of the way Whitman interpreted 'sympathy' and consequently limited his vision by falling into a theory of inaction: "It is not I who guide my soul to heaven. It is I who am guided by my own soul along the open road, where all men tread" (190).

According to Lawrence, it is here that Whitman's vision weakens as he interprets sympathy as only a "feeling for", thereby losing out on its semantic possibility of interpreting it as a "feeling with" (187).

Lawrence explains how it is possible to move away from a theory of inaction to action by taking into account the semantics of both these feelings. With the examples of the "negro", the prostitute and the leper, Lawrence suggests that Whitman's democratic vision, his idea of allness would have gathered a different energy if only he had allowed sympathy its semantic expansiveness. Lawrence gives a clue to what would constitute sympathy in its expansiveness when he discusses slavery:

> If I can help him I will: I will not take over his wound and his slavery to myself. But, I will help him fight the power that enslaves him when he wants to be free, if he wants my help, since I see in his face that he needs to be free. But, even when he is free, his soul has many journeys down the open road, before it is a free soul. (188)

For Lawrence, Whitman falls short when it comes to moving from a "feeling for" state to a "feeling with" state and therefore is unable to imagine a truly democratic future for America. It is perhaps for this reason that Lawrence calls him a post-mortem poet, who could offer powerful critiques of Salvationism and "saviourism" but falls short when it came to offering a roadmap to American democracy. One can defend Whitman for choosing to remain the poet of the open road but his vision of allness flounders when confronted with questions of race and slavery in America.[14]

America has continued to move inexorably in its path of democracy, freedom and equality since the time of Whitman and the masters of American classics. As we heard in the beginning of this paper, contemporary American corporate executives, such as Beinoff and Polman are visibly disturbed by the increasing inequalities in America. They are arguing for a more conscientious capitalism, a system based on the Christian precept: "Treat others and the planet as you wish to be treated" (10). They seem to articulate a need for America to learn from Americans, from the way the Founding Fathers of the American Constitution adopted values from the confederacies of Native Americans. What Lawrence's reading of the American classics has shown is that America and American art until at least the 1920s, worked with the assumption that the only way America could emerge, socially, politically and artistically is by working out its relationship in an oppositional mode to its European past. But, what Lawrence also seems to suggest is that America needs to engage with itself, its own class and race issues, the historical coordinates of which can be found in America, not Europe. Today, in 2020, the two American corporate executives echo the voice of Lawrence who had expressed very similar sentiments in the 1920s:

> Americans must take up life where the Red Indian, the Aztec, the Maya, the Incas left it off...there lies the real continuity not between Europe and the new States, but between the murdered Red America and the seething White America.[15]

It is quite clear that Lawrence's *SCAL* performed a very important function in the 1920s, when it ushered in a new method of reading literature, a method which had no precedence in criticism, formalism being the most dominant critical tool. Besides, Lawrence was fiercely comparative in his critical orientation and was never comfortable working with literature as an essentialist, exclusivist and homogeneous body of writing. This is perhaps the reason why Lawrence's study of American literature is inevitably comparative, both in spirit as well as method. His studies are conducted in the form of a dialogue, between Lawrence as interlocutor and as critic, performing both these tasks with sincerity and fairness. His readings of American authors are conducted in a manner that point to the entanglement of histories and cultures of Europe and America. They also reveal the entangled nature of a whole lot of concepts, such as class, race, gender, religion, freedom and democracy, particularly the ways in which they are imagined in Europe and in America. Nevertheless he remains critical of their careers in both these societies. His *SCAL* can be seen as an example of a comparative and cultural studies kind of research conducted at a time when post-colonial studies, post-structuralism and many of the Western Marxist Studies, even Race Studies were nowhere in the horizon. The tradition of Lawrence criticism remains unfair in its assessment of his creative as well as critical works insofar as it has remained unwilling to read him in the context of his time. He clearly seems to be almost anticipating and predating some of the most powerful critical tools of our time.

Notes

1. Mark Benioff, "We Need To Build a New Capitalism", *The Times of India* (Ahmedabad/Baroda, 22 February 2020), 10.
2. D.H. Lawrence, *Studies in Classic American Literature* [1923]. (New Delhi: Atlantic, 1995), 10. Heareafter *SCAL* in the text.
3. Kim Polman, "Interview", *The Times of India* (Ahmedabad/Baroda, 22 February 2020), 10. For contemporary debates on capitalism in America see, John Mackey and Rajendra Sisodia, *Conscious Capitalism: Liberating the Heroic Spirit of Business* (Boston: Massachusetts, 2013) and Rajendra Sisodia and Michael J. Gelb, *The Healing Organization: Awakening the Conscience of Business to Help Save the World* (New York: Harper & Collins, 2019).
4. D.H. Lawrence, *Studies in Classic American Literature* (New Delhi: Atlantic, 1995). Henceforth *SCAL* in the book. For the tortuous publication history of the book, see Ezra Greenspan, Lindeth Vasey and John Worthen "Introduction", *The Cambridge Edition of the Works of D.H. Lawrence: Studies in Classic American Literature* (Cambridge: Cambridge University Press, 2003), xxiii-lxxiv.
5. Critics have seen SCAL as a major critical work rich with historical, sociological, psychological, and mythic perceptions. For example see Richard Foster, "Criticism as Rage: D.H. Lawrence" in *D.H. Lawrence: Twentieth Century Views*, Mark Spilka ed. (New Jersey: Prentice-Hall, 1963), 160.
6. Lawrence could perhaps be considered the first canonizer of American Literature, as Richard Foster points out when he says that Lawrence was "discussing American 'classic' almost before we knew we had such things", *ibid.*, 161.
7. D.H. Lawrence, "Foreword", *Studies in Classic American Literature* (New Delhi: Atlantic, 1995), n.p.

8. References to tin cans recur in Lawrence's writing as a marker of "sheer mechanical materialism." For an elaboration of this point see Raymond Williams, "Lawrence's Social Writing", in Spilka, 163-64.
9. A similar study of the impact of these almanacs can surely be pursued in the context of colonial India.
10. Besides influencing English reformers like Godwin and Tom Paine, Crevecoeur was a source of inspiration to a whole lot of Romanticists like Hazlitt, Shelley and Coleridge in England and Chateaubriand in France.
11. For critical accounts of how flesh gets undermined by the spirit and how it consequently becomes a source of neurosis and morbidity in Hawthorne and Poe and how it undermines the Genteel Tradition of America, see Samuel Chase Coale, *The Entangled Polarities: The New Criticism* (Wheaton College, Massachusetts: Boydell & Brewer, 2011), 91-115.
12. For a detailed account of Lawrence's quarrel with Christianity and its relationship with human love and democracy, see Graham Hough, "Lawrence's Quarrel with Christianity: *The Man Who Died*", in Spilka, 101-11.
13. For an account of the tradition of reading associated with Melville see, O.W. Riegel, "The Anatomy of Melville's Fame", *On Melville: The Best from American Literature*, Louis J. Budd and Edwin H. Cady eds. (Durham and London: Duke University Press, 1988), 1-9.
14. For an insightful reading of Lawrence and his working class origin as a source of his social criticism see, Williams, 162-74.
15. D.H. Lawrence, "America, Listen to Your Own", *Phoenix: The Posthumous Papers of D.H. Lawrence.* Edward D. McDonald. Ed. and Introd. (London: William Heinemann, 1936), 87-91.

Works Cited

Benioff, Mark. "We Need To Build a New Capitalism", *The Times of India.* Ahmedabad/Baroda, 22 February 2020, 10.

Coale, Samuel Chase. *The Entangled Polarities: The New Criticism*, Wheaton College, Massachusetts: Boydell & Brewer, 2011.

Foster, Richard. "Criticism as Rage: D.H. Lawrence," *D.H. Lawrence: Twentieth Century Views.* Mark Spilka ed. New Jersey: Prentice-Hall, 1963.

Greenspan, Ezra, Lindeth Vasey and John Worthen. "Introduction." *The Cambridge Edition of the Works of D.H. Lawrence: Studies in Classic American Literature.* Ezra Greenspan,

Lindeth Vasey and John Worthen, eds., Cambridge: Cambridge University Press, 2003.

Hough, Graham. "Lawrence's Quarrel with Christianity: *The Man Who Died*", *D.H. Lawrence: Twentieth Century Views*. Mark Spilka ed. New Jersey: Prentice-Hall, 1963.

Lawrence, D.H. *Studies in Classic American Literature.* Delhi: Atlantic, 1995.

_____. "America, Listen to Your Own", *Phoenix: The Posthumous Papers of D.H. Lawrence.* Edward D. McDonald. Ed. and Introd. London: William Heinemann, 1936.

______. "Foreword." *Studies in Classic American Literature*. New Delhi: Atlantic, 1995.

Mackey, John and Rajendra Sisodia. *Conscious Capitalism: Liberating the Heroic Spirit of Business.* Boston: Massachusetts, 2013.

Polman, Kim. "Interview", *The Times of India.* Ahmedabad/ Baroda, 22 February 2020.

Riegel, O.W. "The Anatomy of Melville's Fame", *On Melville: The Best from American Literature*, Louis J. Budd and Edwin H. Cady, eds. Durham and London: Duke University Press, 1988.

Sisodia, Rajendra and Michael J. Gelb. *The Healing Organization: Awakening the Conscience of Business to Help Save the World.* New York: Harper & Collins, 2019.

Williams, Raymond. "Lawrence's Social Writing", *D.H. Lawrence: Twentieth Century Views.* Mark Spilka ed. New Jersey: Prentice-Hall, 1963.

12

Lawrence's Poetry: Humans, Animals, and Plants

Rabindra Pradhan

Highly influenced by the American poet Walt Whitman, Lawrence began writing verse when he was just nineteen. His 45-year-long life may seem short in comparison to the poets who have outlived their generation. But, within this short span of life, he wrote some 800 poems. Like his fictions, Lawrence's poetry was often castigated due to its content rather than style. But, the 21st century has witnessed unprecedented success and critical appreciation for his verse. Lawrence's poetry which has stood the test of time is infused with a philosophical appreciation of the reality of changes in morals and values than the philosophy of his own time. Undoubtedly, he receives enviable recognition as a poet addressing a host of issues such as vitality, instincts, emotional health, human sexuality, and spontaneity. Lawrence's poetry ranges from the base to the sublime. He wrote his poems, as always, as he felt life in its many forms. Although many are simply deep passionate rantings about society and industry; a select few rise above the rest and are recognised as great.

E.M. Forster rightly described him as 'the greatest' imaginative novelist/poet of our generation. He reached the pinnacle of glory for his treatment of numerous themes in his poetry. His best-known poems are probably those dealing with nature in the collection, *Birds, Beasts and Flowers* (1923). This incorporates the *Tortoise Poems* and *Snake*. "Snake" displays some of his most frequent concerns—those of man's distance from nature and subtle hints at religious themes. "Snake", the most famous of this collection, is about a simple story of the poet's encounter with a snake. The poet went to his water-trough on a hot noon. A snake came to drink water from the trough because it was very hot. Lawrence was enthralled by its beauty. He felt it was better to stay on and watch it. He is fearful, awed and honored by the snake drinking out of his trough, but also a bit confused because the snake might be venomous and his education has told him to kill it. Eventually, as the snake leaves, he throws a stick at it, an act he forever regrets because it made it leave faster. Though the narrator understands that the snake would not harm him, he still tosses a stick towards it once it is slithering away to safety. The narrator harms the snake while its back is turned after the snake had trusted the narrator for sharing his water.

Lawrence uses the snake as a complex metaphor for the darker side of humanity. The narrator notices that a snake has come to drink at his water-trough. Though the snake is not bothering him nor showing any signs of danger or aggression, the narrator feels compelled to kill it and desecrate its body. In the end, just as the snake is leaving, the narrator throws a stick at it. Though the snake moves away uninjured, the narrator still deeply regrets this final act of savagery and misjudgement.

What makes the poem special is the way the speaker's observations are interwoven with thoughts and feelings—the content perfectly matches the form. His poem's success is achieved through its form of free verse lines and the use of devices such as sibilance, alliteration and assonance. Enjambment helps to bring suspense and a feeling of strong rhythm. The poet's use of figurative words to help paint a picture of this creature enhances the quality of the poem. The narrator is divided between respect and honour on the one hand and fear and loathing on the other. This sets up a tense energy within the poem lasting almost from the first few lines to the last. The first few lines of the poem reveal on the surface, a man meeting a snake at a water-trough, accepting that the snake 'was *at the trough before me*', so the man must wait. The way the poem develops, with varying metre and alliteration ("*strange scented shade*")—mirrors the slow movement of a slithering snake beautifully. As the man waits voices arise within him and begin to battle for supremacy. Should he kill the snake? Was he a coward for not doing so?

Contrastingly, there is a part of the man attracted to this reptile '*come like a guest in quiet*'. Why should he destroy such a wonderful creature? This poem demands a closer look simply because it is written by a writer who in his time helped redefine social attitudes towards religion, the natural world and sex. In the poem, the snake is not a tempter however, nor is it referred to as evil but the narrator does pose the question of whether or not it should be killed!

There is a tension set up by these various voices within the narrative. One wants to kill the snake, the other wants to honour it. The former is born of superiority, the latter of equality. In the constant war between humans and nature, the snake is seen as little more than vermin, something to fear and loathe and ultimately destroy. Lawrence's poem captures this dilemma and puts it before the reader in vivid human and environmental terms. Coming across a poisonous snake in Sicily is not all that rare; meeting a snake that has come for a drink at a shared water trough is something special. Water is the life giver, the man, the potential life-taker. "Snake" has as its main theme the ongoing conflict between humans and nature. It raises questions about our relationships with animals, of how we are to continue to exist with nature, as opposed to totally destroyed. This poem also raises issues regarding our modern day individual responses to animals often regarded as 'vermin'. There are some powerfully crafted lines in the poem. The syntax and enjambment work together to produce a mesmerising effect.

The poems from Lawrence's poetry collection, *Tortoises,* are considered his best-known poems. It was published in 1921. The book includes *Baby Tortoise, Tortoise-Shell, Tortoise Family Connections, Lui et Elle* and *Tortoise Gallantry.* The *Tortoise Poems* are permeated with philosophical implications but Lawrence does not directly philosophize. What is at work is rather the artistic projection of his ideas through rhythmical images figuring particular moments of time, thus revealing a unique kind of art in which beautiful and enlightening images move harmoniously and defy their temporal inscription by becoming eternally fixed in the readers' or listeners' minds. In effect, the determined tortoise, so vividly portrayed by Lawrence, resembles the poet himself, burdened as he is with ill-health and frustrated by the repressive morality of his age. The tortoise is therefore the medium through which the poet experiences a kind of purification since this animal represents an independent and spontaneous spirit striving to survive in spite of its stifled sexual frustration.

Lawrence's *Tortoise Poems* are presented in a series of images, each image existing within its own time and space while never losing its connection with the others. He succeeds in creating an art form that goes beyond the purely aesthetic experience of art for art's sake by "making us *experience* the experience" (Eggert, 104). As we are immersed in the realm of tortoises, we are allowed to witness and feel their fluctuating movement and their existential struggle. Keith Sagar describes this style as an "almost occult penetration into the being of other creatures" (Sagar, 121). Tortoises are given superhuman dimensions, as Lawrence projects himself into their space. He abandons himself to their natural world, he captures its aesthetic beauty, while concomitantly experiencing his own being in relation to everything around him, all the time conscious of a greater spiritual power: the creative mystery. *Baby Tortoise* describes a tortoise's life as beautiful, evocative, and paints a picture of the tortoise's existence as spiritually empowering. Lawrence compares the tortoise metaphorically to other creatures, such as an insect or bird. He also describes it as a 'traveller', 'challenger', 'like a gentleman in a long-skirt coat and as wearing a wimple'. There are uses of simile throughout, such as 'like a baby'. Most of the verses end with a statement labelling the tortoise with terms such as 'so indomitable', which the speaker later retracts as though they cannot pin down who this tortoise is, unable to affix a single descriptive word to the transience of the tortoise's growth and progress. The repetition of certain words like inanimate, indomitable also demonstrates the speaker's reflective tone, mixed with awe.

Tortoise sets out an enormous sense of movement and flux. This small and feeble creature that is making its initial progress into the world is as powerful and alive as any of nature's creations. Its vitality and liveliness, in fact, resemble that of the poet. The poem with plenteous verbs such as "To open," "To lift," "And reach," "And move" create a sense of immediacy. The tiny baby tortoise is compared to a human baby, although one endowed with an iron strength despite the heavy burden on its back and an 'indomitable will,' that of an "invincible" little "Titan." This small, lonely, newly born creature of the animal order, kin nonetheless to a human baby, makes "slow, ageless progress/ And a baby makes none." Here, Lawrence seems to be establishing a relationship between motion and time.

One can argue that both tortoise and poet move in different time-spaces, and that it is only by moving at extremely high speed in relation to another being that one can enter another time dimension. Lawrence's use of action verbs emphasize the sense of movement. They are mostly fragmented, lacking syntactic form. A predominance of sentences, structured in accordance with standard logical and syntactic form suggests linear time.

The poem is replete with contradictory and unrelated comparisons concerning the tiny baby tortoise, which in some instances appears slow and monotonous, and then strong and active in others. This is suggestive of the order and chaos in the natural world. Yet again, the tortoise's continuous movement is chaotically interrupted by the uncontrollable desire for completion. It was this which had caused Nietzsche to believe that, "one must still have chaos in oneself, to give birth to a dancing star" (Nietzsche, 26). Renewal and rebirth are the refreshing result of chaos. Anais Nin says: "In Chaos there is fertility" (Nin, 118).

Let's consider the different comparisons associated with the tortoise who is at times human, superhuman and animal: a baby, a bird, a traveler, a Titan, a gentleman, a little Ulysses. Such randomly used contradictory and unrelated comparisons highlight the significance of this small creature which is stronger in both its physical and mental abilities.

A series of rhetorical questions further enhance the sense of movement, while adding a musical effect. Some of these are mostly concerned with existence and with a sense of wonder at the tortoise, while others are directed toward the understanding of its nature. They are infused with hyperbolic comparisons to humans, testifying to the poet's desire to understand the creative mystery and existence of this admirable small creature. The final stanza introduces the notion of pain that goes with the sense of the movement of the tortoise like the fragments interrupting the flow of the lines. This is achieved by way of the comparison between the tortoise and Christ carrying the cross.

In *Tortoise Shell*, Lawrence presents his ideas regarding mathematics and the creative mystery through the figure of a tortoise-shell. He starts by way of a description that is both rhythmical and detailed, the combination of these two properties producing a sense of *aliveness*: "life-clouded, life-rosy tortoise-shell." Even its shell is an essential part of its being alive, in the world. The scales on the shell 'are locked in an arch like a bridge,' a bridge that symbolically connects the physical world to the metaphysical world through strange signs which point to the existence of a mysterious creative force. The poet's identification with the tortoise's plight is a significant sign of a certain bonding with this small creature.

The word 'keystone' and the number 'four' are repeated four times in a single four-line stanza. The number four may refer not only to the number of shapes on the shell. In fact, the whole poem is full of numbers and mathematical allusions in a disordered and almost chaotic manner. There are even expressions suggestive of chaos, such as 'the whirligig of dozens.' These reflect the beautiful and wild quality of nature.

Rhythm, here, moves in phase with the poet's description of the shell keeping up with the tortoise's continuous movement. When he lifts the tortoise for a closer appreciation, the reader is given the vision of a 'kicking little beetle' and when the poet once more 'turns him over on his toes again,' we can only imagine how its 'rowing limbs' instantly resume their pace forward. In effect, the poet provides a 3D image of the shell through his words.

Moving from his attempt to connect and identify with the tortoise family, Lawrence again shifts his focus onto the courtship mannerisms of tortoises, highlighting the conflict of forces between the male and the female. We notice at this point the lack of equilibrium between them. The romantic French title *Lui et Elle* is an anthropomorphic expression suggestive of love and romance, with the added ironic personification of the female tortoise as 'mistress.' Moreover, the equilibrium suggested by the two people mentioned in the title contrasts sharply with what is actually revealed in the poem. The 'mistress' or 'Elle' are words that have no relation with the actual intended signifier, here qualified as being "large and matronly/ And rather dirty,/ A little sardonic-looking, as if domesticity had driven her to it." She is large, unsympathetic and aware only of her needs. Unlike the tortoise, Lawrence, the poet and onlooker, feels differently about the female and is 'almost frightened' by her. At this point, he encroaches into her space, offering her food but is bitten in the process. He cries out loud, but his human cry falls into a void and is unheard; she is completely unaware of his pain. It is interesting to note that his shout does not break into her space. Materialistic and down-to-earth, she represents the modern 'sexually self-centered woman' (*Fantasia*, 102), whose concern is more with the preservation of her own desires and with her image in society than with meeting the needs of a desirous spouse.

Lawrence's sadness and pity for the poor little animal, therefore, arise out of a realization that though 'more delicate than she,' the tortoise is doomed to keep chasing the female, "In the race of love-/ Two tortoises,/ She huge, he small." It is also important to note that the scar on the tortoise's shell suggests the female's cruelty, while also strengthening the connection between the poet and the tortoise. Along with Lawrence's identification with the male tortoise, one could also deduce that the scar noticed by the poet on the tortoise's shell is the projected scar of the poet, who had been bitten by 'Elle' when she nipped at his finger while offering her food earlier, "Snake-like she draws at my finger, while I drag/ it in horror away." In spite of this, Lawrence maintains the sense of movement by stressing the male tortoise's obstinate will to keep moving onwards 'with a grim, reptile determination' belonging to 'serpents' long obstinacy/ Of horizontal persistence.' The tortoise accepts his chaotic desire, does not repress his physicals urge and is oblivious to pain. This is poignantly expressed in the following lines:

> The spear is through the side of his isolation.
> His adolescence saw him crucified into sex,
> Doomed, in the long crucifixion of desire, to seek his consummation beyond himself.
> Divided into passionate duality,
> He, so finished and immune, now broken into desirous fragmentariness,
> Doomed to make an intolerable fool of himself
> In his effort toward completion again.

Though a certain measure of resistance is part of the courting act, the female tortoise in this poem exaggerates her withdrawal to a condition characterized by her complete denial of her mate and of her own natural calling. According to Andrew Keese, the issues Lawrence brings up in these poems "revolve around the concept of imposed human morality, which he blames for crippling human societies" (Keese, 136). His pity is not the case of a projected self-pity. What is involved is more the response of one saddened to see humanity, like the female, losing touch with nature and failing to understand the tortoise's natural urges.

Lawrence believes that it is the "the female who sends out her dark summons, the intense dark vibration of sex" to lure the male. Though in *Tortoise Gallantry*, he does formulate the enigma of the male tortoise's desire, "Does she know?" the answer would most probably be affirmative, since the male tortoise is in fact moving in reaction to her signals. Lawrence's question also reflects Nietzsche's belief that woman is 'conscious of man's feelings' towards her, while acting as though she is ignorant in order to exert what he also refers to as 'the will to power.' The female tortoise is 'large and matronly' and 'almost too large,' compared to the male's 'much smaller' stature. Her 'will to power' is therefore stronger, and the more she moves away from him, the greater the attraction he will undergo to submit to her stronger magnetic pull. In fact, by moving deliberately away, the female is also denying her own basic needs. In natural terms, both of them need completion. All their movements should therefore be spontaneously directed towards this moment of fulfillment. When she does finally succumb, the union that results from the force that has pulled the male tortoise forward becomes spiritually uplifting, due to the pain or suffering that has preceded the moment.

Tortoise Gallantry might appear to be a repetition of the earlier courting experience in *Lui et Elle*. However, this is not the case. It is a repetition with a certain difference. There is a barely discernible and yet significant shift in the perspective, from 'the little old man' to that of the 'little gentleman' who has now blossomed and is about to experience the persistent courtship characteristic of a tortoise and who will continue the sorry plight of its predecessor, the father tortoise. Here the tortoise, in his pursuit of the female, "does not look at her, nor sniff at her,/ No, not even sniff at her, his nose is blank." This echoes Lawrence's claim in *Fantasia of the Unconscious* that "Love is blind. Without sight or scent or hearing the powerful magnetic current vibrates from the hypogastric plexus in the female, vibrating on to the air like some intense wireless message." The poem's emphasis on the negative, coupled with the use of the word 'blank,' indicates the lack of any real emotion other than the desire to achieve the fullness of being preceding procreation.

More importantly, the image of the female in *Tortoise Gallantry* is not as ungainly and as invidious as the female in the preceding poem, since we can discern her 'vulnerable folds of skin,' in contrast to the evocation of the 'ugly ankle' of the mother tortoise in *Lui et Elle*. Even more so, in *Tortoise Gallantry*, the female does not seem as completely nonchalant to male advances as the female in the previous poem is. In fact, 'she sprawls along/ In her ungainly pace;' the word 'sprawls' has a sexual connotation as does her 'ungainly' to for unhurried pace.

These differences are suggestive of the change that occurs within cyclical existence along horizontal time, the implication of which is that beings do not have to be mere copies and repetitions of generations. It seems that the female of the next generation does not need to exercise her 'will to power' outwards onto the male and that she is fated to achieve a greater truth to her spontaneous self, to the natural act. Her 'will to power' is now more faithful to her physical need. Her 'ungainly pace' is in equilibrium between her inner and outer material needs and it thus becomes what it should be: the natural act of seduction preceding the mating act, rather than the forced disregard of the inevitable. In fact, the slight change in the female's attitude indicates that the progression of time does not have to be tediously repetitive. Even the title of this poem, *Tortoise Gallantry* is less sarcastic, suggesting bravery and respect for a female who can balance her inner and outer needs.

Rhythm and motion, mixed with a sense of urgent need distract the tortoise. He is unwillingly pulled towards his desired object, as if by a stronger mysterious force. Lawrence succeeds in vividly portraying the natural desire that controls all creatures as a 'grim necessity from within.' The word 'horizontal' is used twice in *Tortoise Shell* and *Lui et Elle* to refer to the linear progression of time. The tortoise's determination is reminiscent of the 'primordial freedom' of Dasein. But this very freedom is a 'delivering over' to one's fateful destiny. Consequently, the tortoises just live each particular experience as part of a whole, with each fragment containing its moments of pleasure or satisfaction after which they once more continue their forward movement. However, the need to persist never ceases and the male tortoise would once more experience a "still more awful need to persist, to follow,/ follow, continue,/ Driven, after aeons of pristine, fore-god-like/ singleness and oneness."

Furthermore, in a series of fragmented memories expressed in rhythmically anaphoric sentences whose motion is tuned to the repeated "Heart-throb, slow heart-throb, persistent for the/ next spasm," Lawrence reveals the different modes of pain and pleasure he has received from different animals and people, including his mother. With each memory causing a heart-throb, the rhythm moves accordingly. Breathlessly and rhythmically, one after the other, memories thus gain momentum, until finally all are forgotten for one single moment of extreme emotion, the climax of all memory, in a final cry:

This last,
Strange, faint coition yell
Of the male tortoise at extremity,
Tiny from under the very edge of the farthest
Far-off horizon of life.

It is this cry which breaks into the poet's space.

What gives these poems their aesthetic appeal is their effective portrayal of what is a real moment in the life-form of tortoises. Through their movement and flux, the poems go beyond the purely aesthetic experience, opening up philosophical and scientific implications. Each poem or image is held together in cosmic, horizontal time by the sense of movement running throughout, and the resulting image of tortoises is a four dimensional one. In the end, what remains in our minds are the timeless experiences of creative beauty: the eternal now of each moment harmoniously enclosed within units of memory.

The snake became a splendid object of Lawrence's attention, and so did the tortoises. It is worth mentioning poems such as *Baby Tortoise* and *Tortoise Shell* on the ground of the simple appreciation of non-human life that Lawrence's poems abound with. *Baby Tortoise* tells the story of "a tiny, fragile, half-animate bean" (*CP*, 352) which is born alone and yet instinctively and courageously struggles on its way towards survival. "It is a contest of life against non-life", where the baby tortoise's descriptions on a small scale seem to embody the whole process of the creation of life and its evolution. This sequential description allows Lawrence to universalise his observations on development in a hostile environment, while the poet at the same time succeeds to remark on their unblemished will to follow their instinct. Here Lawrence's voice seems to argue against the human tendency to complain about life rather than to stand on one's feet and follow the life instinct, the natural flow and Life Force. The baby tortoise, such a small speck of life is comparable to a baby, except that it makes "slow, ageless progress,/ And a baby makes none." Even though Lawrence stresses its smallness and loneliness, the tiny 'slow one', a 'solitary bite' on its 'solitary hunt' stays so indomitable at the same time and is a great 'Challenger' rowing against the huge vast inanimate, incalculable inertia (*CP*, 353).

Lawrence praises the marvellous persistence of life represented by a miniature creature, he broadens out from this realistic base to consider the tortoise, 'no bigger than my thumb' as the Homeric hero, Ulysses, rowing on his wanderings and a Titan, or courageous giant god, sheltering under his shell as battle-shield (Wareham, 5). This monumental space and time which is given to the simple tale of a baby tortoise then shrinks into the real-scale world of the little creature towards the end of the poem: "Fulfilled of the slow passion of pitching through immemorial ages/ Your little round house in the midst of chaos/ Over the garden earth" (*CP*, 354).

We can only admire Lawrence's ingenuity in creating his own kind of art: one that balances aesthetic beauty and existential truth, cosmic and personal time, by way of the poems' harmonious figurings of the tortoises. It can be surmised that the poet's enthusiasm has led us into the wonder of creation, of nature, and into the meaning of existence through the experience of one of the tiniest of the world's creatures. His wondrous gaze upon the tortoise world is an enlightening experience. Thus one can come to terms with temporality through the accession to a harmony with the inner self.

Lawrence effectively developed an art form for his sake. His poems go beyond the habitual procedures and conventions of the poetic tradition, not only through their philosophical and scientific implications, but also through the four dimensional presentation of their poetic images, through which both the tortoise and the poet, each within its specific temporal space, move toward a mysterious beyond and thus towards a mode of experience of transcendence and unity. In effect, like Nietzsche's "Superman," Lawrence teaches men the sense of their existence. The implication would seem to be that if existence could be measured by the units of experiences, it could be known that the quality of Lawrence's varied artistic creations has survived his temporality, that they now exist in harmony with horizontal time.

Whales Weep Not! was published in a collection, curated from Lawrence's notebooks called *Last Poems* (1932). The poem makes its reader dive into a sea of sensory images, mysticism and eroticism. It is a late addition to Lawrence's literary oeuvre and exhibits the hallmarks of Lawrence's interests and style towards the fag-end of his life. Lawrence opens by claiming that while some say the sea is cold, it also contains 'the hottest blood of all' (Line 2). He describes who this blood belongs to in the second stanza: whales—right whales, sperm-whales, hammer-heads, and killer whales (Line 5)—who dive beneath icebergs (Line 4) and rise again, spouting air from their blowholes as they crest the surface (Lines 6-7). He describes whales mating. Like people, they 'reel with drunk delight' and 'tremble with love' (Line 10). In the blue depths of the sea, an enormous bull whale joins with his 'bride' (Line 13). Lawrence concentrates first on the image of the red ocean of blood inside the bull whale (Line 16). The blood inside him propels his erection to 'come[s] to rest' in the female whale's body. The whales are now linked by the bull whale's phallus, which serves as a bridge for oceanic angels, Cherubim, 'archangels of bliss,' to pass pleasure back and forth between them (Stanza 4). This scene is the 'great heaven of whales' (Line 29).

The poem shifts to an image of mother whales suckling their calves and dreaming, open-eyed, in the 'waters of/ the beginning and the end' (Lines 29-30). In hazardous situations, the bull-whales form a protective circle around their 'women' and the baby whales, protecting them like 'great fierce Seraphim' (Line 36). Lawrence reaffirms the setting: This all happens in the sea where God is 'love, but without words' (Line 39), and the Greek sea goddess of sexual desire, Aphrodite, is the happy wife of the whales (Stanza 5). In the sixth and final stanza, Lawrence expands on Aphrodite, this time in her Roman aspect, Venus. Venus skips among the fishes—she is a she-dolphin, then a porpoise, then a female tunny-fish. Venus seems to be transforming before the reader's eyes. She is 'happy among the/ males' and as full of blood as they are (Line 44). The poem concludes with an enigmatic summary image: 'dark rainbow bliss in the sea' (Line 45).

This union between the male whale and the female whale has something distinctly holy about it. The ecstasy of their mutual pleasure is ferried waveringly by angels (Lines 21-29). This theme is continued in the next image, where whale mothers suckle their young in the depths and dream "in the/ waters of/ the beginning and the end" (Line 32). This phraseology imitates the Biblical language of alpha and omega, as both the beginning, end, and everything in-between. But Lawrence's vision of whales is not entirely metaphysical. He quickly returns to more concretely biological behaviors, like the bull whales circling and protecting the female whales and their young at the approach of danger. The whales are not just female whales, but 'women,' and the male whales protect them like fiery angelic Seraphim.

Lawrence is especially interested in using 'real' whale behavior to model idealized human behavior. Here in the ocean, he explains, love can thrive 'without words'. The love of whales is an animalistic love, rooted firmly in sensual pleasure; it is love from a time before civilization, a theme Lawrence returns to time and again. He often rejects modern cerebralism in favor of primordial, animalistic sensuality.

The *Last Poems* use imagery from Greek mythology to paint a poetic universe before the corruptive entrance of civilization. Lawrence describes Aphrodite as the wife of the whales. Then, in the form of Venus, the goddess not only refuses to shy away from male attention; she delights in being in their midst (Line 44). She seems to rapidly transform from one line to the next—she is first a she-dolphin, then a porpoise, then a tuna. Like the male whales, Venus is 'dense with happy blood' (Line 45). In concentrating on her feelings, Lawrence shifts from the male experience to the female experience, ultimately suggesting that both sexes are best served by giving in to their irrational, natural desires. The poem's final image, "dark rainbow bliss in the sea" (Line 45), completes the descent into the deep ocean. Lawrence compares darkness with death and human mortality. But, in "Whales Weep Not!" the darkness has a rainbow hue, evoking the prismatic sparkling of water and its ability to refract color.

In Lawrence's poetic universe, modern man's greatest sin is his desire to allow his mind to subjugate his more animalistic, sense-oriented self. The poet's use of striking, tactile images and lyrically beautiful verse are meant to be provocative to hit the readers out of their patterns of rational thought. "Whales Weep Not!" is a great microcosm of this technique. In the poem's lovely, colorful world, the whales which can be interpreted as idealized humans are directly likened to the Greek gods that swim alongside them (Line 12). While Lawrence looked above to the Greek gods as poetic models for human behavior, he also looked below to the animal kingdom. In his private life, Lawrence was fascinated by the natural world.

The whales also represent an almost Leviathan, spiritual force. Lawrence emphasizes their overwhelming hugeness (and "roll with massive, strong desire," (Line 12); "as mountain pressing on mountain," (Line 15), elevating the whales to a mythological, primordial status. The last portion of *Whales Weep Not!* concentrates on two aspects of the "same" goddess: the Greek Aphrodite and the Roman Venus. Lawrence—like other Modernists—seeks to be a conduit for spontaneous thoughts. Like the works of Wordsworth and Whitman, Lawrence wrote *Whales Weep Not!* in free verse—an open form which does not adhere to any formal rhythm. We can get rid of the stereotyped movements and the old hackneyed associations of sound or sense. In *Whales Weep Not!*, the flexibility of free verse allows the poem to ebb and flow like the sea itself.

Works Cited

Eggert, Paul. "CS Peirce, D.H. Lawrence, and Representation: Artistic Form and Polarities." *D.H. Lawrence Review* 28.1-2 (1999).

Keese, Andrew. "Pansies: Lawrence's Search for the Animal Other in Humans." *D.H. Lawrence Studies*. Oct. 2012.

Lawrence, D.H. *The Letters of D.H. Lawrence*. Eds. Warren Roberts and James T. Boulton. Cambridge: Cambridge University Press, 1997.

———, *Fantasia of the Unconscious*. London: The Big Nest, 2013.

———, *Tortoises*. New York: Thomas Seltzer, 1921.

Nietzsche, Friedrich Wilhelm. *Thus Spoke Zarathustra: A Book for Everyone and Nobody*. Trans. Thomas Common. Pennsylvania State University Press, 1999.

Nin, Anais. *The Diary of Anais Nin 1931-1934*. Ed. Gunther Stuhlmann. New York: The Swallow Press and Harcourt, Inc., 1966.

Pinto, Vivian De Sola, Warren F. Roberts. Complete Poems of D.H. Lawrence. Harmondsworth, Penguin, 1980.

Sagar, Keith. *D.H. Lawrence: Poet*. Humanities-Ebooks, 2008.

Wareham, John. *Birds, Beasts and Flowers: Poems of D.H. Lawrence*. Leicester: The English Association, 1998.

13
Lawrence's Nonfiction Prose

Bibhu Padhi

1

When F.R. Leavis wrote, "Lawrence's genius has very striking manifestations outside his novels and tales," he was probably thinking of the novelist's letters and essays (*Lawrence*, 15). However, Lawrence's nonfiction prose was a product of the same creative process that produced his fiction and poetry. So that Leavis would add, "Lawrence's intelligence in its superlative fineness and vitality, always seems to me—and in the closely argued prose treatise and in the criticism as much as anywhere else—essential genius in terms of a profound ability to see everything as an intrinsic part of a larger pattern, of 'an extraordinary power of relating insights' and recognizing 'complete fields of experience'" (*Lawrence*, 375). Lawrence's intelligence is thus closely associated with his sympathetic imagination—something which made him responsive to the most ordinary details of everyday life and helped him recognize in them the workings of an active universe. His essays, letters and travel books—like his novels and tales—are an attempt at reminding us of the meaningfulness of the created world and of our responsibility in preserving spontaneous life. Writing of the "Theatre" chapter in Lawrence's travel book *Twilight in Italy*, Leavis reemphasized his earlier notions: "It is unmistakable intelligence, and the quick responsiveness of its play suggests a free-flowing fullness of life. It is the greatest novelist and story-teller who evokes with that spontaneity of vividness the circumstances of the visit to the theatre" (*English*, 154-55).

Lawrence's prose asserts the mystery of existence and, in various ways, records his own feeling of wonder in the face of life's innumerable forms. The "mystery" does not exclude humanity, however; in fact, his prose is pervaded by "human" metaphors and draws its essential strength from its intimate concern with human relationships. Even when his immediate intention seems to center around a physical landscape, we strongly sense the presence—or absence—of human beings. In his autobiographical essay "Nottingham and the Mining Countryside," for instance, the topographical details tell us as much about his keen sense of geography as about the people who enjoyed living there. But, as so often in Lawrence, even in the midst of a plain, straightforward description, we are struck by a sudden, nowhere phrase: "I Remember the Great rolls of coarse flannel and pit-cloth which stood in the corner of my grandfather's hop when I was a small boy, and the big, strange old sewing-machine, *like nothing else on earth,* which sewed the massive pit-trouser" (p. 133, my emphasis). The phrase "like nothing else on earth" is not only a substitute for what could have been a simile or a metaphor, but a reminder of the strange ways in which the inanimate object affected the sensitive child. Such phrases, which appear frequently in Lawrence, express the wonder which he saw as the basis of a healthy existence. They form what I.A. Richards in different context calls "a language within a language" (48) and help define the habitual characteristics of Lawrence's prose as well as explain his instinctivist reaction to things and situations. The phrase here tells us a lot about the experience of a man with an extraordinary sensibility—a sensibility which plays upon every natural and man-made object and reveals the essential life that breathes through all things.

A large part of the fluency and speed of Lawrence's prose is due to his instinctual recognition of that essential life, just as his many attempts to describe it with the help of "qualifications" are attempts to come as near as possible to what it exactly is like. In the following example from the same essay, the man working in the pit is described in terms of qualificatory "or": "He was happy: a more than happy, he was fulfilled. Or he was fulfilled on the receptive side, not on the expressive" (p. 136). The miners are Lawrence's instinctual men, always exposed to the cruellest of dangers and always receptive to the vital life manifesting itself in the close physical "touch." They lived in a "curious close intimacy"—"a contact almost as close as touch"; they carried the "*curious dark intimacy* of the mine, the naked *sort* of contact" (pp. 135-36; my emphasis). The phrases of tentativeness refer to the unique nature of the experience of the "contact"—something which gave a vital direction to the miners' life.

The essay "Nottingham and the Mining Countryside" is a looking-back at Eastwood as a typical English village and offers Lawrence an opportunity to take a fresh glance at the present state of things. As is so very much peculiar with him, the past, in a curious, half-romantic way, forces him to make his characteristically sweeping generalizations about the present. The beauty of England has given way to an unbearable ugliness, even as the pastoral sanctity of the English countryside has given way to extensive man-made industrial settlements. Lawrence's style announces, by means of a hammer-like repetition of key words and phrases, his disenchanted state:

> In my father's generation [...] man was not *beaten down*. But in my generation, the boys I went to school with, colliers now, have been beaten down [...]. The men are *beaten down* [...]. The root of all disaster is disheartenment and men are disheartened. The men of England [...] are disheartened. They have been betrayed and beaten. (p. 137; my emphasis)

The ugliness, promoted by the "new" industrialists and mining contractors of the Victorian times, has almost taken a solid, palpable shape:

> The great crime which the moneyed classes and promoters of industry committed [...] was he condemning of the workers to ugliness, ugliness, ugliness; meanness and formless and ugly surroundings [sic], ugly ideals, ugly religion, ugly hope, ugly love, ugly clothes, ugly furniture, ugly houses, ugly relationship between workers and employers. (p. 138)

By a method of repetition and accumulation verging on the childlike or the automatic, ugliness is made almost into a presence; it sounds as though it were everywhere. The paragraphs that follow this catalogue of ugliness in all its particular manifestations, bring in something entirely different. Through a connective that appears recurrently, giving the prose a close-knit, rhythmic form, Lawrence pours forth his hopes and wishes, that which might—and should—have taken place:

> If the company, instead of building those sordid and hideous Squares [...] if they had put a tall column [...]! If they had made big, substantial houses [...]. If above all, they had encouraged song and dancing [...]. If only they had encouraged some form of beauty in dress [...]. If they had given prizes for the handsomest chair or table [...]. If only they had done this, there would never have been an industrial problem. (p. 138)

Although there is some amount of automatism in those repetitions, it is not "tantrum prose"; nowhere do we feel Lawrence's pen running away from him or what Northrop Frye would see as "setting up a mechanical for an imaginative impetus" (p. 328). The repetitions are spiralling around a hard core of beliefs; they suggest a crisscrossing of intensities. Lawrence's feeling of loss, prompted by the miners' inability to assert their own right to enjoy the beautiful things of the world, has made him look further back and view the past as something virgin and untarnished. The phrase "If only they had" (in all its variations) holds a world of possibilities, carrying over as it does the hopes from one sentence to the next. As a whole, the paragraph possesses all the qualities of good rhythmical prose, which urges us into a fuller understanding by underscoring and trying together certain elements of the text.

Repetitions form a large part of Lawrence's rhetorical apparatus. He was as much sensitive to the word-as-sound as to the word-as-sign. In one of his later essays, "Hymns in Man's Life," he recounts the impact of the Nonconformist hymns on his sensitive mind when he was a little boy. He was in love with the sheer sound of the word "Galilee"; for him it was not merely a word or place, but a self-complete and self-fulfilling "world". Lawrence often goes back to certain words with the same passion with which he goes back to certain themes. There goings-back not only lead to an assertion of some relevant particular truth; they also expose us to the inspiration which drew the writer into its magic circle of power. Here is an excerpt from "Hymns in a Man's Life":

> When all comes to all, the most precious in life is wonder. Love is a great emotion, and power is power. But both love and power are based on wonder. Love without wonder is a sensational affair, and power without wonder is mere force and compulsion. The one universal element in consciousness which is fundamental to life is the element of wonder. You cannot help feeling it in the glisten of the nucleus of the amoeba. You recognize it, willy-nilly, in an ant busily tugging at a straw; in a rook, as it walks the frosty grass. (*PII*, 598)

Although there is an argument in defence of "wonder," there is nothing dogmatic about it. Appropriately, the examples that Lawrence has chosen to show where "wonder" resides, are from the region of the non-human. But he is concerned not so much with a particular ant or rook actually doing thing, as with the spirit which guides it; that is, with something that connects the actual with the great sources of nourish-philosophy: "wonder" is no more and no less than what Graham Hough calls "the whole natural order seen in the mode of reverence and delight" (223). The "religious exaltation of tone" is only a natural and necessary extension into language of that "wonder" which is the basis of the Lawrencian metaphysic.

Very often, it is through repetition that Lawrence tries to bring clarity to his own beliefs. In "Morality and the Novel," for instance, he writes about the "true relatedness" which is impossible to achieve without a fluent means of communication; but, at the same times, he *shows*—through the example of his own style—its necessary scope and limits:

> [...] our life *consists in* this achieving of a pure relationship between ourselves and the living universe about us. This is how I "save my soul" by accomplishing

> a pure relationship between me and another person, me and other people, me and a nation, me and a race of men, me and the animals, me and the trees or flowers, me and the earth, me and the skies and sun and stars, me and the moon [...] me for bread, me and the very motion with which I write, me and the bit of gold I have got. This, if we knew it, is our life and our eternity: the subtle, perfected relation between me and my whole circumambient universe.
>
> And morality is that delicate, for ever trembling and changing *balance* between me and my circumambient universe, which precedes and accompanies a true relatedness. (*PII*, 528; his emphasis)

Lawrence's description of "morality" is nowhere near its orthodox definitions, and hence his long catalogue of relationships. The catalogue implies a desire to exclude nothing as irrelevant or insignificant. The repeated "me" does not point toward any egotistical inclination on Lawrence's part; on the other hand, it refers to the multiple directions in which the individual ego might move in order to meet and commune meaningfully with, "all the strange universe," to the myriad ways and forms in which it can achieve a true relationship with the "circumambient universe." Lawrence's related concept, that of the "whole man alive," refers nearly to the same thing: man cannot be whole without being alive to the non-human forces of the universe, nor can he be alive to these forces without being whole. The paradox that the structure of that phrase contains is really self-fulfilling; it suggests a universe where each thing is intimately related to every other thing. In the very process of repetition, Lawrence has been able to offer a shape to his own hald-formed ideas. Repetition is a natural means—and result—of his exploratory intentions. Quoting a letter that Lawrence wrote to Lady Ottoline Morrell on 15 May 1915, James Sutherland contrasts the former's prose style with that of the Victorians: whereas Victorian prose was "comfortably self-possessed" and was at its most characteristic the voice of Omniscience addressing ignorance, Lawrence's is the 'prose of a poet'; his repetitions are those of "a man puzzling over his own experience, and seeking for a clearer definition of it" (85, 105).

But repetitions serve Lawrence's other purposes also, the most significant of which involves a declaration of his established beliefs and intentions. His last letters and essays (particularly, "Au Revoir, U.S.A.," "The State of Funk," and "Pornography and Obscenity") derive their peculiar strength from such repetition. Written just about nine months before his death, "Pornography and Obscenity" reflects a bitterness which has turned into righteous indignation. If problems of style are really problems of personality, this essay is a sufficiently open instance of Lawrence the dying man "embodied I speech." As he suffered more and more from the painful effects of tuberculosis, his earlier high spirit turned "almost terrifyingly savage" (Huxley, xxxi). Aldous Huxley, who knew him from close quarters, wrote sympathetically about the mocking tone of the writing of these last years:

> I have hear him sometimes speak of men and their ways with a kind of demoniac mockery [...]. The secret consciousness of his dissolution filled the last years of his life with an overpowering sadness [...]. It was, however, in terms of anger that he chose to express this sadness. Emotional indecency always shocked him profoundly, and, since anger seemed to him less indecent as an emotion than a resigned or complaining melancholy, he preferred to be angry. He took his revenge on the fate that had made him sad by fiercely deriding everything. And because the sadness of the slowly dying man was so unspeakably deep, his mockery was frighteningly savage. (*Letters*, xxxi)

In "Pornography and Obscenity," Lawrence offers his final, unexceptionable description of obscenity—a description that has, like his many other diagnoses of things and events, something ominous about it. The feeling which the essay expresses—and attempts to arouse in the participating reader—is close to that feeling which produced "the Nightmare" chapter of *Kangaroo* or those hyperbolic passages on war in the long, anecdotal "Introduction to *Memoirs of the Foreign Legion*." In these, as in the essay on obscenity, one listen to a "defensive egotism [...which] records the extreme self-assertiveness that helped Lawrence weather his sudden and severe wartime isolation" (Cavitch, 60). An awareness of imminent death seeps through the following passage, in which Lawrence condemns the vicious "Secrecies" guiding the sex-life of the twentieth-century man. The language breaths the obsessive, hard-driven character of the man who wrote it:

> The vicious circle, the vicious circle! The vicious circle of masturbation! The vicious circle of self-consciousness that is never *fully* self-consciousness, never fully and openly conscious, but always harping on the dirty little secret. The vicious circle of family. The vast conspiracy of secrecy in the press, and at the same time, the endless tickling of the dirty little secret. The needless masturbation! and the endless purity! The vicious circle! (p. 181)

Each repetition is, as it were, a nail driven into the pernicious influence of what to Lawrence is a form of low sex. The passage's rhythm, which is that of a series of hammer strokes, indirectly refers to the "dead loss," the utter lack of "reciprocity" and the "null effect" of the *act* of masturbation itself. The passage ends with the words with which it began, thus bringing that "circle of vice" to completion.

The essay derives its force of appeal from a hymn-like falling back on a single thought, on a structure of echoes and reverberations. It shows how, for Lawrence, anger is just another name for health. F.L. Lucas might find in such essays a "vulgar, horse-whipping style" (94); or Graham Hough might object to Lawrence's preference for "a method of incremental repetition to first-shot precision" (219), but the repetitional style has its strength. It nearly irritates us and turns back as it were; but it achieves it purpose, which is to make us conscious—through indirections, through an insistent reminder of that which is unhealthy—of a direction which is positive and precious. The language of "Pornography and Obscenity" has an energetic, bursting quality—a quality of revelation that is the very opposite of the self-enclosing character of masturbation;

one might say, it explodes the "secrecy" of the "masturbation self-enclosure." Lawrence's own life was a continuous mission against cheapness and indecency; his language bring us nearer to what George Steiner, in partial desolation of our culture, of that which has undermined and that which may restore the resources of insight in modern society (x). While the "angry" repetitional style breathes Lawrence's own private emotions, it also leans toward social criticism and looks anxiously forward to positive social action.

2

Closely related to the repetitions are Lawrence's deletions. Richard Ohmann, in a 1964 essay which has by now become a minor classic, puts forward a basis for Lawrence's personal idiosyncratic style. A large part of the writer's "brusque, emphatic style," according to Ohmann, is due to his "use of truncated sentences, which have gone through a variety of deletion transformations" (275). It is these reduction and abbreviations of the normal syntactic structure that give Lawrence's repetitional style its characteristic emotive force. As in everyday life—where actions and situations repeat themselves with slight variations, while together giving rise to a state of meaningful complexity—so in Lawrence's prose, certain elements remaining constant, others are deleted, added, or recorded, thus creating and impression of complexity and mystery. In the following passage from *Studies in Classic American Literature,* Ohmann finds his example of Lawrence's love for deletion:

> The renegade hates life itself. He wants the death of life. So these many "reformers" and "idealists" who glorify the savages in America. They are death birds, life-haters. Renegade.
>
> We can't go back, and Melville couldn't. Much as he hated the civilized humanity he knew. He couldn't go back to the savage; he wanted to, he tried to, and he couldn't.
>
> Because in the first place, it made him sick. (*SCAL*, 137)

With the replacement of the deleted elements, the passage reads:

> The renegade hates life itself. He wants the death of life. So these many "reformers" and "idealists" who glorify the savages in American [want the death of life]. They are death-birds. [They are] life-haters. [They are] renegades.
>
> We can't go back. And Melville couldn't [go back]. [Melville couldn't go back, as] such as he hated the civilized humanity he knew. He couldn't go back to the savages. He wanted to [go back to the savages]. He tried to [go back to the savages]. And he couldn't [go back to the savages].
>
> [He couldn't go back to the savages] because, in the first place, it made him sick [to go back to the savages]. (quoted. in Ohmann, 275-76)

According to Ohmann, the restoration of the full form with the help of grammar, reveals two interesting things: first, there is a large amount of repetition in the original passage and which accounts for the "driving insistence" one feels in reading it; and second, Lawrentian deletion is "a stylistic alternative to *conjunction*" (275). However, there is something else also—something which is closely connected with an affection for deletion: It is our sharp awareness of a "speaking voice." The sentences, bold and brimming with energy, are punctuated by respiration rather than rules of grammatical or rhythmic structure; their rhythm nearly parallels our natural speech rhythm.

The style of the passage is something of a "tumbling" variety, wherein, as Huntington Brown writes, "the ideas... are...inseparable (in fact, though not in theory) from the words and the emotional appeal is often strong" (55). The "stress-crowded rhythmic units"—a distinctive feature of the tumbling discourse—impart urgency to Lawrence's language and express his "sustained and prevailing point of view" (Brown, 65). The manner of presentation is that of "an unflagging, often aggressive, self-assurance" (Brown, 66). As a further instance of Lawrence' "tumbling" style, one may look at the following excerpt from his essay "Au Revoir, U.S.A.," in which the hard accents, the blunt words, the deletions, and the overall tone of sarcasm induce in the reader what Brown would see as "a state of heightened susceptibility to feeling" (67).

> But look out! The great stone heads snarl at you from the wall, trying to bite you: and one great dark, green blob of an obsidian eye, you never saw anything so blindly malevolent: and then white fangs. Great white fangs, smooth today, the white fangs, with tiny cracks in them. Enamelled. These bygone pyramid-building Americans, who were a dead-and-gone mystery even to the Aztecs, when the Spaniards arrived, they applied their highest art to the enamelling of the great fangs of these venomous stone heads, and there is the enamel today, white and smooth.... You can stroke the great fang with your finger and see. And the blob of an obsidian eye looks down at you. (105)

The passage, with its hurling adjectives, the compound words, the many direct reference to a possible "listener," the deletions, and the repetitions, is a typical example of Lawrence's harsh style. It reflects the obsessive personality of its author—a man of strong emotions, for whom every casual observation is fraught with significance.

It is only a small step from this "tumbling" prose to the prophetic style of essays like "Blessed are the Powerful," "Reflection on the Death of a Porcupine," "On Being a Man," or parts of *Study of Thomas Hardy.* There is a certain quotable, aphoristic quality about their prose—a quality that reminds one of the Nietzschean meditations (although, as is natural to Lawrence's sensibility, they are not as extended and elaborated as Nietzsche's meditations generally are). Their language seems to have captured a prophet's ultimate visionary moments. There is a mark of finality and undeniability about the sentences, which are complete and perfect in their structure. One may consider the opening lines of "Blessed are the Powerful":

> The reign of love is passing, and the reign of power is coming again.

The day of popular democracy is nearly done. Already we are entering the twilight, towards the night that is at hand.

Before the darkness comes, it is as well to take our directions. It is time to enquire into the nature of power, so that we do not crassly blunder into a new era: or fall down the gulf of anarchy, in the dark, as we cross the borders.

We have a confused idea, that will and power are somehow identical. We think we can have a will-to-power.

A will-to-power seems to work out as bullying. And bullying is something despicable and detestable. (*PII*, 436)

Or note the following from "Reflections on the Death of a Porcupine":

Life is more vivid in the dandelion than in the green fern, or than in a palm tree.

Life is more vivid in a snake than in a butterfly.

Life is more vivid in a wren than in an alligator.

Life is more vivid in a cat than in an ostrich.

Life is more vivid in the Mexican who drives the wagon than in the two horses in the wagon.

Life is more vivid in me than in the Mexican who drives the wagon for me.

We are speaking in terms of existence: that is, in terms of species, race, or type.

The dandelion can take hold of the land, the palm tree is driven into a corner with the fern.

The snake can devour the fiercest insect.

The fierce bird can destroy the greatest reptile.

The great cat can destroy the greatest bird.

The man can destroy the horse, or any animal.

One race of man can subjugate and rule another race.

All this in terms of existence. (*PII*, 468)

The single-sentence paragraphs, so common in Lawrence, especially in his nonfiction writings—are almost biblical in their tone and rhythm. The sentences are full of parallelism (the two parts of a sentence being closely alike in structure and separated by a punctuation mark rather than a conjunction) and echoes. Taken as a whole, they read like a hymn, except at those places where Lawrence breaks their onrushing flow with an explanatory "aside"—a parenthetical reminder of the context against which his unqualified statements are to be judged. The sentences contribute to the creation of that illusion of the unbroken process which is the basis of the continuous revelation that Lawrence has in mind. Once again, the appeal is to our aural imagination: we listen to Lawrence *talking* rather than merely read the printed word. The one-line paragraphs are also—like the orthodox prophet's—a device that Lawrence uses against any possible inattention on the part of his reader-listener.

"An assortment of loosely related aphorisms," according to Huntington Brown, "is the essential substance of a work of prophecy. The Force of the whole is the self-contained force of these separate units" (70). Lawrence's prophetic prose lays down "paradoxes as law" and allow "no room for reservations or apologies." Like the prophets again, Lawrence loves to emphasize the brevity of his pronouncements "by making each stand somewhat apart in sense from its context" (Brown, 71). Following the best traditions of the prophetic style, Lawrence, in the closing paragraphs of "Reflections on the Death of a Porcupine," gives the prophet's final warning against the possibility of his "new world" being invaded by evil forces. The final paragraphs are a return from the utopian and the conceptual to the human and the actual. What started as a narrative-descriptive account of the death of a particular porcupine goes through various stages of conceptual growth before ending on a peremptory note on the evil influence of money-values on sources of inspiration and emotional well-being. As elsewhere in Lawrence, the essay develops through a series of "contrasting textures" (Beal, 85); it includes, even within its highly emotional framework, numbered propositions. Like the string, epigrammatic sentences, the numbered propositions are also a rhetorical device used for greater clarity and emphasis.

Rhetorical persuasion is also the basis of Lawrence's unusual adjectives and compound words ("a thick sauce of brown neutrality," "Adonis-blood red," "dawn-lovely Sicily," "shut-in-edness"); novel personifications ("If you try to nail anything down [...] the novel gets up and walks away with the nail"); exclamations; quotation marks around the almost-right words; italics; extended metaphors ("The wild creatures are coming forth from the darkest Africa inside us. In the night you can hear them bellowing. If you are a big game-hunter, like Billy Sunday, you may shoulder your elephant gun. But since the forest is inside all of us, and in every forest there's a whole assortment of big game and dangerous creatures [...]"); literary allusion ("We are such stuff as our grandmothers' dreams were made on, and our little life is rounded by a band"); figures of sound ("The weather is soft and mild, mildly sunny in that hazed, dazed, uncanny sunless sunniness [...]"); the many direct addresses to the "dear, dear reader"; and the question-and-answer scheme. Lawrence has always in mind a sympathetic reader who is also capable of accepting his ideas; consequently, his participation in objects, persons and situations becomes nothing short of an intense personal involvement, often resulting in the sort of vigorous prose that is emotive and lyrical.

3

Perhaps all of Lawrence's travel writings would be called lyrical or poetic, if we understand the word "poetic" as referring to something much broader and more complex than is implied by "metrical composition." It is interesting to see how the particular geographical locations carry Lawrence away from the specificity of an actual place, into the half-lit world of the "unknown." As our interest in the details of observation seems to build up, it is suddenly undermined, as though whatever we were taking an interest in till now were only a remotely relevant part of the truth. There is a diffusiveness about the descriptions, a certain disembodied quality about the objects and persons, all of which seem to dissolve into a feeling or a consciousness. The long, rolling sentences, with their repeated ands, evoke the true nature of the things and the exact state of the mind receiving them, untouched by ratiocination. At the same time, emotional effects are treated as though they were material objects. Here is an excerpt from the opening section of the first chapter of *Sea and Sardinia:*

> Comes over one an absolute necessity to move. And what is more, to move in some particular direction [...].
>
> Why can't one sit still? Here in Sicily it is so pleasant: the sunny Ionian sea, the changing jewel of Calabria, like a fire-opal moved in the light [...].
>
> Why then must one go? Why not stay? Ah what a mistress, this Etna! With her strange winds prowling around her like Circe's panthers, some black, some white. With her strange, remote communications, and her terrible dynamic exhalations. She makes men mad. Such terrible vibrations of wicked and beautiful electricity she throws about her, like a deadly net! Nay sometimes, verily, one can feel a new current of her demon magnetism seize one's living tissue, and change the peaceful lie of one's active cell. She makes a storm in the living plasm and a new adjustment. And sometimes it is like a madness.
>
> This timeless Grecian Etna, in her lower-heaven Loveliness, so lovely, so lovely, what a torture! [...] Where does one go? There is Girgenti by the south. There is Tunis at hand. Girgenti, and the sulphur spirit and the Greek guarding temples, to make one madder? Never. Neither Syracuse and the madness of its great quarries. Tunis? Africa? Not yet. Not yet. Not the Arabs, not yet. Naples, Rome, Florence? No good at all. Where then?
>
> Where then? Spain or Sardinia. Spain or Sardinia. Sardinia, which is like nowhere. Sardinia, which has no history, no date, no race, no offering. Let it be Sardinia. [...] Sardinia then. Let it be Sardinia. (*SS*, 7-9)

Lawrence's style vividly captures the movement of his reflections, uncertainties, and doubts. It is the style of a man talking to himself, explaining to himself his own difficulties in responding to something as mysterious as Etna or Sardinia. Lawrence is not only writing, but meditating at the same time. Language becomes a means of exploration and discovery.

There is a childlike innocence about the cheerful energy that the passage holds, a naïve sensitiveness about the wistful reflections. Lawrence is a part of the material he is dealing with, and, naturally enough, his prose has a loose, rambling quality. It reminds one of the unsymmetrical beauty of a Chinese garden, through which one must walk for a long time in order to be able to contemplate it in its entirety. But it is not self-indulgent writing. What we have here is the language of meditation rather than of action—a language which is concerned with what a thing feels to be rather than what it is supposed to be by some rational prescription. Lawrence's fancy is playful, with childlike possibilities of extending the world, of building up hitherto unknown associations. The "terrible vibrations of wicked and beautiful electricity" that Etna "throws about her": the "wicked witch," Etna, "resting her thick white snow under heaven, and slowly, slowly rolling her orange-coloured smoke": the trees which are "sentiment flesh"—these and several other metaphorical combinations which, on first glance, look careless and capricious, reveal what Keith Sagar would see as "an almost preternatural awareness of the quality of life in the instant moment" (224). Lawrence is feeling into a moment, as it were—participating in the fictional possibilities of definite historical situation. Herbert Read writes of the danger and the impertinence of any attempt to analyse the rhetoric of what he calls, these "speculation[s] with feeling" (144). Much of Lawrence's travel writing defies neat formal categorization. They are travelogues with a difference, which "difference" is what one might see as the essential Lawrence. Unlike the orthodox travel writer, Lawrence is not recording merely the superficial details of a place, but communing with the non-personal, non-human "spirit of the place." The emphatic adjectives—together with the unemphatically-placed nouns—refer to the essential quality of a thing rather than the thing itself.

It is important to note here Lawrence's attitude toward the non-human world vis-à-vis the world of men. He finds much in the people of Sardinia that is revolting to his sensibility; in fact, his characteristic gesture to people is *noli me tangere,* which contrasts well with his encounters with the natural environment. Lawrence's experiences remain private and exclusive; even his wife Frieda (referred to as "queen bee"), who was with him throughout, stands outside the circle of his experience. Here, as elsewhere in his writing (particularly in his fiction), Lawrence treats the individual's experience as something unique, and, to that extent, unshareable (despite his continuous, often desperate, attempts at building up—and assigning significant meanings to—human relationships). The esoteric metaphors and similes, the unconventional adjectives, the slowly accumulating tentative questions, the repetitive falling-back on a single theme, and above all, the buoyant rhythm, point to his strong belief in the unique, non-paraphrasable quality of every honest experience and expression.

4

Running through the entire gamut of Lawrence's writing is his earnest belief that "art must be wholly spontaneous, and, like the artist, imperfect, limited and transient" (Huxley, xvi). His imperfections and weakness are those that life most often forces us to live with; they are the price one pays for remaining human. Huxley, in his Introduction to his edition of Lawrence's letters, wrote that of all building material, Lawrence liked adobe best, whose "extreme plasticity and extreme impermanence" contrasted favourably with the "indestructible solidity" of stone (xvi, xvii). For a man who rarely made "minor" correction in his works but, occasion demanding, completely rewrote them, it was but natural that a highly conscious and carefully evolved style—like the great building of stone—would be an oppression. His own prose style is an example of his aesthetic principles in actual practice. Written during a time of intense moral crisis, his strong and unpretentiously passionate prose is a radical humanist's agent, set against barbarous modes of communication, against the tyranny of the sophisticated, over-formalized modes of articulating "murderous falsehood" (Steiner vii).

In his Introduction to Giovanni Verga's *Cavalleria Rusticana,* Lawrence indicates the energy and characteristic movement of that prose in his own comments on Verga's style, which, as he wrote to Catherine Carswell, he found "so fascinating" (106):

> The emotional mind [...] is not logical. It is a psychological fact, that when we are thinking emotionally or passionately, thinking and feeling at the same time, we do not think rationally; and therefore, and therefore, and therefore. Instead, the mind makes curious swoops and circles. It touches the point of pain or interest [...]. There is curious spiral rhythm, and the mind approaches again and again the point of concern, repeats itself, goes back, destroy the time-sequence entirely, so that time ceases to exist, as the mind stoops to the quarry, then leaves it without striking, soars, hovers, turns, swoops, stoops again, still does not strike, yet is nearer, nearer, reels away again, wheels off into the air, even forgets, quit forgets, yet again turns, bends, circles slowly, swoops and stoops again, until at last there is the closing-in, and the clutch of a decision or a resolve. (249-50)

In a surprisingly effortless way, the mind becomes the metaphorical bird before it is transformed back to itself. Once again, it is impossible to separate Lawrence from the material he is dealing with. One strains to find out whether this marvellously evocative prose only refers to the quality of Verga's style, or is a spontaneously rendered example of Lawrence's own style at its best. Lawrence's intelligence has so sympathetically played upon Verga's works, that it cannot but be itself. The urgency and the clean imaginative sweep; the passionately imitative rhythm, recreating, in verbal language, a flight that has something curiously "artistic" about it; the metaphoric exuberance; the continuous suggestion of the soul's liberation through the body: these are not only about Verga, they are the essential Lawrence.

They are a fulfilment in practice of his long-cherished aesthetic intentions.

Works Cited

Beal, Anthony. *D.H. Lawrence.* London: Arthur Baker, 1950.

Brown, Huntington. *Prose Style: Five Primary Types.* Minneapolis: University of Minnesota Press, 1966.

Cavitch, David. *D.H. Lawrence and the New World.* New York: Oxford University Press, 1969.

Frye, Northrup. *Anatomy of Criticism: Four Essays.* Princeton: Princeton University Press, 1957.

Hough, Graham. *The Dark Sun: A Study of D.H. Lawrence.* London: Duckworth, 1956.

Huxley, Aldous. "Introduction." *The Letters of D.H. Lawrence.* Ed. Aldous Huxley. New York: Viking, 1932.

Lawrence, D.H. *The Letters of D.H. Lawrence*: Volume IV: June 1921-March 1924. Ed. Warren Roberts, James T. Boulton, and Elizabeth Mansfield. Cambridge: Cambridge University Press, 1987.

———. *Sea and Sardinia.* Ed. Mara Kalnins. Cambridge: Cambridge UP, 1997 (*SS*).

———. *Studies in Classic American Literature.* New York: Viking, 1964 (*SCAL*).

———. *Phoenix II*: *Uncollected, Unpublished, and Other Prose Works by D.H. Lawrence.* Ed. Warren Roberts and Harry T. Moore. New York: Viking, 1968.

———. *Phoenix: The Posthumous Papers of D.H. Lawrence.* Ed. Edward D. McDonald. London: Heinemann, 1936.

Leavis, F.R. *D.H. Lawrence; Novelist.* Harmondsworth: Penguin Books, 1973.

———. *English Literature in Our Time and The University.* London: Chatto and Windus, 1969.

Lucas, F.L. *Style*, London: Pan Books, 1964.

Ohmann, Richard. "Generative Grammars and the Concept of Literary Style", *Linguistics and Literary Style.* Ed. Donald C. Freeman. New York: Holt, Rinehart and Winston, 1970.

Read, Herbert. *English Prose Style*. London: Bell and Sons, 1956.

Richards, I.A. *How to Read a Page*. London: Routledge and Kegan Paul, 1967.

Sagar, Keith. *The Art of D.H. Lawrence*. Cambridge: Cambridge University Press, 1966.

Steiner, George. *Language and Silence: Essays on Language, Literature, and the Inhuman*. New York: Atheneum, 1967.

Sutherland, John. *On English Prose*. Toronto: University of Toronto Press, 1957.

Index